# DISCOVERING
## YOUR SOUL
### MISSION

# DISCOVERING YOUR SOUL MISSION

## How to Use Karmic Astrology to Create the Life You Want

## LINDA BRADY
## and EVAN ST. LIFER

Three Rivers Press • New York

Published by Three Rivers Press, a division of Crown Publishers, Inc., 201 East 50th Street, New York, New York 10022. Member of the Crown Publishing Group.

Random House, Inc. New York, Toronto, London, Sydney, Auckland
www.randomhouse.com

THREE RIVERS PRESS is a trademark of Crown Publishers, Inc.

Printed in the United States of America

Design by Rhea Braunstein

Library of Congress Cataloging-in-Publication Data
Brady, Linda.
    Discovering your soul mission: how to use karmic astrology to create the life you want / by Linda Brady and Evan St. Lifer.—1st ed.
    Includes index.
    1. Astrology. 2. Karma. I. St. Lifer, Evan. II. Title.
BF1543.B73    1998
133.5—dc21                                    98-12739

ISBN 0–609–803603

10  9  8  7  6  5  4  3  2  1

First Edition

*To my mother, Irene Blackburn,*
*who taught me the power of words.*
*To my husband, Michael Brady,*
*who is my best "creation." L.B.*

*To my mother, Lola St. Lifer,*
*whose affection and love burn*
*bright within me. E.S.L.*

# ACKNOWLEDGMENTS

**LINDA BRADY**

This book is a testimony to all the clients I have worked with for more than twenty-seven years. Without them it would not have been possible. I would like to acknowledge all my interns: teaching them has allowed me to sharpen my philosophy and my ability to convey it. Many of the insights shared in the book were derived from internship lectures over the last few years. My interns spurred me to be clearer, more organized, and more profound. I would especially like to thank my friends, clients, and students who took the time to write the personal anecdotes that are scattered throughout the book. Their keen awareness and poignant insights have helped give the book life.

I would like to thank three of my graduates who are teachers of the internship program: Richard Hoshal, Suzan Miller, and Sandra Lin Parker. They took the bull by the horns and taught classes for me while I stole away with my laptop and my notes and wrote the book.

My husband, Michael, was always there being supportive, generous, and helpful. I would like to acknowledge him for being understanding when I was unavailable or preoccupied. He literally took charge of all the mundane details of my life, freeing me up to work. My housemate, Richard Hoshal, needs a thank you also. He spent weekends planting, weeding, mulching, and sweating over the new gardens that I wanted. They are our pride and joy.

Lynn Van Gilder in Baltimore and Candy Bodle in Seattle spent hours at their computers, transcribing audio- and videotapes and correlating astrological information. Thank you both—you made my work so much easier!

And I would also like to publicly acknowledge my coauthor, Evan St. Lifer. He patiently taught me to understand what being a writer really is. I have learned so much throughout our relationship.

## EVAN ST. LIFER

On hot beach days and crisp autumn school mornings, on thawing playground days and icy, wintry lonely nights over a span of four years, through the births of our sons Alex then Luke, my wife Diana gave me the time I needed—after dinner, before work, on weekends—to transform *Discovering Your Soul Mission* from the seed of an idea to reality. Above all, she deserves a special thank you, for without her support and willingness to allow my work to intrude on almost every aspect of our lives, I would have been unable to write this book. I am also indebted to author Charles Panati, whose insight and perspective were critical during the formative stages of the book. I would like to acknowledge my colleagues at *Library Journal,* in particular Fred Ciporen, John Berry, and Francine Fialkoff, and Nora Rawlinson at *Publishers Weekly,* for their support and encouragement. My thanks to Jeff Zaleski at *Publishers Weekly,* who was extremely helpful, offering salient advice and plenty of opportunities for commiseration as the book wound down to its conclusion. I also want to thank my immediate family—my father and sister—for their support and enthusiasm, as well as my wife's immediate family.

Both Linda and I would like to extend our gratitude to our agent, Liz Ziemska, who had the foresight and vision to believe in this book from the moment she read the proposal and who had the courage to jump into a heretofore unfamiliar genre. We also appreciate her advice and good sense on the shaping of the book. We feel extremely fortunate to have worked with Laura Wood, our editor at Harmony, whose talent and strong editorial direction and instincts help meld the book into a much more cohesive work. To

Leslie Meredith, we express our gratitude for giving us the opportunity to be part of the Crown family.

Lastly, I would like to thank my coauthor, Linda Brady, not only for being responsible for eliciting in me a higher level of consciousness, but for gently guiding me toward my soul mission and helping me fulfill it.

# CONTENTS

Our evolution toward becoming spiritual adults began thousands of years ago. You've probably heard of the Age of Aquarius. Our souls have experienced many ages as the procession of the equinox slowly moves through the astrological constellations. Every two thousand years or so—at the beginning of each new age—we have taken a major step toward heightened spiritual awareness and maturity. However, when we cling to emulating the majestic personages of previous ages—Moses in the Age of Aries (2500–300 B.C.) and Jesus Christ during the Age of Pisces (300 B.C.–A.D. 1998)—we prevent ourselves from taking advantage of this divine spiritual cognizance.

The Ages of Aries and Pisces both valued sacrifice. Becoming a martyr was, in some way, God-like. Persecution was natural. Today we see this attitude in our propensity to blame others for our misfortunes. In previous ages, because we were spiritually younger, we needed a clear-cut philosophy that would keep us on the path of righteousness. A simple paradigm evolved: to be perfect we must be good. This system yielded sharp distinctions between good and bad, right and wrong. While we learned some of the most fundamental life lessons during those historic epochs, we were also imbued with certain behaviors and habits that are no longer appropriate if we are to thrive in the emerging Age of Aquarius.

During the Piscean Age, for example, when we were unclear about our choices, we had spiritual leaders and the Bible to choose our path to righteousness for us. It was comfortable to live within this predictable, unvarying model. We led an almost childlike existence: we didn't have to think as much, and we didn't have to take responsibility. Those who strayed from the conventional, black-or-white thinking of mutual exclusivity were thought of as unsettling, unconventional, and dangerous. We learned that being perfect was the ideal and that to be Christ-like, we too needed to strive for perfection. The brass ring, after all, was heaven.

## A NEW BEGINNING

The Age of Aquarius has no need for martyrs. Instead, Aquarius has as its canons equality, personal responsibility, and self-creation. During this time we will discover that personal creation leads to internal balance. Blaming others for the misfortunes of our lives demeans our respective spirits and causes us to feel hopeless and powerless. Too often we relish the feeling of righteous indignation that comes with victimhood. Thousands of years of indoctrination and socialization are slow to change.

Taking the ultimate responsibility for our creations and learning from them is a day-to-day experience of empowerment, an approach to life drastically different from the doctrines that we accepted for so long. It's certainly easier to be a victim. But although it's natural for us to blame someone else for the condition of our life, it weakens the fabric of our being and makes us fearful.

Our lives today are increasingly complex and confusing, with a mind-numbing array of variables more diffuse than ever before. We can no longer afford to apply simple, pat solutions to the conflicts of modern life. Growing up clinging to the dusty rule that every situation can be measured in an either-or framework becomes limiting, stressful—even maddening. It's not surprising that people seek counseling simply to hear that more than one option exists. A counselor or therapist may say, "Have you thought about doing this?" and suddenly life doesn't seem as bleak. It sounds simple enough, but breaking out of the absolute mode of mutual exclusivity is terrifying, because thinking creatively means taking personal responsibility for our new options. And other people might not approve. Often we find ourselves pressured by family members, classmates, peers, coworkers, or fellow members of a congregation or tribe to conform to the norm, to stay inside the creative boundaries each respective group has set for us.

Although the Age of Aquarius officially began in January 1998, the Age of Pisces had already been winding down for some time, as evidenced by the decentralization of big government, cataclysmic changes in corporate America, and the explosion of online information and networking. The gradual integration into the medical orthodoxy of holistic practices is further evidence that the Age of Aquarius has begun to manifest itself.

Poised to enter and embrace the Age of Aquarius—the age of spiritual adulthood—we recognize that no biblical scenario will be played out for us; no spiritual leader will symbolize the meaning of this era. Being Aquarian is about being equal, about groups of people who are like-minded with a common goal, sitting in a circle with no leader. Community is the cornerstone of this new Age of Aquarius. There is no stronger proof that the Age of Aquarius has already dawned than the proliferation of the Internet, a technological breakthrough affording people the world over unprecedented networking capabilities and access to information they never could have obtained otherwise. Virtual communities organized around grassroots causes are the ultimate Aquarian symbol. It is no accident that the Age of Aquarius coincides with what has been coined by the scholarly and research community as the emerging Information Age.

## YOUR SOUL: NOT A MYSTERY BUT A SPIRITUAL COMPANION

The Aquarian Age symbolizes our ability to understand God with more maturity by integrating his power into our hearts and minds. It is an awesome responsibility, but we are preparing for it. This new time will provide us with the tools to create a life free of old restrictions. We will become cognizant of the past life memories that have kept us immobilized for so long. We will take appropriate actions to create internal balance, and to heal pain left over from the past. We will create our own divine paths to spiritual freedom by actively considering the full spectrum of possibilities that exist for each of us. We will claim our soul, not as a mystery, but as a spiritual companion. We will listen to its messages and follow its mission. Through that process, we will be co-creating our life with God. This book provides the philosophical grounding and hands-on blueprint to turn these Aquarian expectations into everyday reality.

*Discovering Your Soul Mission* offers seven fundamental goals to help you uncover and maintain your soul's own sacred covenant for a fulfilling and meaningful life:

Encourage an awareness of personal responsibility as a vehicle to self-empowerment. When we take personal responsibility, we no longer blame others; we no longer create victimization; and we are able to make lucid decisions about what we want and desire.

Create a distinction between perfection as a goal and the experience of intrinsic perfection. Cultivate an understanding that our soul always creates our life to be perfect at any given moment.

Promote an optimistic belief system that life is meaningful and full of unexpected events that lead to soul growth, and that all of life's experiences have the potential to be life-altering.

Instill a philosophy that values the soul. Recognize that our soul creates our life experience, and that if we have karmic balance, our lives will be free of paranoia, internal conflict, sadness, and fear.

Learn the meaning of the symbols we create that give us information about our karmic past.

Gain access to our soul and its mission.

Teach methods leading to greater access into the unconscious through astrological evaluation.

## HOW THIS BOOK WILL HELP YOU

*Discovering Your Soul Mission* will assist you in your pursuit of the ultimate destination of your soul road. Its collection of exercises will foster a deeper understanding of your soul as well as help you maintain your soul mission once you discover it. This book will also help prevent you from repeating past mistakes and teach you how to use your past as an elixir to heal your life. By the end of the book, you will be amazed at how much you know about your soul and its purpose for you.

*Discovering Your Soul Mission* presents applications that will spur you to make the most of your soul's energy, to keep your soul and personality in alignment daily, as well as to explore your relationships and experiences symbolically. In order to maximize the techniques and practicums designed to help you integrate your soul into your life on a daily basis, we suggest you purchase a blank journal that has special meaning to you. The journal will enable you to actively participate in the exercises, and review what you've learned. You are now an active participant in this book. Your soul is with you, helping you glean the information necessary for you to discover your soul mission.

Although this book represents our best collaborative effort, we felt it necessary and entirely appropriate to cast the book in Linda's first-person voice in order to truly relate the intimacy of her client relationships and the salience with which she espouses her philosophy.

Thank you for allowing us the opportunity to continue our own soul missions. As we help you reframe your old beliefs, we are rethinking our own. As we help you see your karmic past, we are reviewing our own. As we inspire you to seek your soul mission, we are pursuing our own. Our commitment is to be as clear and as concise as we can. We welcome you to make whatever commitment is necessary, so that reading *Discovering Your Soul Mission* becomes a personal and transformational experience for you.

—Linda Brady and Evan St. Lifer
September 1998

When people come to me for a counseling session, they usually want answers to their life questions: "Should I change my career? Why can't I find the right relationship? Why am I unhappy? What is my purpose in life?" It doesn't take me long to help them realize the fundamental reason they've sought my help: to discover their soul's direction and align their personality with it in order to create harmony in their lives.

Through my use of karmic astrology, I serve as a soul translator, to remind them about what their soul has created for them in their life and why. I am not a predictive astrologer; I will not tell anyone's future. I will, however, use an astrological chart to gain information about their past, their relationships, and their soul mission. As a practicing astrologer for almost twenty years, I am constantly amazed at how perfectly an astrological chart captures the feelings, concerns, memories, hopes, and desires of the people I serve. As a commentator, I make no judgments and offer no advice that isn't already present in their chart.

For thousands of years astrologers have read charts, determined planetary positions, and analyzed how the alignment of the stars affects people's lives. In fact, astrology's origins can be traced as far back as 2000 B.C. to Babylonia, in what is now the southeastern portion of Iraq. To this day, people continue to go to astrologers in the hope of regaining some control over their lives by hearing how their life will be played out: to brace themselves for a malady or to prime themselves for incipient good fortune. Implicit in those meetings is the immutability of that future. Their fate is supposedly sealed, written in stone. Nothing can be altered; they can only anticipate what will befall them. That the power of predictive astrology originated from some external force in the heavens above fits neatly into our fundamental religious belief that God was an external power separate and apart from us.

Traditional astrology's value to us lies in its ability to help us understand ourselves. But the practice implies that our life choices are made by someone or something else. Traditional astrology maintains that our chart—with its houses, planets, and aspects—is the determining factor in our lives. This deterministic claim has led to astrology being mocked in recent times. But astrology—as a symbolic language—helps cultivate a deeper understanding of the connection between the inner and outer worlds—nature and the heavens. As Will Keepin, Ph.D, says, "Astrology [is ridiculed] because it bridges the implicate and explicate orders more clearly than any other esoteric science that I know of."

Karmic astrology is about making informed and expanded choices, on the assumption that our soul is the primary force behind us forging our destiny and is never-ending. While traditional astrology implies that we abdicate responsibility for what befalls us to the cosmos, karmic astrology equips us with the understanding to shape our life the way we want it to be.

On her audiotape series "Inner and Outer Space," Caroline W. Casey explains that astrology is a language of self-possession, revitalizing and connecting us to all creation. She says astrology can help us unleash our own distinct energies so we can be creative agents for positive change in the world.

> "Men at some time are masters of their fates:
> The fault, dear Brutus, is not in our stars
> But in ourselves, that we are underlings."
> William Shakespeare, *Julius Caesar*

| Traditional Astrology | Karmic Astrology |
|---|---|
| 1. planet centered | 1. person centered |
| 2. predictive | 2. creative |
| 3. event oriented | 3. process oriented |
| 4. fate | 4. free will |
| 5. implies external power | 5. implies self-empowerment |
| 6. scientific | 6. multisensory |
| 7. Old Age/representing an external God | 7. New Age/representing the God in all of us |

Perhaps the best metaphor for comparing traditional astrology with karmic astrology comes from Casey's citation of the late quantum physicist and Albert Einstein colleague David Bohm. An airplane, Bohm said, uses radio waves to guide it, but the radio waves do not cause the plane to turn. The radio waves simply supply the pilot with information upon which he or she must act. Similarly in karmic astrology, unlike the common perception of traditional astrology, the planet and stars in the firmament don't force fate upon us, causing us to behave in certain, deterministic ways. On the contrary, they provide us with symbols that feed our intuition, helping to connect us to our soul path.

## ALIGNING YOUR PERSONALITY WITH YOUR SOUL

Each of us has a personality with a corresponding road to travel and a destination to reach within our given lifetime. The journey will be filled with relationships, work, challenges and obstacles, trials and triumphs. Each of us also has a soul with its own destination and a road to follow, a road that began in the distant past and will continue forever. However, the soul has a plan, a purpose for our personality in this life. The soul's intention is to assist the personality in its life journey, to help it reach the destination that the soul intends for it.

Too often these roads are divergent. The experiences of our lives—enacted with our families, our relationships, and sometimes our jobs—often influence our personality's direction, sometimes causing it to stray or simply veer off altogether from the path our soul intends for it. Most of us, in fact, are beset with inner conflicts arising from a clash between our soul and our personality, a phenomenon that can manifest itself as sorrow, depression, anger, a gnawing unfulfillment, or deep emptiness. The challenge for us, as budding spiritual adults, is to find the soul road on which our personality can prosper. I call this process soul/personality integration, and I have dedicated my life to understanding it.

My own personality path, for instance, is to be a loner, a recluse, venturing out only to teach astrology. My personality would be very content if I were a traveling astrologer: doing a quick session here and there with no lasting relationships would be just fine. But my soul path is quite different. Its mission is to create and commit to long-term relationships, and to inspire my students to deal with their spiritual and emotional lives. For my soul, there is no being a recluse, no being alone.

My evolution into spiritual adulthood began when I starting learning astrology. I was trained in experimental psychology and behavior modification. I have a bachelor's degree in psychology and a master's in educational administration. I believed in what could be measured, analyzed, and charted. I also believed in Christ, the Episcopal church, and its mysteries in a childlike, naive way. I did not question; I had faith. But life has a way of intruding on faith, and my faith did not stand the test.

I began my study of astrology in an earnest quest to disprove it, but I found instead that it gave me answers. Even more important, it gave me questions. The idea that the stars wielded the energy to create the perfect chart for me had always made me uncomfortable: it meant that I was not in control of my life and that I could blame the stars for my problems, including my struggles with my weight. (I have a moon in Pisces—it loves rich foods.) As my understanding of astrology grew, however, the answer became quite clear: my soul had created my astrological chart. My soul knew the symbolic meanings of all the astrological signs and planets and the relationships between them. It had created an astrological mandala to provide me with the tools I needed to experience my life.

My soul knew my past; it had been there. My soul knew what this life needed to be as a continuation of what was left from other lives. My soul, in other words, understood my karma. Although this word has been maligned, ridiculed, and misunderstood, *karma* has a relatively simple meaning for me. It means if I take an action, I set up a reaction. We have all heard this rephrased in the axioms "What goes around, comes around" and "We reap what we sow." It is an energetic, universal, and physical law. Karma continues from one life to another. If I betray you in a past life, I can expect that you will betray me in our next one.

Karma is complete only when we have balanced our previous actions through consciousness, commitment, and new actions. Our soul knows these situations and relationships and will create opportunities for us to resolve them. Our astrological chart, created by our soul, provides us with information about these karmic experiences as a spiritual reminder, a road map to understanding.

Even with all of these philosophical insights, I remember the conflicts I had when I first began to entertain the real possibility that all my life experiences were perfect and for my ultimate good. My personality and ego ranted and raved for days. I was a litany of "what about this" and "what about that." I thought about the scores of hardships and tragedies, the rampant pain and injustice in our world. Why would a loving God and compassionate soul put us through such trauma? The answer becomes more apparent when we see our lives as part of a larger whole.

Sometimes, in order to create a karmic balance and to rectify a past life injustice, we "create" experiencing pain. I have often thought of the childhood and life that Adolf Hitler would have to create to begin his process of karmic retribution. Without karmic understanding, the tragedies of life—pain, disease, accidents, violence, loss, and betrayal—appear arbitrary. With it, life is fair. Always. We can't whitewash an agonizing experience, but if we are aware that it will yield us a better understanding, a better sense of why, it doesn't seem as arbitrary.

My soul was in the process of teaching me something that my ego did not want to understand. I had spent forty years believing that I was basically imperfect—a belief fostered by my family and society at large—and that the only way to change that was to strive for perfection. It never occurred to me that perfection could exist at any given moment. I had spent eighteen years in schools that had measured me by a strict criterion. I knew the ecstasy of straight A's and the agony of a D in high school chemistry. Now my beliefs were in serious conflict. How would I motivate myself to excellence with a conviction that I was imperfect?

Becoming bored with the same conflict, I decided to review what striving for perfection had really done in my life. What I learned shocked me: striving for perfection had taught me procrastination and feelings of inadequacy, failure, and fear. It had put me on a treadmill, always searching and never finding. It had taught me to value the end product and disregard the process. I made a decision to let the old belief die. Perfection goals are not so perfect! I transformed this old belief into a commitment to being the best that I could be, valuing the process of life, and entrusting my soul to create my life perfectly.

What is the perfection that my soul wants me to see in its many creations? How would that experience serve me? When I was 31, I decided to go back to school and earn a doctorate in psychology. I was accepted at a fine university and held a great evening position at a local hospital. I was poised to advance my career. Two months before I was to begin my Ph.D., however, I was involved in a head-on automobile collision. The accident left me with a back injury and vision problems. I was unable to start school in the fall.

During that time my surrogate father died, I separated from my second husband, and I sank into a severe depression—it was not a "perfect" three months. The truth is it was the most crucial, most important turning point of my life. After I recovered from both my mental and my physical wounds, my soul led me back to an institution for the mentally handicapped where I had worked several years before. I became a diagnostic specialist and later vice principal. I saw my first aura there. I began my process of understanding reincarnation there. I met my third husband and soul mate there. I became an astrologer while I was there. My soul created that automobile accident to change my life's direction and to put me on the path to my soul mission.

Think about your own life. Try to recall one particularly painful experience. Feel the emotions that the memory evokes. Now ask yourself the following questions: Why did I bring this experience into my life? What opportunity for growth and awareness did it provide me? What did it teach me about myself or someone else? How did it change my life for the better? By asking yourself these sensitive questions, note how your perspective changes, and think about some of the new insights you may have developed.

## Your Soul

Your soul is the common thread that weaves all of your personalities from your past and present lives together, the multidimensional part of you that transcends this life, that exceeds the here and now. Your soul is your continuity expert, ensuring that each of the personalities from various lifetimes performs its essential role in your grand drama. It supplies you with the past life link you need in order to understand your karmic responsibilities in this life, and it helps you carry them out.

> *"The soul is the captain and ruler of the life of mortals."*
> Sallust

Your soul provides you with a plan, revealing it to you through dreams, symbols, your unconscious mind, your relationships, and your experiences. The soul holds the reason for your personality to exist and grow. It is the essence of your spiritual core, the energy of truth and love unfettered by the external stimuli that affect your personality.

> *"Now I lay me down to sleep,*
> *I pray the Lord my soul to keep;*
> *If I should die before I wake,*
> *I pray the Lord my soul to take."*
> Prayer from
> *The New England Primer,* 1784

While we have become inured to reciting the words *soul* and *spirit* in our prayers seemingly by rote, their meanings continue to be misunderstood. The two words mean the same thing, but religions tend to use the word *spirit* in the context of the afterlife, while *soul* has a more secular usage in the context of living a fulfilling and meaningful life. Soul/personality integration is about improving the quality of your life now by embracing and nurturing your soul on a daily basis.

> *"Either death is a state of nothingness and utter unconsciousness, or as men say, there is a change and migration of the soul from this world to another.... Now if death be of such a nature, I say that to die is to gain; for eternity is then only a single night."*
>
> Plato

### What We Know About the Soul

Generally, the soul is:
- Immortal: It is energy that cannot be created or destroyed.
- Perfect: It is our gift from God and is intrinsically connected to the Universal Order.
- Love: It is the opportunity during our lifetime to change fear to love.
- Our spiritual creator: It provides perfect experiences for our karmic growth.
- A filter: Through it information comes from the higher realms.
- Transcendent: It is transcendent both before and after this lifetime.

Personally, the soul is:
- Your spiritual companion and best friend.
- Your creator of your soul mission.
- Your guide to directing you to your soul's mission.
- Your continuity expert, keeping track of your past and creating your future.

## Your Personality

Your personality is the specific lens through which you see your current lifetime. Its lucidity and focus are constantly being adjusted almost instantaneously by your vast and varied experiences. Through this lens you react to the world and make judgments about it. It is the part of you that responds, often impulsively, to the ebbs and flows of life, at various turns fortified and scarred by the ups and downs of your emotions. Your personality is your social and emotional template, helping you distinguish who you are. It encompasses your thoughts, morality, feelings, senses, motivations, and dreams, and it carries the indelible stamp of your family history.

On an unconscious level, your personality links you to your seminal belief system learned from your parents; the hidden child within you; memories and pain not dealt with in your conscious life; and your night dreams, fears, and phobias. At this deep level, it also remembers personalities you've had from other lives and important information about who and what you have been. These memories of the thoughts, actions, and feelings of previous personalities share a common thread with you now, and they become the source of much of your unconscious motivation, impulse, angst, and relationship challenges. Unlike your soul, your personality does not transcend this life.

*"Your personality is that part of you that was born into, lives within, and will die within time. To be a human and have a personality are the same thing. Your personality, like your body, is the vehicle of your evolution."*
Gary Zukav, *Seat of the Soul*

## COSMIC TWO-BY-FOURS

Suppose you lose your job. Your spouse or partner leaves. You get sick. Your journey on the personality road winds to a crawl. You get scared, stuck, and stressed out. You get depressed. The skills that delivered you to the roadblock in the first place don't help. Nothing works. Your personality doesn't know what your soul requires—it only knows that it doesn't want you to change, which leaves you mired in a powerful soul/personality conflict. You should view this turbulence, rattling you to the core, as a signal that you've arrived at a junction. Now you can discover solutions to issues that have long vexed you, by using an approach that differs drastically from the one that delivered you to the roadblock in the first place.

It is usually at this crisis point that people show up at my office for the first time. Imagine their surprise when I smile and say, "Congratulations." I am, in fact, reframing conflict into opportunity. Their souls have adroitly created the necessary roadblocks, with perfect timing. These obstacles are their souls' way of providing them with a deeper awareness of the other road they need to travel.

I frequently refer to these roadblocks as cosmic two-by-fours, which are meant to get our attention and prepare us for a major karmic insight. A cosmic two-by-four is actually an experience created for us by our soul to stop us in our tracks and draw our attention to a behavior or habit we were unable to detect previously.

According to Swiss psychologist Carl Jung, the more we repress a behavior, the more likely we will be to create the behavior outside ourselves as chaos or conflict. A cosmic two-by-four is my name for the chaos and conflict to which Jung referred. It is our soul's way of giving us a new perspective on our life, enabling us to see what heretofore had been invisible. The impact of a cosmic two-by-four varies in severity from a reminding tap on the shoulder to what feels like a mind-splitting whack across the head. Since most of us are not conditioned to notice the smaller, less pronounced taps, cosmic two-by-fours become increasingly powerful until one finally gets our attention. Experiencing a cosmic two-by-four affords us the opportunity to stop, collect ourselves, and hopefully alter our behavior. My husband Michael describes the more extreme instances we encounter as "getting our worlds stopped."

When you become cognizant of how untenable your current path is, and when you realize there might be a more fulfilling road to travel, you are ready to discover your soul's purpose on a conscious level. As you read on, you will not only discover that road to fulfillment—your raison d'être—but you'll learn how to embrace it and live it every day.

# PART I

## Soul Creation: Taking Control of Your Life

# CHAPTER 1

# Creating Our Own Lives

Do you believe that you possess some measure of responsibility for the way the experiences and events in your life unfold? When I ask my clients if they "create their own lives," more often than not they say yes. After all, personal accountability is a spiritually correct philosophy currently on the rise. However, when they experience a specific tragedy in their own lives—a divorce, the death of a loved one, the loss of a job—many of the same clients respond by saying, "But I didn't create *that*."

A general misperception exists about the theory of creation. Many believe it is a conscious and intellectual experience: creating goals and committing to them, as well as planning proactive stratagems for organizing and affirming them. Some of us believe—and many recent books reinforce the point—that if we visualize a positive outcome, create a mantra and concentrate on it consistently, and take actions that support the creation, we will get what we want.

Others believe that life creation is an unconscious process whose rudiments lie in our psychology. Jung, for instance, believed that we tend to repress and store in our unconscious the emotions and beliefs with which we are the most uncomfortable. Later, at a time it deems appropriate, our unconscious mind brings those averse feelings to the fore of our conscious mind and creates them externally. In other words, Jung said, we project an unconscious part of ourselves onto the people in our lives. For instance, if you've repressed all of your aggressive anger, then you would project that aggressive anger onto one of your close friends or a family member, whom you would see as having those same aggressive qualities, so that you could learn from them. While our unconscious, intellect, and emotions all play important roles in creating our lives, I believe they are complements to the fundamental role that our soul plays in life creation. Why do we create our lives to be the way they are, with their distinct experiences and relationships? Because our soul yearns for us to have that life in order to learn new lessons and evolve to a higher spiritual order. Soul creation is the practice of taking ultimate responsibility for the way our lives transpire. Our souls create exactly the lives we need.

The difference between our intellect, our emotions, and our soul, however, is that our intellect and emotions are related only to our personality and its current life experiences. The task of creating our life comes from our soul, a dimension that transcends this life and its permutations.

> *"Welcome, O life! I go to encounter for the millionth time the reality of experience and to forge in the smithy of my soul the uncreated conscience of my race."*
> James Joyce, *Portrait of the Artist as a Young Man*

I know how difficult it can be to distinguish the domain of our souls from the orientations and motivations of our minds and bodies; I see this challenge almost every day in my work with my clients and interns. A workshop I conducted for an AIDS support group in Washington, D.C., in 1987 made me painfully aware of how difficult it can be to discern the role of the soul in creation. Ironically, the surge in interest in the mind/body connection has somehow made this process even more confusing.

The AIDS support group consisted of nine men—all infected with HIV—who had been using a holistic orientation to treat their illness. They had adopted macrobiotic diets and used visualization and meditative techniques as part of their belief and exploration into the mind/body connection and its healing potential. They met on a weekly basis to discuss and review the progress being made in alternative treatments.

In my workshop I explained to them that what was missing in their mind/body philosophy was the understanding of their souls' creation of reality. Our soul creates our life with a certain purpose, I said, and thus there were reasons why they had "created" their illness. In other words, I continued, our soul presents us with life possibilities, and sometimes illness is one of those possibilities. I posited that having AIDS was an event that each of their respective souls had needed them to experience. Having AIDS enabled each of them to meet new people that their souls wanted them to meet and to follow a path that they wouldn't have taken otherwise.

They reacted angrily, taking my brief explanation to mean that they had "created" AIDS consciously, a notion that would only add to their guilt and shame and further damage their already fragile physical and emotional well-being. They thought I was implying they had deliberately brought on their own illnesses. They could not tolerate that belief, which they found demeaning and offensive. I understood why these young men were so upset—and justifiably so. The medical community, and to a greater degree the media, have perpetuated the notion that AIDS is a behavioral by-product of promiscuous gay male sex and/or intravenous drug use. Since contracting the disease is sometimes tied to behavior, they were deeply offended at what they thought was my inference that they had purposely gone out and contracted AIDS.

It was not their fault, I told them. They shouldn't feel guilty about having AIDS, and they shouldn't judge their previous behaviors that might have led to their contracting the disease. I spoke about the soul and the reasons why it might create illness. As soon as they were able to detach themselves from their shame and guilt and understand their souls' respective motivations from a karmic standpoint—that their souls were perhaps balancing past life experiences with their encounter with AIDS in this life—they were able to see the bigger picture and were more receptive to my message.

"If our souls are loving and compassionate, why would they do such a terrible thing?" they wanted to know, a question all my clients ask when confronted with tragedy. I explained that as soon as we are better able to comprehend our lives in the context of a grander scheme, we begin to see our experiences not as good or bad but as inordinately fair lessons that our souls need in order to evolve to a higher order. I wasn't seeking to diminish the emotional and physical ramifications of AIDS. Rather, I was trying to explain how they could make some spiritual sense of their disease: how to learn and grow from the experience, to consider what impact it has had on others, and what has happened in their lives as a result. Difficult lives are not punishments, but rather opportunities for astonishingly spiritual growth.

> *"We're here to participate joyfully in the sorrows of the world."*
>
> Joseph Campbell

A few of the men began relaying stories of powerful transformational experiences that they had encountered since finding out they were infected with the disease. One of the men, Tim, 27, said that getting AIDS was "the most significant thing that ever happened" to him. He offered this observation after discovering that his soul had "so many things in mind for me." He was a vice president of a Washington, D.C., bank and he hated being a banker. After contracting AIDS, he left his job to become an artist.

Most important, the disease allowed Tim to become more honest and open with his family. Prior to becoming HIV positive, his relationship with his family had been serviceable at best. It's not that they didn't know he was gay; they just didn't readily acknowledge it. His relationship with them was safe and anesthetized: his parents buffered themselves from the pain and disappointment of having a gay son. Once he got sick and his mother and father realized they might lose him, their attitude changed. Their burdensome judgments over who Tim had become and the choices he had made dissipated, and they began to cherish him for what he was: their "only boy." Now he is more emotionally connected to his parents than ever before. They discuss treatments with him and are curious to know more about AIDS. His father makes periodic trips to the nearby college's medical library to research the disease. Tim talked about how the disease had liberated him: he and the other men began to see how getting AIDS was leading them to their respective soul missions. Considering their future with this new philosophical outlook gave the men power, hope, and a sense of completion.

Another man from the AIDS support group, John, had subsequent sessions with me; he recounts the progress he has made and how his life has been different since participating in the workshop:

*Shortly before I began working with Linda, I learned I was HIV positive. I was twenty-eight, single, and working in a job that neither challenged me nor helped me realize my potential. I was depressed and generally feeling defeated and fatalistic toward life. My doctor had me convinced that I should wrap things up and prepare to die in less than two years (a common diagnosis for someone with HIV in 1987).*

*By learning and adopting the fundamentals of soul creation, of taking responsibility for all the misfortune in my life—including AIDS—I was able to see that I held the choices I needed to turn these things around. I had to make changes in my personal and family relationships, own my sexuality, redesign my finances and career thinking, and in general adopt a thought process and life philosophy that, at the time, scared the hell out of me. I had to learn to jump off cliffs that were higher than I could possibly imagine. I had to take the risk of revealing myself not only to those I encountered, but to myself as well, and that was the most difficult part. "Creating my own reality" meant learning to love this new image of myself.*

*In time I learned how to let my intuition guide me to people and situations that I never guessed were out there. I found new work, new relationships, and new ways to manifest my creativity as well as a profound understanding of how my world worked. I am now thirty-six. I haven't died of AIDS. In fact I have empowered myself and many others to live far beyond our medical deadlines. My immune system is stronger than ever due to my growth and understanding of alternative therapies and self-healing techniques. I have been in a relationship for more than six years. I live in Tucson and look out of my home to mountain views and magnificent sunsets. I do the kind of work I want and don't limit my options. I had spent most of my life trapped inside myself not knowing if I was crazy or not, unclear about who I was and what I had to offer. Not anymore.*

*I had to allow myself to act intuitively and fully trust that the risk of speaking to anyone from the soul and heart was worth taking in order to find the joy that is available to all of us. The healing from this is a great reward, the prosperity endless. However, this journey is a great challenge, and it isn't over yet. I am just over the first big hill; and with any luck I will find many more. I have created a splendorous and expansive reality. I didn't give up and surrender to the great weakness or spirit that sabotages us. I didn't die from AIDS.*

> *"You want to live your longest healthiest life? Find your way, your path. Be in touch with your soul."*
> Bernie Siegel, M.D.

## SEEING SERENDIPITY

We often become discouraged in the pursuit of our goals and dreams when we fail to exact the results we had envisioned. When things don't go our way, we stop striving, unceremoniously cutting short what could have been a fulfilling and meaningful journey. We turn a deaf ear to the realm of possibility.

Unless we accept serendipity as an invaluable link to our potential, we are hard pressed to live with verve, to celebrate and revel in our soul missions. Good things seem to happen to some people, while we sit on the sidelines. But who are those people who land the big job that we can't seem to get, who have the intensely passionate relationship that we envy? They are the ones who have faith that something good will come from serendipitous events, whether it be a learning experience or a positive twist of fate. But when we are paralyzed by our own fear of failure, limited by our own internal rules, we exude negative energy and obsess over why things didn't turn out the way we planned.

Serendipity is an unexpected outcome that stems from taking an action. The only way we can adopt serendipity as a personal creed is to let go of committing ourselves emotionally to a single desired outcome. The outcome we expect comes from our intellect, our conscious mind. Too often we are restricted by the myopia of our intellect, by its willingness to accept only one anticipated scenario. Looking at the spectrum of choices with our soul allows us to diversify our expectations, to realize that the possibility of the unexpected—with some adjustments—can be better than anything we imagined.

I agree with today's cadre of self-help experts who say we need to set goals and take decisive action through vision and commitment. The key to ensuring success, however, hinges not on the exact result itself but on our ability to learn from and stay pliant during the process, no matter what the outcome. Successful people gain by rebuilding, revamping, and reconfiguring. We may see them as lucky, but they've been busy building on their own serendipity, embracing it as a springboard to accomplishment. So remember: stay receptive to other possibilities.

By enhancing the communication between your personality and soul, you are creating a conversation that gives you an expanded positive view of the meaning of your life's experiences. Here's an example. Your boss calls you into his office. His face has a look of urgency that you haven't seen before. You sense this isn't going to be a pleasant chat. You sit down, and he adjusts his tie, and without looking directly at you, he tells you that he's "letting you go." You're fired. You've heard him, but you deny it inside. You feel scared. Your mind races. You think about the new house you just bought. How will you pay the mortgage and the kids' bills? Now you're angry. How dare he fire you! You've always been a very conscientious worker, totally committed to the company. Then you begin to feel guilty and ashamed: *What could I have done wrong to deserve this?*

The range of emotions—anger, fear, shame, guilt, embarrassment—that flow forth is typical of your personality's response to a traumatic event, in this case, the news you've been fired. Now imagine you are practiced at bringing your soul's perspective to your experiences. Here's how your soul might orchestrate a conversation with your personality:

*I know you're really upset about this, as well you should be. It's okay that you're intensely emotional about being fired. But let's start to work on finding the meaning, purpose, and serendipity of the situation. Try to answer these questions. It's all right if you're too upset to answer all of them now. Just try to ask yourself these questions, and you can figure out the answers later:*

- *Why have I (your soul) created this situation for you, and what can you learn from it?*
- *How will this experience ultimately help you achieve your soul mission?*
- *What is the possible serendipity of this challenge?*

## WHY WE HAVE TROUBLE BELIEVING IN SOUL CREATION

Like the men in the AIDS support group, most of us have difficulty coming to terms with the fact that the spiritual part of us has a role in creating an event or relationship that knocks the wind out of us. However, our souls play just as essential a role in our encounters with the fantastic and the enchanting. Again, to reiterate: our souls base an experience not on whether it is good or bad, but on what lessons we can learn from it.

*"I only believe what I can see.*
*Or what I know is true.*
*Argument against what I can see:*
*Electricity, emotions."*
                                        Linda Brady, 1997

Soul creation is an effective process that helps us eliminate feelings of victimization. Yet many of us still experience those feelings on a daily basis. I have been engaging in soul creation conversations with myself every day for the last fifteen years, but on occasion, even I can't help feeling like a victim—one of the most basic and reflexive of human emotions—when I feel I've been misunderstood or disrespected.

That's why you must practice being aware of soul creation every minute of every hour of every day. As you ingrain it into your belief system as a prevailing philosophy, you will minimize your tendency to react like a victim. While I acknowledge that it can be tiring to maintain such an intense self-awareness, it's important for you to keep practicing soul creation. You will stumble, and like all of us, you will have bad days when you can't help but feel victimized. However, the end product—the quality of your life and the degree to which you are happy and fulfilled—will take care of itself.

Darlene went through a period when she figured that the calamities in her life entitled her to feel like a victim. However, her ability to adopt a belief in soul creation helped her embrace a different, more liberating path:

*In 1975 at the age of twenty-five, I felt like a victim of the world, powerless to alter my life circumstances. On some level, I was waiting for the money pressures, heart trouble, lung trouble, lower back trouble, diabetes, negativity, depression, and boredom that were part of my family history to be mine. In October of that year, my mother hung herself in our back yard. She was forty-eight. Later that same year my fiancé ended our five-year relationship, and my grandmother had passed on the year before on New Year's Day. Now I had even more ammunition for believing the world was out to get me. I had some great excuses for self-pity. Who could blame me?*

*For a number of years I was resistant to the belief that we create what happens to us, because it meant I would have to change. This new philosophy asked that I find my soul's direction and purpose, commit to it, and live life in that direction. When I finally began to adopt creation theory, these changes were quite scary and often confusing. It meant a change in my identity and the way that I had lived my life until then. No more excuses! No more blame! It wasn't easy. During that confusing and transitional time, it was easy to accept the creation of the "good" things—not so easy to "own" my creations of the painful. Now my life would be my personal responsibility.*

*Two months after I had begun working with Linda, I was in an automobile accident. I called her from my hospital bed, expecting, I suppose, to be told that this would be an exception to the creation "rule." After a few minutes of making sure I was okay, she asked me the big question: "Why do you think your soul created this, Darlene?" I didn't know the answer then. It took weeks of reflection and struggle. Finally I came to understand that the accident represented a turning point for me. It was an opportunity to truly practice what I had been learning. I created that accident to learn in a powerful way that my soul did, in fact, create my life. It was a chance to leap out of my personality and ego and leap into the unknown abyss of what was best for my soul. Staying in old patterns, although familiar and comfortable, would have been even more painful. I took the risk and accepted my soul's creation of the accident. I healed very quickly, did not blame the elderly gentleman who was driving the car that hit my car, and learned a valuable lesson.*

*From there, events in my life flowed more easily, and I felt a tremendous sense of freedom. I was no longer stuck. It has been fifteen years since I came to realize that I have the power to create exactly what I want from life. It required only that I decide what I wanted. I finally learned to see obstacles as challenges. I embrace even the most painful experiences, because it means I am alive and doing my soul's work. I see my relationships, my work, and my health as conscious choices. I approach life from a more aware and empowered perspective. I am no longer a victim. I have inner peace.*

## Your Soul's Impact

Answering some of these questions will help you to see the more obvious instances in your life where your soul has made a palpable impact.

- Have you ever had an experience that was so weird that you couldn't explain it?
- Have you ever felt déjà vu?
- Have you ever known someone was going to call you and they did?
- Have you ever felt watched over or protected?
- Have you ever felt the presence of someone who has died?
- Have you ever heard a little voice inside you say something that you had never contemplated before?
- Have you ever felt a gentle caress when no one was there?
- Have you ever taken a wrong turn that led you to an unexpected experience?
- Have you ever felt energy from a person, a plant, or an animal?
- Have you ever felt strongly attracted or repulsed by a person you just met for no logical reason?
- Have you ever felt strongly attracted or repulsed by a color, a gem, or a flower?
- Have you ever felt irresistibly drawn to a country, or a time in history, for no reason?
- Did you have any childhood experiences that were unusual?
- Have you ever just known that a situation or a person was "right" for you and acted on it?
- Have you ever felt deep emotions about something without a reason?
- Have you ever been stopped from doing something that you later discovered would have been harmful to you?

Cliff, 38, had been referred to me by a longtime client of mine, Wendy. She had told me he would see me but warned me he would be "tough." He didn't believe in religion, astrology, or anything else. But Wendy was worried about him: he was at the tail end of a painful separation from his girlfriend, Sylvia, and was not handling it well. He had seen a psychiatrist for a few weeks, but he felt the therapy wasn't working. He was depressed, hopeless, and angry.

Cliff made an appointment with me a few days later. As he sat down on the sofa in my office, he smiled wanly and said: "I'm really doing this under protest, you know. Wendy wouldn't stop nagging me until I had at least one session with you." I retorted, "So I have one shot to convince you of something. Okay, Cliff, I'll take that challenge. Tell me how you felt when you met Sylvia. Your first impression, your first thoughts."

Cliff paused a moment and then said. "You know, I felt like I had met her before. I felt so strongly about her. I can't believe it's over. I felt like I had finally found the woman I would live with forever."

When I asked him about his parents, he said that his mother had died when he was 21. "Have you felt her presence since she died?" I asked.

"Not really," he answered, "but I always wear her wedding ring on my small finger. Sometimes I swear I can feel a gentle wind gliding over it. I'm sure it's my imagination, but it happens sometimes."

"Cliff, this may sound like a strange question for me to ask, but is your favorite color lavender?" I knew from his chart that lavender was his soul color.

Cliff was befuddled and agitated. I thought he was going to get up and walk out.

I reached over and touched his arm. "Lavender is your soul color, Cliff, and judging from the way you look right now, it has some significance to you, doesn't it?"

Cliff poised himself, straightened his body, and answered, "It was my mother's favorite color. I made sure the flowers at her funeral were predominantly lavender. I planted lilacs in my backyard to remind me of her. This is getting very weird. I really don't know how to feel about any of this."

"Cliff, you said when you walked in that you only believed in what you could see. I'm trying to help you realize that there are

other things in your life that have been very powerful and important that have nothing to do with physical reality. The experiences
that you recounted have to do with an energetic or spiritual reality.
They are just as significant, just as real as anything that you can see
or touch. We could hypothesize that they were all orchestrated by
your soul, couldn't we?" I asked.

Cliff answered a little haltingly. "Okay, so let's say I agree that
it's a possibility. How could it help me?" he asked.

"Well, for one thing it could help you understand why the color
lavender is so important," I said. "Understanding your soul could
provide you with inner peace. It could help you deal with your
depression, lessen your conflicts, and make sense of what has happened in your life. It could also help you make sense of your relationship with Sylvia. Why it felt so familiar and why it ended. You
might even find out what other karmic experiences you've had
with Sylvia that led to this breakup. Wouldn't that help you right
now?"

Cliff nodded. "I am in so much pain that anything you can do to
help would be appreciated. I can tell you that for some reason I do
feel better. I'm willing to give this a try."

We scheduled our next meeting, and Cliff left a little happier
and more at ease than when he arrived. In the ensuing sessions we
concentrated on his painful breakup with Sylvia. We worked
together for more than a year on a regular basis. Three years later I
met his new love and did her chart. Now I counsel them together as
clients. They are committed to each other and their soul missions.

## SOUL CREATION AND CHANGE

Belief in soul creation challenges not only two thousand years
of history but even, to some extent, our principles and morality.
Many of us will consider migrating from the status quo only when
our circumstances have become so horrible that anything would be
better. Having nothing to lose sometimes gives us everything to
gain, because at that point our fear of change has diminished and
change is the only thing that will transform the situation.

I have clients whom I've sent home, requesting they not call me again until their lives are unbearable. As heartless as this may sound, many of us won't even entertain the notion of making changes in our lives until we reach such a point. How often have you heard about a smoker who passionately adheres to his right to smoke, until he almost dies of a heart attack? Most of us have the same unhealthy tendency to cling to what is familiar until it almost ruins us. Yet to achieve our soul mission, we must embrace change—and to understand soul creation, we must practice it.

One new client, Ann, was referred to me by her sister. Ann was 40 years old and continued to live with her mother in the same house she was born in. Her most distinguishing characteristic was her reticence. She was so nervous to be in our first session alone that her sister had to stay with us. Through her sister I learned that she was still living at home, caring for her elderly mother. Her mother was relatively healthy for a woman of 70 but endured occasional spells of vertigo. In fact, about ten years earlier Ann had been offered a promising job in a neighboring state. She had wanted to take the job but turned it down when her mother complained that her vertigo was worsening.

Ann took an office job near her home instead. She spent her free time watching television with her mother. Her sister was worried that she was wasting away her life, but Ann said she was perfectly content. In fact, Ann was comfortable and felt safe. She admitted to hating anything that disrupted her routine. She listened politely when I described her soul mission but had no response. Surprisingly, however, she made another appointment. At the third session I suggested to her that she not come back. I finally elicited a minor response: she was surprised by my comment. I told her that her life was not difficult enough for her to want to alter anything, and that her greatest fear was of change. When she was better prepared to take action, I would love to see her, I said.

It took Ann two years to return. Her mother had met a man, and they were going to be married. They had asked Ann, in so many words, to move out. She was devastated and scared—and furious with her mother. Now we could make some progress. She listened to what I said about her soul mission and began to create her own freedom by leaving her comfort zones and moving into the world. She planned her first real vacation, a critical step in gaining the courage to finally embrace her own experiences and independence. She soon overcame her fear of leaving home, unshackling herself from the only life she knew. Her progress helped her overcome her anger toward her mother. She was brighter, more vibrant than I had ever seen her. She received a promotion at work.

In my own life my fledgling belief in soul creation was put to the test in 1980. My boyfriend Michael and I had been living together for two years and had just moved into our first house. Then one night Michael told me he had had an affair. I felt as if I had been thrown from a horse. Michael was my soul mate. For twelve hours I cried and screamed at him for doing this to me. The pain that I felt was unbearable: I was angry, scared, and confused.

I remember sitting in our backyard, staring at an old oak tree, silently screaming at my soul. The whole concept of soul creation was new to me then; I was just beginning to understand it, and now my soul had done this. It was so unfair, I couldn't stand it. The next morning Michael reluctantly went to work. I was alone with my pain. I sat for a long time trying to make sense of it all. In the end I finally understood that my soul had created this crisis so I could prove to myself that I truly believed what I said about soul creation. I profoundly changed that day, my new practice safe from my own doubt.

I canceled my evening appointments, grabbed my dog Ti, and drove to the hospital where Michael worked. We met in the picnic area. I told him that I knew my soul had created this situation and that although it would take a while, I would figure out all the details of that creation. Our relationship survived, and we were married six months later. Our marriage is strong today because of that moment. We both live in our relationship now, knowing that we are soul mates and confident that our souls will continue to provide us with experiences to strengthen it.

My belief in my soul as the creator of my reality and as my spiritual companion got me through that experience with Michael, and it will get me through others. Change and new experiences are what our souls require to help us migrate to the exciting, powerful, and joyful lives we want. One of the emotions we feel when we are confronted with change is fear. But being afraid to do something yet doing it anyway is called courage.

Despite our inert tendencies, change is the ultimate reality. Every day we change, internally and externally. Cells die, hair grows. We think or feel something we haven't thought or felt before. The change may seem negligible, but it's dynamic nonetheless. Weather changes, the earth changes, seasons change, our scenery changes. The tree in our backyard changes, politics change, the news changes. We witness change on a daily basis, yet most of us are unaware of it. Our souls know the truth, and each day they seek to teach us that basic principle.

## TAKING RESPONSIBILITY

Many of us would agree that life doesn't seem fair. In my case, it was the sheer randomness of the world's inequities that moved me to study reincarnation as a viable possibility. I had had a notion of God as being fair and just, like a loving, wise father. I believed in a perfect universal order and a benign God. But as a logical person, I couldn't understand why God would allow so many people to be subjected to such rampant tragedy and misery. It didn't make sense to me that this loving father would give his children only one chance to learn and to right their lives. Providing them with many chances, many opportunities, made more sense to me. This conclusion helped me come to terms with the theory that there is a uniform fairness and justice in all our experiences, whether we perceive them as good or bad. We have many lives in which to practice, many lives in which to rebalance, many lives in which to become more God-like.

Those who dismiss soul creation and discount the possibility of reincarnation often exhibit an either/or mentality. Some believe in heaven or hell as the ultimate reward or punishment. Others have martyristic leanings, believing that fulfilling certain honorable duties in life affords one a higher standing in death. Fairness, to followers of this mutually exclusive philosophy, is measured by the barometer of how much good fortune comes to those who do good things. When bad things happen to good people, these people often become disillusioned. Their beliefs are broadsided, and they become confused, jaded, and angry. Many others adopt a fatalistic approach: they take life as it comes, believing that you live, you die, and that's it. They may not even entertain the abstract concepts of justice; they are too busy surviving their daily adversities. I know that when I was a young adult, struggling to get through school and pay my bills, I had no time or energy to be philosophical about the meaning of life and to deal with the more abstract theories of justice. I met life every day on a pedestrian level, because it was what I had been taught to do. Many of the people I see are angry at God for allowing "bad things to happen."

*"Only when we realize that there is no eternal, unchanging truth or absolute truth can we arouse in ourselves a sense of intellectual responsibility."*
Hu Shih

I'm sure that you would tell me that *you do* take responsibility. You could probably list a hundred things for which you are responsible. But think about the last time you blamed someone else for something that happened to you. Perhaps it was earlier today, or yesterday. I did it five minutes before I sat down to work on this chapter. I have worked for years to stop blaming others, and yet I still find myself doing it.

*"We do not do what we want and yet we are responsible for what we are—that is the fact."*
Jean-Paul Sartre

If we're blaming others, we aren't taking personal responsibility. Write down your account of the last time you blamed someone, and your thoughts about it now. If you feel justified, beware. We love feeling justified—in fact we need to—and so we continue to assign blame. But only when we let go of blaming others can we examine what else stands in the way of our inability to accept responsibility.

But taking responsibility doesn't mean simply shifting blame for everyone else to yourself, either. It doesn't mean beating yourself up and second-guessing yourself over every incident and relationship in your life that doesn't play out exactly the way you had planned. The primary reasons we take responsibility are so we can identify and learn from our experiences.

I acknowledge that taking responsibility requires work—a discouraging prospect. We work at our jobs, we work on our relationships, we work on our physical health, we devote time to our children, and on and on. Now I'm proposing that you do even more: that you take a leap of faith and commit to being responsible for your actions, reactions, and life experiences for one month. Write about the difficult circumstances in your journal. Reframe your reactions by asking the following questions:

- Why did my soul create that situation?
- What can I learn from it?
- What actions do I take to rectify it?

Write down what you've learned. At the end of the month, take a hard look at your work, relationships, children, and health. I bet they've improved. This exercise probably won't give you the same level of short-term gratification that you derive from blaming, but it will give you insights that will help you alter your behavior. In time, your relationships will show some subtle changes, and you'll feel better.

Judy knew she had the capabilities to fashion a successful career: she was well educated, intelligent, and creative. But by her early forties, she had failed to produce anything more than a string of short-lived and unsatisfying jobs and several failed entrepreneurial ventures. Soul creation helped her redefine what career success really meant to her and helped her thrive in the process:

*I love my work. I feel privileged, gratified, challenged, and inspired by the opportunity it gives me to express myself, and to make a difference in people's lives. Looking back over the years, I can see how all the pieces came together perfectly to propel me forward into this glorious future. Of course, I can see that now in hindsight. I wasn't always so visionary. Ten years ago, I walked into Linda's office feeling defeated, victimized, and badly in need of foresight.*

*Linda helped me to understand my career as a "calling," to consider it my "life's work" or "soul mission"—a possibility I hardly considered in my pursuit of money and reputation. My astrological chart identified key elements to the success of my mission: a commitment to service, communication skills, and the promotion of avant-garde ideas. We addressed my fear of failure. Like many "late bloomers," I had needed time to gain wisdom and maturity. I easily grasped the concept of self-creation because I had already seen evidence of the relationship between past crises and opportunities for self-awareness. However, taking responsibility for creating my whole life was a larger leap: one that proved very cathartic. Trusting the wisdom of my soul allowed me to release old anger, blame, and regret. I left my first session with Linda pointed in the right direction, and hopeful.*

*My test of faith continued. Could I own all of my experiences? Could I remain patient and optimistic in the space between the appearance of a problem and its resolution? Could I create my future consciously? By living in these questions, I gradually shifted my values. Activities I had once regarded as "unproductive," including personal growth and volunteer work, moved up from footnotes into the main text of my experience. A sense of purpose replaced my former angst. I more quickly recognized the gifts in adversity. I treasured the journey and surrendered the results.*

## DEALING WITH GRIEF AND LOSS

Many clients come to me grieving the loss of a loved one. They tell me heartwrenching stories involving the tragic death of a child, father, mother, brother or sister, or friend. My goal is to help those who are grieving overcome their sense of guilt, by imbuing them with a spiritual perspective.

Death in and of itself often seems distressingly arbitrary: only when we explore its meaning through soul creation can a sense of its fairness begin to take shape. On a mundane level, we can't explain why, for example, a 3-year-old girl would be gunned down during a drive-by shooting. But on a spiritual level, we can begin to understand why the little girl's soul needed her to have that violent experience. Since our souls are the continuity experts for our lives, they know everything that has come before and what experiences we need to create in this lifetime in order to continue to evolve and learn. If we could understand the soul contracts (discussed in Chapter 2) that this child had with her parents, and the past lives she brought to this short life, perhaps we could make some sense of the tragedy.

The soul gives me this information through the language of karmic astrology. The astrological chart provides us with the insights we need to understand such things.

We all are confronted by choices that are based on what our soul knows we need to learn. And while our souls create certain choices for us, we make the final creative decision at the critical point when the path needs to be chosen.

# CHAPTER 2

# Soul Mates and Soul Contracts

The contemporary surge in spirituality and New Age philosophy has ushered the term *soul mate* into our culture's lexicon primarily as a term of endearment. Some of us consider our soul mate to be a partner to whom we are bound by a love and understanding that transcends our material world: our ultimate relationship. I have a more in-depth explanation of what a soul mate is.

All the relationships we enter into—including those involving soul mates—are karmic. By initiating a relationship, we set in motion a soul contract with that soul to learn a lesson and resolve an issue from a previous life. A soul mate represents a karmic relationship that we have resolved: a deep conflict that has been settled, an obligation that has been fulfilled, and love that has replaced fear and anger. We recognize a soul mate by the supreme level of comfort and security we feel with that person. That doesn't mean that there aren't issues that remain to be ironed out. Rather, it means we know intuitively that we can resolve issues with our soul mate without losing his or her love and respect. When feelings of abandonment and betrayal arise with a soul mate, they do not last. Once soul mates achieve an ultimate level of symbiosis and serenity with each other, it remains forever.

> *"We should help people discover their vocation in life, their calling, fate or destiny. This is especially focused on finding the right career and the right mate."*
> Abraham Maslow

Having a soul mate is not necessarily a rare occurrence. It's just that few of us have the understanding or the tools to recognize whether the significant person in our life is indeed a soul mate. One must be evolving spiritually to have this awareness: cognizant of love as the basic fabric of life. Soul mates tend to find each other during their respective pursuits of their soul missions. Creating a soul mate could be seen as a spiritual reward that we give ourselves, after pursuing many soul contracts rife with discord.

A soul contract is an agreement we make with souls whom we've known previously from other lifetimes to work through situations in this life that need special attention. Soul contracts occur between all of us, all the time. We incarnate with a certain group of people, who represent different things to us, from one life to the next. They are companion souls off whom we can "bounce" our life's experiences. They agree to "play" with us to help make us aware of the lessons we need to learn. As part of the contract, we agree to do the same for them. Some of these people are closer to us than others, but all are important in helping us discover who we've been and how to learn our next major lesson.

Edgar Cayce, renowned in spiritual circles for creating a better understanding of reincarnation and psychic healing during the post-Depression era, said souls reincarnate with others to whom they are closely related for three reasons:

- to overcome conflict
- to repay an obligation
- to perpetuate love

Lee came to see me as a last resort. She had undergone a lot of psychotherapy but still could not overcome her guilt over her brother's death. She was jaded by the counseling process, having been to more than her share of therapists and psychologists. She told me matter-of-factly that her brother Dan had committed suicide ten years before, at the age of 17. It had come as a complete shock to Lee and the rest of her family. Each member of the family, in his or her own way, had assumed blame for his death, preventing them from resolving the issue and moving on with their lives. Lee, who had been 14 at the time, had loved her older brother but was very jealous of him. Dan had been active in sports and had won the admiration of her father in a way Lee could not. She remembers hating Dan for "taking her father away" from her. The day before he died, he had won a state-level tennis competition. Lee had left Dan's celebration party upset and angry because of the attention he received from her mother and father. The next day Dan shot himself in the head. He left no note, gave no explanation. Lee blamed herself for it. She felt that her jealousy and anger had driven him to take his own life.

When Lee was finished telling me this story, I asked her why she would create a soul contract with a brother prone to suicide. My question visibly jolted her. I explained that through the contracts that our souls forge with each other, we create the experiences and relationships from which we need to learn. Lee, who was just getting started in social work, was already adept at controlling her emotions, but I could sense her anger and disbelief as she pulled a couple of pillows up to her stomach, barricading herself. "Why would my soul do such a thing to me or my brother?" she asked. "That would be so unfair—worse, it would mean that I really did kill him," she said, tears now streaming down her face.

I explained to Lee that on a personality level, she had nothing to do with her brother's suicide. Making a contract with someone else's soul to learn a lesson—even if it included an aspect of death—did not make her or her soul an accomplice in a criminal act. On a soul level, she knew even before she and Dan incarnated in this life that he could choose to end his life. She had decided to be his sister for her own reasons. In essence, they had agreed to go through this tragedy together.

As Lee listened, she started to calm down. "Do you mean that my brother knew that he was going to kill himself when he came into this world?" Lee asked. I answered carefully, telling her that her brother's *personality* had not known. His soul, however, knew that suicide was a possibility and his soul also knew the reasons why it might happen.

Although aspects of Lee's and Dan's story have the trappings of fatalism, the truth is their souls did give them choices. Soul creation and fatalism diverge at one of the fundamental tenets of soul creation: that ultimately, the choice of which path to follow lies with us. The older we get, in fact, the more choices we have. Dan had choices, and suicide was one of them. Perhaps he was too young to see the other possibilities that his soul was showing him. Many souls deliver people into this world, aware that suicide may be a potential event from which they will need to learn. But plenty of them choose a different path perhaps because their soul determined that they had already learned the desired lesson from another experience or relationship.

Lee and I reviewed Dan's astrological chart and found some possible reasons why he might have chosen to leave the earth plane early. His chart was dominated by female energy. He was sensitive, creative, emotional, and spiritual. Even though he was a natural athlete and a competitor on the tennis court, he was gentle and compassionate. He would often agonize over how his opponents might feel after losing to him. After a tennis match he would go to his room and stay there for hours, refusing to eat or talk to anyone. He had wanted to quit sports and concentrate on writing but was terrified to confront his father, who strongly supported his tennis career. After his death, his mother found a journal of poems he had written. In several of them he wrote of a palace that was white and crystal, with fountains surrounded by white marble courtyards. Beautiful music and tinkling bells made this palace truly magical. The family saw these poems as a manifestation of a side of Dan that he had kept hidden. I saw them as a description of the other side beyond death and as evidence of Dan's yearning to go home. I believe—and I shared this with Lee—that Dan longed for the other side and never felt comfortable with his life. Before I even knew of the content of these poems, I had described the other side similarly to Lee, so she was able to truly believe that her brother had chosen to return to his spiritual home.

Lee now began to look at death in a more secure, thoughtful way. As a small child, she had been terrified of death. She had always hated the nightly prayer she was required to say: "If I should die, before I wake . . ." conjured up dreams of dark places with eerie monsters. At 14, Dan's death had brought back the fear and the nightmares. Her religious training was spotty, and she did not have a spiritual base to help her deal with death or offer her an afterlife. The only thing she could relate to was the darkness and the monsters. One of her first thoughts after Dan died was that he had gone into "that black hole and was living with those terrible monsters." Talking to me about the soul, the other side, and soul contracts helped diminish her terrible fear of dying. She began to see the real possibility that her brother had gone to a peaceful and beautiful place.

For the first time in ten years, Lee could have a conversation about her brother's death without feeling guilty. Guilt no longer interfered with her grieving process. Now she is able to help her family deal with it on a different level. In fact, Lee now volunteers at a hospice and helps other families deal with the death of their loved ones. She is able to love Dan and honor him for helping her to transform her own fear of death. His death, Lee learned, enabled her to discover and utilize her ability to help others learn about the dying process and share her own life experience, the essence of her soul mission. That experience, for Lee, was the basis of the soul contract she had made with her brother's soul.

One day Jill, a woman in her early forties, called me from Seattle in tears. Carl, her husband of fourteen years, had just told her he was leaving. There was no other woman, and he said he still loved her. He told her that he "needed to be free," to relieve himself of the collective burden of all the responsibilities they had accumulated during their marriage. As Jill and I worked together on her problem, I found information in her astrological chart that indicated that in another life she had been very commitment-phobic. By doing a chart comparison (in which I analyze one person's chart against another), I discovered that in another life she had been in a relationship with a man (probably a previous incarnation of her present husband) but felt she could not marry him. She had left him abruptly and never given the relationship the closure it deserved. In fact, she hadn't even said good-bye.

Because Jill had an unresolved issue with Carl left over from that previous existence, her soul brought them back together in marriage in this life so she could experience him leaving her and learn from it. She was able to see that she needed to repay this old obligation by dealing with Carl's needs. After a few sessions she decided to "let him go," to allow him to find the freedom he craved with impunity. This decision helped her eschew anger and blame, our most common reflexive tendencies. She refused to consider herself a victim. A few months later Carl came back, Jill's old karmic obligation having been paid in full. The two of them were now free to explore the next level of their relationship.

Cayce's law about needing to resolve left-over conflict sounds similar to his law of needing to meet a remaining obligation, but there is an important distinction: a conflict need not create obligation and demand repayment; rather, it may require some form of resolution. The conflict can be anything from a personality conflict where two people simply do not like each other, to a couple of colleagues vying for the same promotion.

Tom knew the moment his son David was born that something was wrong. The unadulterated joy that most fathers experience upon witnessing the birth of a child, the sheer euphoria, was absent. It wasn't the prospect of impending parental responsibilities and commitments that overwhelmed him, nor was he worried about what kind of father he'd be. Instead, Tom felt a deep, visceral, free-floating paranoia.

Too ashamed to tell his wife, Tom tried for several months to deal with his ambivalence toward David on his own. Finally, as a last resort, he came to me. An investigation of both Tom's and David's charts illuminated a past life conflict between the two of them. David had been in a position of great power and had had control over Tom's very existence. Tom had lost the only security he had, his land, which had taken him years of hard work to acquire. The culprit had been David. In that past life Tom had died an angry, frustrated man, never recovering the land that he felt was rightfully his and blaming David for his misfortune.

Thus Tom's conflict in this life centered on his inability to control his fate, his sense of feeling victimized—and his real desire to love his child. But now, in this life, through his newborn, he would have an opportunity to resolve the conflict by loving and caring for him. By being in control of his relationship with his son in this life, he was resolving that past life experience of powerlessness and, in effect, creating a karmic symmetry: just as Tom's fate had previously been in David's hands, David's fate was now in Tom's hands.

How did Tom and I know this past life experience was legitimate? The only way we ever know is by sensing how it feels. When we began talking of his possible karma with his son, Tom began to cry. The information felt right, and his body was responding to the truth. The most powerful part of the session was its result: Tom left no longer feeling conflicted, no longer afraid of the feelings that his little boy had catalyzed within him. Once he understood the soul contract he and his son had made—to overcome his feeling victimized by resolving the conflict and creating a life of love—he was free to be the open, generous, loving father he had always wanted to be.

Resolving major conflicts and fulfilling obligations leaves us with unconditional love, a hallmark of a soul-mated relationship. Discord will continue to surface periodically—our soul ensures it—but love and commitment become the prevailing tools of resolution.

## KARMIC WARNING BELLS

While we enjoy karmic relationships with all the various souls with whom we share soul contracts, they are not necessarily our soul mates. However, just because two people in a relationship aren't soul mates doesn't render their soul contract any less important.

Most of us have experienced the heady emotions, the passionate rush, that accompany our initial foray with someone special. All the signs are there: the energy, the sexual electricity, the infatuation. While these symptoms are commonly known as emotions of the heart, I refer to them as karmic warning bells. Upon meeting someone to whom you are attracted, you may really be falling in love—or you may be getting a wakeup call. What feels like love in many cases is really a cosmic two-by-four meant to get our attention and prepare us for a major karmic insight. In such cases we create the intensely amorous feelings in order to keep the relationship going long enough for us to discover the past life connection, alter it, and change ourselves. The relationship ends once we have the reflections we need. Sometimes it's difficult to draw a distinction between love and a karmic warning bell. Usually, with the latter, one feels a vague sense of familiarity and a strong "here-I-go-again" dread.

When Olivia came to see me, she was totally stressed out. At 42, she was happily married and had two young children, but she had fallen in love with another man—despite knowing that the relationship imperiled her marriage. While she loved and respected her husband, Olivia found the appeal of a younger, good-looking man intoxicating. He was arrogant and indiscreet—and to make matters worse, he worked with her husband. Olivia was putting her whole life on the line, and she couldn't figure out why. She said she "couldn't help it." She felt like she was "addicted" to this person, a rare emotion for her, considering that she exhibited not even the slightest indication of addictive tendencies. Her lust for George allowed her to overlook the fact that he was a heavy drinker.

We needed to find out the karmic implications between her and George, and we needed to do it quickly: Olivia was terrified that George, in a drunken stupor, would tell her husband what was going on. When I explained to Olivia that she was in this bizarre relationship with George in order to learn something important about herself and that these intense feelings were her soul's way of keeping her in the relationship, it made sense to her. As a matter of fact, it was the only thing that did make sense. From looking at Olivia's and George's astrological charts, we learned that in a previous life George had been in Olivia's employ. Her arrogance had demeaned and threatened him, but as a subordinate, he had felt powerless to confront her. As a result, Olivia now had an obligation to repay, and George had a conflict to resolve. They had come together in this life to balance their karma. As soon as Olivia recognized her previous ties to George and the need to balance their karma, she was able to talk to him, and end their relationship. She even convinced him to go to Alcoholics Anonymous. Her karmic warning bells stopped ringing, and the intense feelings dissipated. This obsessive kind of falling in love is particularly intense, yet its intensity can be altered just as quickly when it is understood. Olivia was able to preserve her family and move on with her life.

We spent a few sessions figuring out why her soul had needed her to understand her arrogant behavior from the past. We discovered more about who she had been in that life: she had been autocratic and had misused her power. She also felt that her life had been ended rather abruptly either by accident or murder at the hands of someone she had abused. A deep-seated fear had plagued Olivia for years: she had always been afraid of being center stage, had dreams of being assassinated, and on several occasions had a paranoia about someone being "out to get" her. Understanding this past life helped her make some sense of those fears. Her karmic relationship with George had given her the opportunity to discover herself at another level. At my suggestion, Olivia wrote George a thank-you note explaining all she had learned.

Too often our friends and family members, we ourselves— even society's most notable and accomplished people—engage in behavior that seems unexplainable. They make seemingly bizarre choices that defy their better judgment. Even the most emotionally grounded, commonsensical person you know could be drawn into a relationship completely incongruent with their sapience. But although this behavior is incomprehensible to our personalities, our souls understand it. Olivia knew George acted like a "jerk" but was able to stop seeing him when she realized that the relationship was showing her issues about herself.

## KARMIC VERSUS SOUL-MATED RELATIONSHIPS

The distinction between soul mates and other people with whom our souls have contracted relationships is that the issues between ourselves and our soul mates have come to some form of resolution, while issues in karmic relationships have yet to be resolved. Soul mates tend to cooperate, while those in karmic relationships tend to compete. Still, we can learn just as much from our experiences in both types of relationship. Conflicts among soul mates are more stimulating and creative because there is an attitude of expansion and a knowing that the conflict will be resolved. Often a soul-mated relationship serves a spiritual purpose. As soul mates, we sometimes help each other explore and find our own spiritual missions. Sometimes we work together to accomplish important life goals.

I know that if I had not been spiritually prepared, I wouldn't have attracted my husband into my life. Michael's support and unfailing generosity have aided me to become the person that I am and given me the time to dedicate myself to my work, even time taken away from our relationship. Years ago I was caught in an emotional quagmire. I knew that I had old anger festering within me. I knew it was unhealthy to bury it, but I couldn't find a way to express it. The morning after Michael told me about his affair, we were in the kitchen arguing. For one instant I literally saw red. For the first time in my life, I lashed out. I shoved him up against the refrigerator. When I finally stopped my raging tirade, I looked at him, and he was smiling. It was so incongruent: I was angry; I was close to being abusive; and he was smiling. I didn't know whether to laugh or cry. At that moment I knew I had broken through my inability to vent—I had actually gotten angry. Only a soul mate would have smiled.

## SOUL CIRCLES OF LIFE

Some people are disappointed to learn that our soul mates are not the only people with whom we have shared our past. In fact, we each have a very large group of people, hundreds or more, who are linked to us from one life to the next. Some relationships are closer than others, and their type may vary from life to life. You could be married to the person who was your mother-in-law in a previous life; your child could have been your father in another life—the combinations are endless. The homeless person now asking you for some change may have been your boss in a previous incarnation.

## SOUL CIRCLES OF LIFE

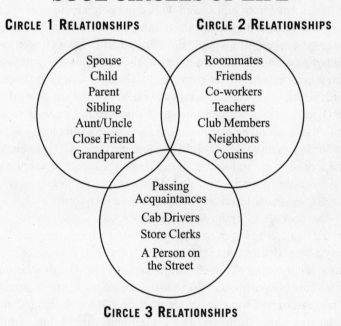

**CIRCLE 1 RELATIONSHIPS**

**CIRCLE 2 RELATIONSHIPS**

Spouse
Child
Parent
Sibling
Aunt/Uncle
Close Friend
Grandparent

Roommates
Friends
Co-workers
Teachers
Club Members
Neighbors
Cousins

Passing
Acquaintances
Cab Drivers
Store Clerks
A Person on
the Street

**CIRCLE 3 RELATIONSHIPS**

Imagine yourself in the middle of three concentric circles. The first circle contains the people whose karmic relationships with you are most important for your growth in this life: your parents, children, lovers, soul mate, husband, wife, beloved pet, counselor, spiritual teacher, or any other family member or intimate who has played an important role in your life experience. These circle-one relationships are intense, passionate, powerful, and sometimes disruptive because they are formative.

The second circle, one step removed from the intimacy and intensity of the first circle, comprises people whose karmic relationships with you have provided some interaction but are less significant. They could include an important teacher who helped you realize your career, a teenage romance that began an important relational pattern, a boss who challenged you, or possibly a friend who left your life after several years of an enriching relationship.

The third circle comprises people whose karmic relationships with you have been punctuated with some poignant moments but lack the sustained potency and vitality of the first two. Circle-three-type relationships could involve a sales clerk with whom you shared a profound, intimate moment; the man who ran into your car; the doctor who operated on your gall bladder. One of my circle-three relationships was with a postal clerk. I was at the post office last spring talking with her, and she helped me decide what mode of delivery would be best to deliver my book contract to my agent as quickly as possible. As she was stamping the mailing envelope, she looked at me and said, smiling, "Now I'm a part of your book too." People in circles two and three can have a very powerful impact on you in the midst of an experience with them.

The concept of group karma explains why certain people are linked together to experience poignant life situations together. You may have ended up in one history class rather than another, or been stuck in an elevator with certain people. Maybe you, or someone you know or read about, missed that doomed plane, while several other passengers went down. Or perhaps you were stranded at a diner in a snow storm and had a meaningful interaction with a stranger. Try to recall an event in your life when you ended up with a group of people, even strangers, who seemed vaguely familiar to you. Try to envision it as a group karmic experience. Think about what you learned from it and how it affected your life.

I will never forget getting caught in a terrific hailstorm on the Southern Illinois University campus in Edwardsville, Illinois, in the summer of 1973. I was close to finishing my master's degree and was in the process of deciding whether to join my husband, who had been transferred to the Philippines, or return home to Baltimore. About ten of us were waiting out the storm, making idle chatter. I mentioned that my husband was serving a two-year tour in the Philippines. One person in the group related a story about a friend in the Philippines whose dog had been stolen and was later found skinned in a marketplace in Manila. That was all I needed to hear. My dog's safety had always been an obsession with me. I did not go to the Philippines but came back to Baltimore—and began the most significant transformational period of my life.

## DETECTING SOUL MATES

Soul-mated relationships are distinguished by their deep feelings of permanence and comfort. Soul mates are secure in their knowledge that there will never be a situation they can't handle. Another indicator is how soul mates feel when they initially meet. Instead of karmic warning bells, they feel a low-level hum. The new person in their life seems familiar; they feel that they have "known" each other before. In essence, they are saying hello again.

My interest in the distinction between soul-mated and other karmic relationships grew as a result of my clients' fervent inquiries about soul mates. They wanted to know when they would find their own and how they could make it happen soon. As I explored dozens upon dozens of my clients' existing relationships, I came to the conclusion that many of them already had soul mates but didn't know it.

A story I often tell my clients is that our soul mates are waiting on our soul path. The more committed we are to what is in our soul's best interest, the more likely we are to find them. I had known my soul mission for several years before Michael appeared. His soul path was the same as mine. Although we are socialized to idealize soul mates as the stuff of storybook romance, soul-mated relationships come in many forms.

Many years ago, when I taught school, the administrator for whom I worked was also my mentor and my friend. In retrospect, I "knew" John from the moment we met. He left the school, but he never left my memory. I haven't talked to him in twenty years, and I probably never will again—at least, not in this life. Yet he fits the criteria of a soul mate. We were comfortable and at ease with each other. We could argue and know that we would resolve the conflict. We were constantly exploring a win-win model. He and I never had a social relationship outside the school; we were not lovers. We were two people who worked together for a common purpose, and we had a bond that I will always cherish. He was one of my soul mates.

As you think about your relationships, try to broaden your concept of what a soul mate is. You may be surprised and thrilled to find you already have one or several in your life. To clarify the difference, look at the following chart and review a few important relationships in your life.

| Soul Mates | Other Karmic Relationships |
| --- | --- |
| Win-Win | Win-Lose |
| Cooperative | Competitive |
| Peer relationship | Hierarchical relationship |
| Comfort | Agitation |
| Expansive | Constrictive |
| Inspirational | Antagonistic |
| Stimulating | Challenging |
| Creative | Draining |
| Integrated | Isolative |
| Ease of flow | Disruptive |
| Secure | Exposed |

Karmic relationships are challenging and therefore offer us opportunities to ascend to new heights in our spiritual growth. We have the potential to change their inherent difficulties by understanding and being aware of the gifts they bring. Soul-mated relationships have their own share of conflicts and arguments. The differences lie in the attitude of cooperation and in the deep inner knowledge that we will resolve the problems. Soul-mated and karmic relationships are synthesized at exactly the right time to enable us to learn about those sacred truths at our emotional core. Since our soul coordinates all our relationships, it presents these situations to us when the timing is right. What we do with these situations is our choice.

Imagine yourself as a soul on the other side. You are preparing to incarnate back to the earth plane. You meet with other souls to plan the relationships you need to fulfill your life's purpose. You talk to your circle-one karmic relationships first. Circle two and circle three come next. You speak to the soul, for instance, who is to be your father in your next earthly existence. Together you recall your previous life experiences, as well as the conflicts that will need to be resolved and the obligations that will need to be met. You acknowledge the love that has endured throughout time. You decide on the context of the relationship you will share to help both of you evolve. Your souls cocreate a soul contract. You have many meetings like this one, to consummate all the contracts you need to evolve and grow spiritually in your next life.

Your soul then integrates your soul contracts into your astrological chart. Information in the chart reminds you of the contracts and the souls with whom you've contracted. That vague sense of "knowing" or familiarity we experience when we meet new people can be attributed to the fact that we usually don't recognize the personalities behind our soul agreements, but we always recognize their souls. Our soul knows the people we're going to bring into our lives. Our astrological chart only serves as a blueprint of what our soul intends for us to help us evolve. We might not recognize someone immediately, but if we have some notion of what our soul needs us to learn in this life, the reasons for their presence in our life will become more readily apparent. This rationale also explains the common experience of meeting under the flukiest of circumstances—while asking for directions, at a school or job orientation, on the plane while traveling, in a doctor's office—someone who becomes a central influence in your life. These "chance" meetings are not at all random.

Many people have asked me why we do not remember our past lives. The reason is that our soul has all those experiences recorded and brings them forth when they are needed. Many karmic experiences create poignant emotions that we have difficulty confronting because we do not understand where they come from. Until we have a philosophic context in which to deal with these feelings, they stay repressed.

All karmic relationships are familiar to some degree. We have known the person for whom we've developed strong feelings many times before. That's how we know we are entering into a relationship to complete what we failed to complete before.

It is important to distinguish between comfort and familiarity. The comfort of a soul-mated relationship is different from the familiarity of a karmic relationship. Familiarity could involve myriad types of relating. For instance, if in previous lifetimes you created abusive relationships, then an abusive relationship will seem familiar to you now. Falling back into the well of familiarity is the easiest thing for us to do. Being in a relationship created by old behavior characteristics is like being on automatic pilot.

Unfortunately, many people repeat the same behavioral patterns countless times without alteration. I've seen it over and over again in my practice, and it truly saddens me. Ultimately our souls do give us opportunities to alter our lives. If we ignore these opportunities, we end up taking these unresolved issues into our next life. We will learn sooner or later—our souls are infinitely patient.

## THE GIFT OF REFLECTION

Knowing this truth has helped my clients—as well as myself—make tremendous inroads into learning more about themselves. Yet we all have painful memories that we consciously do not want to unearth. Scores of my clients have undergone extensive past life therapy and remember lives where they were persecuted, victimized, and betrayed. But few remember lives where *they* were the persecutor, the abuser, or the betrayer. We wish to bury these memories, and we do.

Some of my clients create major cosmic two-by-fours over and over again. They get increasingly stronger until sooner or later we can no longer ignore them. The more blocked we are, the stronger the two-by-fours. Consider the statements you make repeatedly: they reflect an unconscious memory, waiting for you to interpret and understand it.

All significant relationships provide us with information about our blind spots. Jung thought that the more deeply we repress our thoughts and feelings about ourselves, the more intensely we create them outside ourselves as conflict and chaos. We will attract another person to show us precisely what we don't consciously know about ourselves. Once we understand that we bring all our relationships to ourselves for learning and balance, we can alter and transform the behaviors that need changing.

Take a moment to think about an important person in your life. Now isolate a behavior from that person that irritates you, scares you, or causes you pain. That person's action may cause irritation or fear in you, but it may hardly bother another colleague, family member, or friend. If this is the case, could it be that you actually behave in that irritating or painful way yourself? If so, my guess is that you've experienced an extreme reaction to that behavior before. Try claiming that behavior as your own, and make a commitment to change. Suddenly you may find that it alters the reaction you have toward that other person. That person may not change what he or she does; what has changed is your perception of that person's behavior by changing your own.

## BIG SOULS AND LITTLE SOULS

God and the universe have a perfect order, and that perfect order filters down through us. We don't have to strive for perfection, because we share the energy of God. Most people scurry about trying to prove that they're perfect, but they don't see that they are part of God, and that God has already given us the greatest gift he can give us: our soul.

When we are in communication with our soul, our relationship with it exemplifies growth and healing. But people who are not in sync with their soul are more often sick, tired, angry, frustrated, frayed, and jaded than those who are. We've all encountered people who are jaded; they seemingly have everything but sound as if they have nothing. They don't have spirit, they don't have joy, they don't have drama, and they don't have the zeal to celebrate life. Above all, they don't believe in their soul. I'm better today than I've ever been because I'm in concert with my soul, and this sacred connection is bringing me to personal and professional heights I never thought possible twenty years ago. My soul helps me do more important things, endeavors that have significant meaning not only for me but for countless others.

We all have a big soul and a little soul. Our big soul is connected to God. In fact, God and the big soul are one. The big soul is our container for the total human condition, our orchestrator of life's events, our continuity expert from one life to the next, our total awareness and knowledge as a people. For those who believe that God "keeps track" of our lives, the big soul is his reference point. The big soul knows everything about us, everything we have done, and what we will need to do in the future to learn and evolve. It creates our experiences here on this material plane.

The big soul, in its infinite wisdom and love, gives to each of us a little piece of itself, which I call the little soul. The little soul is our spiritual companion, a function of our daily existence. It is the essence of God that is within each of us, as if he were holding each of our hands. It aids our personality, pushing us to fulfill our potential, and helps us evolve by confronting us with the encounters and relationships from which we need to learn. Our little soul is the impetus behind our realizing our soul mission and our purpose in life. It is our deepest strength and our greatest joy, and with it we are never alone. The little soul and the big soul are always connected, and the big soul is always connected to God.

The big soul guides the little soul in its respective relationship with us. It deals with issues of a larger scope, like choosing a particular generation with a specific path to significance and a large group karmic track. Each generation is different, but a common thread runs though it, a similarity of karmic lessons and a major need to transform them. Each generation has a larger purpose to fulfill that will advance its evolution and awareness. The big soul also coordinates the massive number of soul contracts into which each of us has entered. For instance, my interns are part of my own karmic group, each for their own individual reasons. Some come to learn from me and stay connected; others decide to separate from me. I know that I have created meeting all of them to push me toward a better understanding of my soul's work. The big soul is more connected to the bigger picture.

## KARMIC AMALGAMS: YOUR KARMIC JIGSAW PUZZLE

Karmic amalgams are aggregate images of the people who are most meaningful to us. Drawing a karmic amalgam is a dynamic process that helps us figure out how to learn from the new, interpersonal situations we are constantly creating in our lives. They are effective because we've already known the people we attract from other lives, having entered into soul contracts with them. A karmic amalgam gives us the opportunity to see ourselves through the people we create. For instance, if I had been a dogmatic father in another life and my soul needed for me to understand the devastating effects that being dogmatic had on my family, I would likely ask my son in that life to be that kind of father to me in my next. If my "son" takes on that contract, he is helping me by being dogmatic and unrelenting. Then we can resolve the conflict we had in our last life.

Whenever we experience a new, important relationship, we must adjust and revise our karmic amalgam. Adding each new, essential relationship as it evolves enables us to understand what that relationship symbolizes and provides us with insights to learn from it. Once we understand that our souls seek to confront us with all our own relationships as a learning experience, we can alter and transform the behaviors that need changing.

In the workshops I conduct to help people glean powerful information from their relationships, I use an exercise based on a theory that we enter this life with a jigsaw puzzle without pieces. Every karmic relationship we create becomes a pertinent piece of the jigsaw puzzle. The completed puzzle shows us in a very profound way who we have been and what memories we may have hidden from our conscious understanding of ourselves.

Circle-one relationships are our biggest jigsaw pieces. Your mother and father may encompass as much as one-third of your puzzle. Your soul has chosen them to provide you with very significant karmic information. Understanding how your parents serve you through their reflections back to you is the first step in cobbling together your karmic amalgam. The power and importance of a reflection is judged by the emotional impact it has on us. I always admired my mother for her compassion, her deep desire to serve humanity, her charm and graciousness, her love of books, and her writing skills. She was a career woman who worked her way up the career ladder. Having had a major influence on the evolution of volunteerism in this country, my mother was an inspiration for me. She was open-minded and totally supported my need to leave the traditional world of education and become the holistic teacher that I am today.

Still, as a young girl, it used to frustrate me when my mother was committed to her work responsibilities at my expense. I felt abandoned and scared. As a teenager, my frustration and fear turned to anger. It upset me that she could so easily sacrifice herself and her role as my mother for her career. But as I got older, I saw that I was doing the same thing. I was a workaholic. I sacrificed myself for my work. I had chosen my mother to show me myself.

Our parents' interactions with us help us to remember the soul contracts we have made with them. This Parents Exercise will highlight the important role your parents played in helping you learn more about yourself and the "perfection" of their service to you.

### Parents Exercise
- Think about your mother. Write down in your journal five things that you admire about her.

- Now write down five things about her that frustrate you.
- Do the same thing with your father.

Often in our previous incarnations, we were much more extreme versions of our parents. In essence, we make our parents bigger than life so that we can get in touch with that karmic part of us. We create a soul contract with them to show us that part of ourselves.

Nadine, a 43-year-old writer from Hercules, California, was able to come to terms with her mother only after realizing that their volatile, angst-ridden relationship was providing her with a life-altering lesson:

*"You picked your parents." Linda's words ricocheted off my ears, only to boomerang back later. Instinctively and almost defensively, I felt a chill and thought to myself: "No way in hell." And then I thought, "Maybe that accounts for all of my previous poor judgments and decisions."*

*Sometime after the humor wore off, I finally understood. Ironically, what has taken me almost my entire adult life to understand has left me feeling grateful that I finally "got" it. Now I can spend the rest of my life making a real difference. This coming to terms—or maybe better, coming of age—happened after three years of living with my mother in a volatile relationship, then not speaking to her for another three years after that. After more than six years of external and internal turmoil, I finally came to terms with . . . me.*

*First I realized that a gift is not only what we have been given but what we ultimately do with it. Since the gifts my mother gave me were not conscious and certainly did not come from a loving place, it took me a while to validate them. The gift became my own growth out of a fiery place.*

*I have not only reconciled her back into my life, I have clearly gained more respect for her journey. The added benefit is that my compassion for others is now more evident in my daily life.*

*We all have a profound need to look deeply inside—to go beyond the conventional rhetoric and teaching, to find our own truth and accept our appointed tasks, our purpose for living. But before that, it's really only about love. Once you give yourself compassion, you see the world through loving eyes. That moment of understanding transformed the course of my life forever.*

Traits we display in our significant relationships show us not only the behaviors we tend to repress but the jigsaw puzzle pieces of ourselves as we were in other times. The following exercise will walk you through the process of finding the personality pieces that will allow you to learn about the puzzle that is you.

### Exercise: Karmic Amalgam for Female Energy

This exercise will provide information on characteristics you have had in the past as a woman. If you are a woman in this life, it will supply you with more information about your past. If you are a man, it will inform you about your female side as well as provide you with insights about what qualities you are attracted to in women. The female amalgams you "create" will give you important insights into your hidden female side.

## STEP 1

Choose and list in your journal five women with whom you have had an important relationship. (Always use your mother as the first one, since she is a circle-one soul contract.) If you don't have five, list as many as you can. Here are five examples: your mother, a childhood friend, a supervisor, a professor, and your grandmother.

## STEP 2

Examine the personalities of the five women you've chosen. Look for their attributes that have deeply affected you. Identify and journalize roughly half a dozen strong and weak or challenging characteristics for each of the women you've chosen. Your selection of attributes as positive or negative should not imply a judgment about them. What is significant is how you view them and the effect that their behavior has had on you.

## STEP 3

List the strengths that most of the five women have in common. These strengths now can become pieces of your jigsaw puzzle: they are characteristics that you may not have realized that you have yourself.

## STEP 4

List the weaknesses that most of the five women have in common. As with your strengths, you can now add your aggregate weaknesses to your karmic jigsaw puzzle. Chances are these weaknesses are aspects of yourself that you've chosen not to identify. They could offer a glimmer of information about who you've been in past lives.

### Exercise: Karmic Amalgam for Male Energy

This exercise will provide information on characteristics you have had in the past as a man. If you are a man in this life, it will supply you more information about your past. If you are a woman, it will inform you about your male side as well as provide you with insights about what qualities you are attracted to in men. The male amalgams you "create" will give you important insights into your hidden male side.

## STEP 1

Choose and list five men with whom you have had an important relationship. (Always use your father as the first one, since he is a circle-one soul contract.) If you don't have five, list as many as you can. Some examples: your father, your uncle, a first love, your husband, a married lover.

## STEP 2

Examine the personalities of the men you've chosen. Look for their attributes that have deeply affected you. Identify roughly half a dozen strong and weak characteristics for each of the men you have chosen. Your selection of attributes as positive or negative should not imply a judgment about them. What is significant is how you view them and the effect that their behavior has had on you.

## STEP 3

List the strengths that most of the five men have in common. These strengths can become pieces of your jigsaw puzzle: they are characteristics you may not have realized you possess yourself.

## STEP 4

List the weaknesses that most of the five men have in common. You now have six more characteristics to add to your karmic jigsaw puzzle. Again, the weak or challenging traits you've elicited may indicate parts of yourself that you've chosen to repress. They could also offer you some insight into the type of person you were in previous incarnations.

Your karmic jigsaw puzzle will ease your heart, expand your consciousness, and give you a sense of continuity that you have never before experienced. It will give you vital information on why you've chosen your soul contracts. You will be free to love and honor your parents and all the others who have joined with you on a soul level to teach you what you have needed to know. You will feel more empowered because you will no longer need to create others to show you what you already know. You will be able to put karmic memories in perspective and discriminate their value. You will be less vulnerable to the chaos created by unconsciousness. Finally, you will be operating in partnership with your soul.

# PART II

## Journey to Your Soul Mission

# CHAPTER 3

# From Who You Are
# to Who You Want to Be

Having a fundamental working knowledge of your soul and your personality and being aware of their spiritual dynamic will help you align them in such a way that you can experience living your soul mission. You gain access to your personality through your intellect, your sensations, and your feelings. You gain access to your soul through your intuition.

> *"When the personality comes fully to serve the energy of the soul, that is authentic empowerment. This is the goal of the evolutionary process and the reason for your being. Every experience that you have and will have upon the Earth encourages the alignment of your personality with your soul."*
>
> Gary Zukav, *The Seat of the Soul*

When your soul and personality are aligned, you will finally be able to devote yourself to your soul's mission, your life's work. You will experience an unparalleled level of satisfaction and purpose, leading to a fundamental inner peace. In *Seat of the Soul,* Zukav discusses the relationship between personality and soul:

> *"When a personality is in full balance you cannot see where it ends and the soul begins. That is a whole human being."*

Your soul mission is always that which you say you cannot do. It is your growth path—the singular, distinctive purpose that represents your fulfillment. Your soul mission becomes your journey to reaching your fullest potential, to become something you haven't been before. It is diametrically opposite to your comfort zone.


## YOUR NORTH/SOUTH NODES

The North/South Node process is fundamental to learning and living your soul mission. Through your North and South Nodes, you uncover words and symbols that you will use to bridge the gap between past lives and this one. You don't have to believe in reincarnation or past lives to benefit from the North/South Node process, but if you believe life has some purpose and meaning, it's easier to grasp the concept.

The nodes are points in the heavens where the moon intercepts the earth's orbit around the sun. Your North and South Nodes are thus represented by astrological signs that diametrically oppose each other in the cosmos. If your North Node is Cancer, your South Node would be Capricorn; if your North Node is Taurus, your South Node would be Scorpio, and so on.

The South Node, which we will refer to as your Soul Pattern, embodies the type of person you are when you exhibit your old, predictable habits and behaviors. It represents your most familiar thoughts, feelings, and beliefs. It tells you the past lives you need to remember, karmic debts you need to repay, and relationships that will support your vision. (A karmic debt is an unresolved issue from a previous life.) It shows you your unresolved themes from the past that are causing you pain and frustration in this life.

Martin Schulman, author of *Karmic Astrology*, describes the Soul Pattern (South Node) as

symbolic of man's past. [The South Node] is not symbolic of one incarnation, but [rather] a combination of events, ideas, attitudes and thoughts from every incarnation whose accumulated unresolved effects have created the current life. For some the South Node can be limiting, while for others whose past foundations are firm and large it can be just the factor which brings the present life to fruition and achievement.

You must evolve from the habits and tendencies confirmed by your Soul Pattern to reach the possibilities signified by your North Node, which we will refer to as your Soul Potential. In the simplest terms, your Soul Pattern represents your past, while your Soul Potential represents your future, your soul mission.

Each of us brings specific tendencies or issues from one life to the next because they are unresolved. Once you learn the lessons your soul wants you to learn, you need not carry that "karmic baggage" into your next incarnation. Your Soul Potential offers you a road map of words and concepts helping you to understand who you need to be to achieve your soul mission. It could be described, fundamentally, as what scares you the most, eliciting feelings of insecurity or fear, because it seeks to take you into new, unfamiliar terrain. We are all drawn to our Soul Potential, as a moth to a flame, yet we are terrified of it at the same time.

Once you embrace it, your Soul Potential will provide you with a clear path to a life of profound joy, purpose, and congruence. Schulman explains one's Soul Potential (North Node) as

> the symbol of the future. It represents a new experience as yet untried. For the individual this is the new cycle to which he is looking forward, carrying with it all the apprehensions of the unknown and as yet untried experiences. This nodal position nevertheless has a curious, magnetic allure, pulling the soul to its future growth. . . . It symbolizes the highest area of expression to be reached in the current life and therefore must be interpreted by the highest qualities of the sign and house in which it is placed.

The best way to begin to learn about your soul journey is to consult your Soul Pattern. Like your Sun sign, your Soul Pattern sign is determined by your date of birth, providing you with information about your past lives and showing you how you've manifested certain past life tendencies in this life (see the charts in Chapter 4). Your Soul Potential, on the other hand, represents your soul mission, and symbolizes your future. It gives you a conscious understanding of your life issues that have—up until now—been dormant. By confronting certain life issues via your Soul Pattern and extracting the negative habits and behaviors that have held you back from pursuing your dreams and goals, you can focus on traveling the road to your Soul Potential, to live the kind of life endeavored by your soul.

## WHY BREAKING OLD HABITS IS SPIRITUALLY THERAPEUTIC

> *"To fall into a habit is to begin to cease to be."*
> Miguel de Unamuno

Your soul is on a perpetual growth path. It wants you to evolve to a higher order, learning lessons cumulatively from one lifetime to the next. It wants you to encounter new experiences. Remaining stuck in an old and familiar Soul Pattern hinders your evolution. Your life circumstances may feel familiar for now, but your Soul Pattern will eventually arouse you by creating an unpleasant or life-jarring experience.

Most people, when they are content with the status quo, do not make wholesale life changes. They change only by having to confront a problem—specifically, one they created themselves via their Soul Pattern. At some point in each of our lives, our soul says to us, "You've got to do something different now." But leaving your Soul Pattern behind for the good of your soul mission is at best uncomfortable and at worst downright terrifying.

> *"Ill habits gather by unseen degrees—*
> *As brooks make rivers, rivers run to seas."*
> John Dryden

Unlike your personality, your soul is not judgmental. It assesses your experiences not in terms of whether they are positive or negative but rather if they are new or old. Your soul is interested in exposing you to discovery, in plying you with new experiences and insights that will lead you to your next incarnation.

## WHY WE FEAR CHANGE

The fundamental reason we fear change is that, consciously or unconsciously, we equate it with death. Our mortality is the ultimate transformation, but most of us see it as a finality rather than as a new beginning.

> *"The sun . . .*
> *In dim eclipse, disastrous twilight sheds*
> *On half the nations, and with fear of change*
> *Perplexes monarchs."*
> John Milton

Those who fear change often say they feel as though they have lost touch with their spiritual center. But being in touch with our spiritual energy is part of our soul journey of discovery, change, and novelty. If we don't allow ourselves to continue on that journey, we get stuck. A journey implies movement, and those who refuse to take action are paralyzed by their fear of change, of finding themselves in territory that is unfamiliar.

In order to follow our Soul Potential, we need to trust our soul and take a leap of faith. Many of us, as youngsters, were fearful before we took that first dive into the pool, and we see the same terrifying feeling in our own children as they take their first dives. The same apprehension prevents us from seizing new, promising business opportunities, making dramatically different career moves, or cultivating meaningful and fulfilling relationships. Nothing could reduce our fear of entering the water headfirst but the actual first dive itself. Our Soul Potential is about not knowing, but trusting our soul that it's right. Invariably it is.

*"In spite of illness, in spite even of the archenemy of sorrow, one can remain alive long past the usual date of disintegration if one is unafraid of change, insatiable in intellectual curiosity, interested in big things, and happy in small ways."*

Edith Wharton

Influenced by the misguided adage "Don't rock the boat," many people have been conditioned to believe that dramatic change is not worth affecting. Most of us were raised by parents in a society that valued security. In the history of the world, the individuals who are now considered agents of change—from Plato and Galileo to Susan B. Anthony, Margaret Sanger, and Martin Luther King—were often condemned and ridiculed for their visionary beliefs in their respective times.

Greek officials shut down Plato's learning academy because he was teaching innovative aspects of physics that they determined to be "dangerous." Galileo was arrested and ostracized for his adoption of the Copernican belief that the sun, not the earth, was the center of the solar system. Because of their ground-breaking efforts in furthering the causes of women's suffrage and birth control, respectively, Anthony and Sanger both suffered at the hands of society's mainstream: Anthony paid with her life and Sanger was jailed. At a time when blacks did not share the basic inalienable rights that America's forefathers had mandated for its citizens, King emerged as a voice of love and reason and, most of all, change. His efforts cost him his life.

Three Reasons Why We Fear/Loathe Change
1. Most of us equate it with fear of dying.
2. We've been taught not to rock the boat.
3. It is not a logical process but an emotional one.

## WHY INTUITION IS ESSENTIAL TO YOUR SOUL MISSION

In our culture we are taught to value and trust logic in making decisions. We look askance at our intuition, considering it "weird" when we receive a major revelation. Logic is based on what we already know, but intuition defies what we already know. A stop-the-world moment, intuition itself can drastically alter our lives. Insight creates change, and insight that comes from intuition yields the greatest change.

According to Jung, we see our environment through four filters: intellect, emotion, sensation, and intuition. While intellect, emotion, and sensation are the filters related to our personality, intuition is the filter to our soul. It transcends the other three filters, allowing us to interpret and understand life's events with more clarity and a deeper perspective. I call it a divine spark, a moment in time when a thought you've never had before helps you see things differently. A passel of growth workshops and self-help seminars can help yield you some insights—or "ahas," as I sometimes refer to them—but insight that is not developed and acted upon fades away.

## SOUL PATTERN: OLD PREDILECTIONS

From your Soul Pattern you can glean information about the areas in your life where you persistently hold on to your past. Your Soul Pattern may be so familiar, you've become inured to the fact it even exists. Your behavior, intentions, attitude, and perspective—traits of your personality—are as much a part of you as the color of your eyes, the sound of your voice, and the way you walk, personal aspects you hardly consider in daily life. Mining these habitual characteristics through Soul Pattern exercises can yield a rare introspective look at yourself. Investigating your Soul Pattern allows you to peel back the layers of your psyche, to help you identify qualities about yourself that could be keeping you from achieving your soul mission. In fact, you'd be hard pressed to achieve the soul mission that your Soul Potential has laid out for you without discovering the personal mysteries of your Soul Pattern.

Those with a Soul Pattern (South Node) in the sign of Capricorn, for example, tend toward rigidity and perfectionism. Having their South Node in Capricorn signals their strong need to be responsible, as well as their penchant for rules. Their bias toward order may hamper their ability to achieve their soul mission, which often is about taking a less restrained approach to life. But unless they become consciously aware of their rigid inclinations, they will continue to repeat the same behavior, fueled by the same obstinacy.

Four Things You Should Know About Your Soul Pattern
1. It provides you with your spiritual starting point, and tells you where and what you've been before, alerting you to your toxic tendencies.
2. It identifies what is safe, predictable, and familiar to you.
3. If you are not aware of your Soul Pattern, you will tend to create problematic relationships based on it.
4. If you don't tend to your Soul Pattern, it will, at some point, rear itself as a major crisis.

## SOUL POTENTIAL: WHAT YOU CAN BE

Our soul mission terrifies us, like a hair-raising roller-coaster ride, because our soul takes us into unfamiliar terrain, full of unknown twists and turns we couldn't possibly anticipate. Your soul reveals itself through your Soul Potential, evincing its personality, color, passion, energy, and essence. Those with a Soul Potential in the sign of Cancer, for example, would aspire toward understanding their emotions and learning how to be nurturing. Having one's Soul Potential in Cancer signals the need to become the consummate mother, who expresses her creativity through caring for others with sensitivity and compassion. Needing to be needed by those they love is vital to their self-esteem.

Four Things You Should Know About Your Soul Potential
1. On a spiritual level, your Soul Potential represents the light at the end of the tunnel.
2. It provides you with information about the type of energy, characteristics, and traits your soul wants you to manifest.

3. It represents a "stretch" in ambition, pulling you to do things that you are not inherently comfortable or confident doing but that will be fulfilling once you overcome your anxiety and "take the leap."

4. Your Soul Potential is not a destination to reach, not a static end product, but the journey your soul wants you to take, a dynamic ongoing process.

## Embracing Your Soul Potential

When you aspire to live your soul mission, you commit to becoming more than you think you are. You glean happiness and fulfillment not only from realizing your soul mission, but from the process of striving for it. Life itself is a process, not an end product. Thus, we are always in the process of becoming what our soul wants us to become. The more we are able to stay on our soul road, the happier and more content we are, regardless of whether we ever definitively reach our soul mission. Staying on our soul road keeps us motivated and connected to our life's possibilities.

Pursuing your soul mission and striving to live your Soul Potential take work and commitment. But the process doesn't end when you reach your perceived destination; in fact, as you try to refine your soul mission and attain its highest levels, it takes on a different type of spiritual obligation. Once you identify your soul mission, you should try to do things that mesh with it but that you don't think you can do.

> *"Most people live, whether physically, intellectually or morally, in a very restricted circle of their potential being. They make use of a very small portion of their possible consciousness, and of their soul's resources in general, much like a man who . . . should get in a habit of using and moving only his little finger. Great emergencies and crises show us how much greater our vital resources are than we had supposed."*
> William James

Once you have discovered its path, maintaining your soul mission becomes easier over time. As you grow older, you become increasingly conscious of eschewing your Soul Pattern and are more committed to embracing the life endeavors articulated by your Soul Potential. Achieving your soul mission can be elusive; the key is to continue to strive for it so that you never lose track of what it is.

When you are aware of your Soul Pattern and what it represents, your soul no longer needs to create obstructions to clue you in to your problem areas. Your daily life will look a lot different: more peaceful, less chaotic, happier, healthier, and more prosperous. The cosmic two-by-fours will dissipate, and when you do encounter a problem, you'll be able to negotiate it with greater ease, channeling it into an opportunity for personal growth. Remember, realizing your soul mission is all about the quest for it.

## Committing to Your Soul Potential

It's essential that you make a meaningful commitment to reaching your Soul Potential, a commitment that will be reflected in a more positive way of life with a greater sense of purpose. Whether you succeed is predicated not just on making the commitment but on evaluating the actions that stem from that commitment—actions that your soul wants you to take. You have to ask yourself: Do your actions represent your Soul Potential (your soul path) or your Soul Pattern (the path from your past)? You know you're committed to your Soul Potential when you find yourself asking how you would utilize the energies surrounding your Soul Potential to handle an opportunity or problem.

Achieving your Soul Potential is the result of a conscious choice, but it is also comparable to the experience of buying a new leather coat: each time you wear it, it feels more comfortable and looks better. Similarly, the more you commit to and practice the soul mission symbolized by your Soul Potential, the better it feels. Your Soul Pattern, on the other hand, is comparable to your skin: it is ever-present, and wearing it involves no conscious choice.

Jim, whose Soul Pattern is in Pisces and whose Soul Potential is in Virgo, is a recovering alcoholic who hadn't had a drink in ten years. When alcohol was part of his life, he remained in darkness and pain, unable to escape his spiritual agony. Although he had a college degree in music, he was employed as a janitor. A very talented musician, he couldn't perform in public because he was so withdrawn.

Devastated and suicidal, Jim came to see me after his girlfriend left him for another man. I suggested he see a psychiatrist, but he refused. He wanted nothing to do with therapists and medication. I learned that most of his relationships had turned out the same way this one had: he would wear down his partners with his needful and codependent tendencies, and they would leave. In this latest affair, he had lost himself, having given up all personal boundaries.

We talked about Jim's Soul Pattern in Pisces, about his being extraordinarily sensitive and vulnerable to the energies of those who entered his life. We talked about how fragile and pure of spirit he had been in his past lives. I told him that his previous personalities had cowered from arguments, that he had been repulsed by expressions of anger and hatred. In one life he had lived deep in the woods, far from people and the savagery of his culture. He had been so empathic that he absorbed the energy from others and could not separate himself from them. However, his musical talent was a common theme, an emotional outlet for him in many lives, a means of expression by which he could honor himself. In previous lives he had been a healer, a priest, a nun, and a physician: all lives of self-denial and martyrdom. In this life, instead of living in the woods, he had sealed himself off from having to interact with people by abusing alcohol and working as a janitor at night.

Spiritually Jim remembered the beauty, harmony, and peace of the other side and had not been able to feel secure on the earth without his addictions. He had to learn the lesson of his Soul Potential in Virgo: to value the earthly plane and not try to escape from it. We talked a lot about the beauty of the earth, and soon he began to feel a little more secure in it. He was amazed when I was able to show him how judgmental he had been of the earth and the people on it. As he learned to value the earth, he learned to develop more physical structures in his own life, and to create boundaries by being more discriminating. He worked on other skills relating to having his Soul Potential in Virgo, including prioritizing and organizing his life.

Jim was thrilled to discover that he did have a logical mind. Soon, his emotional paralysis gave way to long-denied emotions. His shyness began to dissipate when he committed himself to helping people without totally losing himself in the process. He decided to return to school and become a music teacher. Teaching music enabled him to use his creative talent as well as be a healer again, this time with more solid personal boundaries and stronger priorities.

Bob, whose Soul Pattern is in Taurus and whose Soul Potential is in Scorpio, worked in a bank for fifteen years—his whole adult life. He came to me when he was 37, unhappy, stuck, and resistant to any form of change. His wife had given him a gift certificate to see me one year before he actually made his appointment. He admitted that he was afraid that I might induce him to change, which was anathema to him.

Bob's life at the bank, however, was becoming increasingly restrictive and depressing. He came to me as a last resort, and I noticed immediately that he had come from many lives as a personality that valued the earth and all that it represented. Security and safety were old foundations that he believed would protect him. I mentioned that Taurus is the sign of the builder on the earth plane: before Bob chose to study finance in college, he had almost become an architect in this life. I shared with him Taurus's fear of change, its need for stability. We talked about money as a symbol for that security. He admitted that he derived great comfort from going into the bank's vault and just looking at the rows of money. He didn't need to have it; he just liked knowing it was there. Taurus collects things as a form of protection.

Bob began to realize how frightened he was of anything that

was transitional. He had even hated the interval between leaving college and finding his job because he loathed uncertainty. He would connect with people, showing a great deal of loyalty to them. He still communicated with a childhood friend, even though he really didn't like him.

We zeroed in on a past life where he had been a housewife to a farmer in the Midwest. She had loved her uncomplicated pastoral life and had been a wonderful gardener and cook. Her life was good, Bob remembered, because it was predictable, unchangeable, and secure. His Taurean belief was that life had to continue unchanged if he were to be secure and safe. He recalled another past life as a settler whose farm had been burned and destroyed by a tribe of marauding Indians. That memory impressed upon him how quickly security can be destroyed by sudden, momentous change. In this life, familiarity and a need for predictability became his foundations, and the bank served as a symbol of that security. But now the old ways were becoming problematic for him. He was in the throes of a significant conflict.

Bob's karmic issue around fear of change is very consistent with the energy of Taurus. Taurus needs the earth under its feet, and it values steadfastness and other endurable qualities. Many people with a Soul Pattern in Taurus have had lives as builders, bankers, farmers, potters, and architects. They are comfortable working within the boundaries of the material plane. But sometimes they get caught when the earth turns into mud. Taurus is symbolized by the bull, in its strength and in its stubbornness. It is the farmer who has the patience and the wisdom to know the growing seasons. And it is the banker who is obsessed with the money accruing in his vault. Bob's career was the perfect symbol for his Soul Pattern. He stayed in the bank for years, even when he felt unhappy and stuck.

When I told Bob that he needed to become more Scorpian, to emulate his Soul Potential, he was appalled. His father had been a Scorpio—and was a violent and vengeful man who had done irreparable harm to his family. The last thing Bob ever wanted was to be like his father. However, I helped him understand another side of Scorpio: a gentler, more sensitive, more emotional, transformative side.

This new side of Scorpio made more sense to Bob. His wife had complained for years that he held back his feelings, both emotionally and sexually. Once Bob learned more about his Soul Potential in Scorpio, he soon realized that becoming more Scorpian would be in his best interest. I explained to him that Scorpio stands for having the courage to confront issues and probe one's emotions. For Bob, that meant forgiving his father.

I describe those with Soul Potential in Scorpio as "the Sherlock Holmeses of the universe," because they are very interested in probing their own unconscious, to learn more about their emotions, desires, and needs. They also have a propensity for helping others transform and regenerate themselves passionately. Interestingly, Bob followed along this path, seeking not only to uncover layers of himself but to help others do the same. He has been studying psychology for some time now and is close to completing his Ph.D.

Bob's journey to realizing his Soul Potential took him from a mundane existence to investigating the full range of emotions, both in himself and in others. Scorpio is about what "I want" and what "I need" and is unafraid to pursue its aspirations. From a person who was terrified of change with his Soul Pattern in Taurus, Bob evolved to a person who recognized that change is the only reality, a promising indicator of his Soul Potential in Scorpio.

# CHAPTER 4

# Learning About Your Soul Pattern and Soul Potential

As we have mentioned, your Soul Pattern and Soul Potential signs are diametrically opposite each other. Thus, if your Soul Pattern is in Gemini, your Soul Potential is in Sagittarius, or vice versa. The other five pairs are: Taurus/Scorpio, Aries/Libra, Pisces/Virgo, Aquarius/Leo, and Capricorn/Cancer. In order to determine which signs correspond to your Soul Pattern and your Soul Potential, consult Chart 1, referring to the day, month, and year you were born.

### Chart 1: Soul Pattern and Soul Potential Signs

| Date Interval | Soul Pattern | Soul Potential |
|---|---|---|
| Jan.1, 1900–Dec. 28, 1900 | Gemini | Sagittarius |
| Dec. 29, 1900–July 17, 1902 | Taurus | Scorpio |
| July 18, 1902–Feb. 4, 1904 | Aries | Libra |
| Feb. 5, 1904–Aug. 23, 1905 | Pisces | Virgo |
| Aug. 24, 1905–Mar. 13, 1907 | Aquarius | Leo |
| Mar. 14, 1907–Sept. 29, 1908 | Capricorn | Cancer |
| Sept. 30, 1908–April 18, 1910 | Sagittarius | Gemini |
| April 19, 1910–Nov. 7, 1911 | Scorpio | Taurus |
| Nov. 8, 1911–May 26, 1913 | Libra | Aries |
| May 27, 1913–Dec. 13, 1914 | Virgo | Pisces |
| Dec. 14, 1914–July 2, 1916 | Leo | Aquarius |
| July 3, 1916–Jan. 19, 1918 | Cancer | Capricorn |
| Jan. 20, 1918–Aug. 9, 1919 | Gemini | Sagittarius |
| Aug. 10, 1919–Feb. 26, 1921 | Taurus | Scorpio |

| Date Interval | Soul Pattern | Soul Potential |
|---|---|---|
| Feb. 27, 1921–Sept. 15, 1922 | Aries | Libra |
| Sept. 16, 1922–April 4, 1924 | Pisces | Virgo |
| April 5, 1924–Oct. 22, 1925 | Aquarius | Leo |
| Oct. 23, 1925–May 12, 1927 | Capricorn | Cancer |
| May 13, 1927–Nov. 28, 1928 | Sagittarius | Gemini |
| Nov. 29, 1928–June 18, 1930 | Scorpio | Taurus |
| June 19, 1930–Jan. 6, 1932 | Libra | Aries |
| Jan. 7, 1932–July 25, 1933 | Virgo | Pisces |
| July 26, 1933–Feb. 12, 1935 | Leo | Aquarius |
| Feb. 13, 1935–Sept. 1, 1936 | Cancer | Capricorn |
| Sept. 2, 1936–Mar. 21, 1938 | Gemini | Sagittarius |
| Mar. 22, 1938–Oct. 9, 1939 | Taurus | Scorpio |
| Oct. 10, 1939–April 27, 1941 | Aries | Libra |
| April 28, 1941–Nov. 15, 1942 | Pisces | Virgo |
| Nov. 16, 1942–June 3, 1944 | Aquarius | Leo |
| June 4, 1944–Dec. 23, 1945 | Capricorn | Cancer |
| Dec. 24, 1945–July 11, 1947 | Sagittarius | Gemini |
| July 12, 1947–Jan. 28, 1949 | Scorpio | Taurus |
| Jan. 29, 1949–Aug. 17, 1950 | Libra | Aries |
| Aug. 18, 1950–Mar. 7, 1952 | Virgo | Pisces |
| Mar. 8, 1952–Oct. 2, 1953 | Leo | Aquarius |
| Oct. 3, 1953–April 12, 1955 | Cancer | Capricorn |
| April 13, 1955–Nov. 4, 1956 | Gemini | Sagittarius |
| Nov. 5, 1956–May 21, 1958 | Taurus | Scorpio |
| May 22, 1958–Dec. 8, 1959 | Aries | Libra |
| Dec. 9, 1959–July 3, 1961 | Pisces | Virgo |
| July 4, 1961–Jan. 13, 1963 | Aquarius | Leo |
| Jan. 14, 1963–Aug. 5, 1964 | Capricorn | Cancer |
| Aug. 6, 1964–Feb. 21, 1966 | Sagittarius | Gemini |
| Feb. 22, 1966–Sept. 10, 1967 | Scorpio | Taurus |
| Sept. 11, 1967–April 3, 1967 | Libra | Aries |
| April 4, 1967–Oct. 15, 1970 | Virgo | Pisces |
| Oct. 16, 1970–May 5, 1972 | Leo | Aquarius |
| May 6, 1972–Nov. 22, 1973 | Cancer | Capricorn |

| Date Interval | Soul Pattern | Soul Potential |
|---|---|---|
| Nov. 23, 1973–June 12, 1975 | Gemini | Sagittarius |
| June 13, 1975–Dec. 29, 1976 | Taurus | Scorpio |
| Dec. 30, 1976–July 19, 1978 | Aries | Libra |
| July 20, 1978–Feb. 5, 1980 | Pisces | Virgo |
| Feb. 6, 1980–Aug. 25, 1981 | Aquarius | Leo |
| Aug. 26, 1981–Mar. 14, 1983 | Capricorn | Cancer |
| Mar. 15, 1983–Oct. 1, 1984 | Sagittarius | Gemini |
| Oct. 2, 1984–April 20, 1986 | Scorpio | Taurus |
| April 21, 1986–Nov. 8, 1987 | Libra | Aries |
| Nov. 9, 1987–May 28, 1989 | Virgo | Pisces |
| May 29, 1989–Dec. 15, 1990 | Leo | Aquarius |
| Dec. 16, 1990–July 4, 1992 | Cancer | Capricorn |
| July 5, 1992–Jan. 21, 1994 | Gemini | Sagittarius |
| Jan. 22, 1994–Aug. 11, 1995 | Taurus | Scorpio |
| Aug. 12, 1995–Feb. 27, 1997 | Aries | Libra |
| Feb. 28, 1997–Sept. 17, 1998 | Pisces | Virgo |
| Sept. 18, 1998–Dec. 31, 1999 | Aquarius | Leo |

After you find your Soul Pattern and Soul Potential signs, consult Chart 2 to learn more about the energies and characteristics associated with them.

### Chart 2: Soul Pattern Energetics Model

| Aries | Taurus | Gemini |
|---|---|---|
| defiant | opinionated | deceptive |
| dominating | greedy | nervous |
| brash | fearful | always tense |
| tactless | retentive | unreliable |
| arrogant | lazy | inconsistent |
| uncooperative | materialistic | moody |
| combative | indulgent | distracted |
| self-absorbed | jealous | gossipy |
| selfish | stubborn | easily bored |

### Aries
accident prone
angry
impetuous
hot-headed
unreliable

### Taurus
fearful of change
slow
overvalues self
undervalues self
stingy

### Gemini
unfocused
manipulative
scattered
lost in present
high-strung

### Cancer
too sensitive
crabby
manipulative
obsessed with past
clingy
too reserved
childish
passive
needs being needed
smothering
insecure
negative
easily hurt
timid

### Leo
fearful of aging
needs attention
requires applause
demands respect
melodramatic
dictating
self-centered
vain
needs center stage
pretentious
autocratic
conceited
patronizing
disdainful

### Virgo
tends to blame
judgmental
obsessive
too logical
perfectionistic
sometimes petty
melancholy
martyristic
too analytical
fussy
fears disease
work-obsessed
dissecting
needs to be right

### Libra
ambivalent
wishy-washy
superficial
fears conflict
avoids anger
overly compromising
too relational
passive
peace at any price
status conscious
apathetic
dishonest

### Scorpio
raging
fanatical
manipulative
withholding
secretive
too intense
loves chaos
jealous
possessive
revengeful
judgmental
caustic

### Sagittarius
preachy
academic
outspoken
claustrophobic
hot-headed
restless
too abstract
too generous
impatient
afraid of commitment
unrealistic
too futuristic

| *Libra* | *Scorpio* | *Sagittarius* |
|---|---|---|
| vain | distrustful | overly expansive |
| procrastinating | paranoid | irresponsible |
| fickle | intimidating | impractical |

| *Capricorn* | *Aquarius* | *Pisces* |
|---|---|---|
| materialistic | overly logical | timid |
| rigid | too detached | feels inadequate |
| overly ambitious | oblivious | martyristic |
| obsessed with past | intolerant | escapist |
| pessimistic | meddlesome | addictive |
| unresponsive | cold | easily deceived |
| stern | remote | illusionary |
| disciplinarian | repressed | codependent |
| always needs rules | impersonal | fearful |
| overly cautious | radical | introvert |
| arrogant | opinionated | indolent |
| stubborn | too unpredictable | impractical |
| brooding | erratic | sacrificing |
| insensitive | aloof | wounded healer |

These characteristics are the tendencies that each Soul Pattern may repress and then project into the world. Most of our past life themes are unconscious, and therefore we project them outside ourselves. These words give you an opportunity to bring your memories to light and deal with them on a conscious level.

## SOUL PATTERN: PUTTING WORDS AND SYMBOLS INTO CONTEXT

When you look at the Energetics Model for the words concerning your Soul Pattern sign, they may well elicit in you an emotional response ranging from anger to ambivalence. The emotional reaction you're experiencing tells you that an unconscious theme has just been catalyzed. The stronger your reaction, the more significant is the past life memory.

### Soul Pattern Exercise

This five-step exercise gives you an opportunity to access your past life memories, bring them to light, and deal with them on a conscious level. Once you are conscious of your past, you can value the emotions you feel and utilize them to more clearly understand your past lives.

## STEP 1

Identify the words in your Soul Pattern sign in Chart 2 that elicit in you the most negative emotions, that make you feel uneasy, uncomfortable, or annoyed.

## STEP 2

Take the words you've just selected, and create a short story from them. Using these words will help you provide a structure for the story and kindle your memory. The karmic story you write will come from your reservoir of past memories. Don't be concerned that you're only "making it up" and that it won't be valid. Do not discount the information because you feel it came from your imagination. Of all the thousands of stories you could have written, there is an important reason why you created that particular one. It could explain why you are stuck in patterns that keep you from creating the love you want and pursuing your soul mission.

## STEP 3

Using your imagination, set your story in a specific time and place. Think about a historical period you've been interested in, and place your story in that time. Using the words you have chosen, decide if you were a man or a woman. Keep true to the words, and develop a story.

Years ago when I did this exercise, I chose July 3, 1863, in Gettysburg, Pennsylvania, because as a small child I had been fascinated by Pickett's Charge. I would go to a special place, a hundred yards from the bloody angle near the stone wall that was held by the Union, and play there. When I got older, I felt drawn to Gettysburg for a different reason: that day and place held an important past life memory. Because of the words I had chosen from my Soul Pattern (*rebel, revolutionary, individualistic, out of sync*), coupled with my past life memory, I concluded that I had been a male, a rebel, and a Confederate soldier.

## STEP 4

If this story you just scripted was an actual past life of yours, would it explain issues with which you are experiencing difficulty in this life? My memory of being a Confederate soldier began my search for a past life that finally cleared many of my current life phobias and guilts. I have always been reluctant to be a leader, preferring to stay behind the scenes, to such a degree that I created a speech problem so that I would have to stay reclusive. But this reclusiveness was explained by the fact that I had been a commander in Pickett's Charge, leading my men into a battle that left most of them dead or wounded. It also explained my current terror that my dogs would die because of some imagined carelessness of mine. I learned that, in that battle from a past life, my prized horse had also died. Knowing these past life stories helped me work through my fears in this life. Think about an unexplained anxiety or fear that you have had, and see if it dovetails with your story.

## STEP 5

If you could, how would you change one aspect of the story you just wrote? To make that change, write down a commitment you are willing to make now. Take action on that commitment for three weeks, and see what happens. I have made many such commitments based on my past life story.

## SOUL POTENTIAL: ENERGIES YOU NEED TO BRING INTO YOUR LIFE

After finding your Soul Potential sign in Chart 1, consult the Soul Potential Energetics Model in Chart 3 to learn more about the energies and characteristics associated with that sign.

## Chart 3: Soul Potential Energetics Model

*Aries*
assertive
values the physical
independent
self-aware
initiating
likes novelty
risk-taking
spontaneous
prefers actions
eager
competitive
self-motivated
courageous
explorer

*Taurus*
values self
creative
a builder
resolute
patient
a finisher
loves the earth
sensual
warm-hearted
reliable
loyal
creates security
serene
loves home

*Gemini*
curious
present to the now
self-expressive
literary
open-minded
gathers information
social
reflective
versatile
intelligent
shares information
articulate
quick
clever

*Cancer*
nurturing
sensitive
intuitive
emotional
focuses on home
maternal
empathetic
devoted
values family
faithful
supportive
tenacious
protective
romantic

*Leo*
whimsical
self-confident
leader
dramatic
generous
fun-loving
courageous
commanding
exuberant
heart-centered
inspiring
dignified
influential
willing to act

*Virgo*
service-oriented
analytical
health-aware
ordered
conscientious
practical healer
efficient
methodical
discriminating
industrious
productive
organized
practical
studious

*Libra*
loves beauty

*Scorpio*
seeks to transform

*Sagittarius*
honest

| *Libra* | *Scorpio* | *Sagittarius* |
|---|---|---|
| needs balance | sexual | philosophical |
| mediating | understands power | globe-trotter |
| touts honesty | magnetic | loves freedom |
| just | self-controlled | values nature |
| diplomatic | intense | loves animals |
| refined | passionate | futuristic |
| cooperative | strong-willed | goal directed |
| harmonious | piercing | optimistic |
| fair-minded | investigative | straightforward |
| social | ingenious | seeks truth |
| charming | deals with death | loves physicality |
| wishes to please | confrontational | ethical |
| desires peace | loves mysteries | teacher |

| *Capricorn* | *Aquarius* | *Pisces* |
|---|---|---|
| self-sufficient | humanistic | adapting |
| responsible | individualistic | psychic |
| paternal | values equality | romantic |
| wise | inventive | intuitional |
| ambitious | social activist | devoted |
| hardworking | intellectual | musical |
| conservative | tolerant | forgiving |
| traditional | friendly | spiritual |
| meticulous | broad-minded | generous |
| enterprising | imaginative | emotional |
| economical | objective | introspective |
| disciplined | altruistic | poetic |
| committed | idealistic | visionary |
| goal directed | progressive | charitable |

Examine the words in the Energetics Model under your Soul Potential sign. Do any of them elicit in you an emotional reaction? The words that cause the most fear or anxiety are usually the most important, because they are the characteristics that you probably feel unable to integrate into your life. Ironically, many of my clients have said that those words describe their friends, lovers, or family members. The truth is that we have attracted those people to ourselves to show us what we can become. You can "fake it until you make it," or alter your external behavior until you finally realize that it is right for you. Certain words represent new experiences and energies for you. Have faith in your soul's direction that you can become something that you think you can't be. Keep practicing until it becomes more natural to you.

Living your Soul Potential is not much different from learning to hit a backhand in tennis. Initially it doesn't feel right, and the first few experiences are frustrating. But as you practice and become increasingly comfortable with the new stroke, your confidence will build, and you will hit the ball more consistently and with more authority.

## WHY ASPECTS OF YOUR SOUL POTENTIAL MIGHT RANKLE YOU

At first glance, the words associated with your Soul Potential may not seem entirely appealing to you. Although we are loath to admit it, we often don't like what we can't emulate; we often become resentful. In fact, you might look at your Soul Potential characteristics and say, "That's not who I am."

Remember, your Soul Potential is not about who you are but rather who your soul wants you to aspire to be. Thus the words that you say "aren't you" actually refer to the type of energy your soul wants you to bring into your life. For instance, you may be a supremely ambitious person who has drawn a lot of satisfaction out of succeeding in a career or in a business. Now your Soul Potential tells you that you need to be more nurturing, more devoted to home life. At first glance, the notion of "domestication" may make you wince in discontent. In actuality, that initial aversion is your soul's way of telling you it wants you to experience an aspect of life that has heretofore been unfamiliar to you.

The evolution of the soul from one life to the next is all about learning and discovery, about taking on new experiences. Your soul, unlike your personality, does not judge experiences based upon whether they are negative or positive, but upon whether there is a lesson to be learned from your exposure to a new or unfamiliar experience.

## Soul Potential Exercise

### STEP 1

The words in the Soul Potential Energetics Model are positive aspects of the astrological sign that bespeak your potential. They are words that your soul wishes to bring into your life as part of your soul mission. Choose several words that inspire and excite you. Emphasize the words that refer to what you would like to become but feel you cannot. These are directions you need to take in order to follow your soul path.

### STEP 2

Choose one of the words, and create a goal around it. Write it down in your journal to confirm your commitment. Take action on the commitment for three weeks, until it becomes more of a habit. Many of my clients have noticed that the more they take action on a goal, the easier it becomes, because it is aligned with their soul's intention. Being on the path means your soul goes with you.

### STEP 3

Educate yourself about your Soul Potential and the astrological sign that symbolizes it. Learning everything you can about it is extremely important. Many of my clients have done extensive research on their Soul Potential sign, making it easier to live it. The more you know about your Soul Potential, the easier it is to fulfill. Use the Internet, the library, bookstores. Become well versed in your Soul Potential sign.

### STEP 4

Pay attention to people whose Sun sign is the same as your Soul Potential sign. They are invaluable. Ask them how they would handle various life situations. You will be amazed at how different their responses are from what yours would be. Since my Soul Potential sign is Leo, I've made it a point to learn everything I can from my Leo friends. They have taught me more about Leo than anything I've read.

## STEP 5

Each astrological sign has a color, a stone, a metal, an herb, an animal, and much more that symbolizes its energy. Become aware of the symbols that remind you of your Soul Potential. Since my Soul Potential is Leo, I wear gold, and a lion ring. I have a collection of lions that constantly remind me of the lion's courage, power, and regal qualities.

## STEP 6

Evaluate the results. Keeping a journal is very important. It will make you more aware of your progress.

### WINDOW TO YOUR SOUL

Think of your Soul Potential as a window through which you can see your soul. Through its attributes, you can understand your soul better. It's as if your soul were saying to you, "This is who I am in this life for you, and I am making it easier for you to understand that by assuming these characteristics." The following information for each of the twelve signs will give you a good head start toward learning more about your Soul Potential and considering how to integrate it to improve the quality of your life. Remember, you may not identify immediately with the description of your sign because it does not correspond to what's familiar to you. Rather, it signifies who you need to be and the energies your soul wants you to bring into your life to make it more fulfilling. Your Sun sign contains characteristics that are more familiar to you and more aptly describe who you are now. After you read about these energies, consider incorporating them into your life and then see how you feel about it.

## SOUL POTENTIAL SIGNS

### ARIES

The spiritual warrior. Those with Soul Potential in Aries are natural athletes, pioneers, and leaders. They are also self-aware, creative, masculine, confident, and competitive. They enjoy action, speed, and taking risks. They may be assertive and bold, and they don't mind being alone because of Aries' extraordinary self-value. Archetypes: the Native American warrior; the sportsman who competes with self; the beginning of spring.

### TAURUS

The spiritual gardener. Earthy, sensual, loyal, and practical, those with a Soul Potential in Taurus represent self-worth. Patient and determined, they follow their goals to completion. As builders, they put one block on top of the next to create stable and secure earthly foundations. They represent serenity and peace, warmth and love. Home is important because it represents security. Archetypes: the architect; the gardener; the singer; the farmer.

### GEMINI

The spiritual messenger. Those with a Soul Potential in Gemini are bright and versatile and are exceptional communicators. Their curious, versatile, and intellectual tendencies make them effective information gatherers who enjoy writing and speaking. They have the gift of being able to revel in the moment. Archetypes: the news journalist; the radio personality; the wordsmith.

### CANCER

The spiritual mother. Emotional, sensitive, maternal, and home-loving, with an Earth Mother orientation, those with a Soul Potential in Cancer often want to create a nest for nurturing and tending to those they love. Highly intuitional, they are devoted to supporting the child in all of us and are able to express their deepest feelings, unafraid of showing their vulnerability. Archetypes: the mother; feminine nature; the guardian of the home; the summer; and the gourmet cook.

## LEO

The spiritual king. Proud, regal, dramatic, and a leader, those who have the sign of Leo representing their Soul Potential honor and respect themselves, are inspirational, and have a powerful presence. They are joyful, spontaneous, and playful, yet they can be sophisticated at the same time. Another Leonine quality is having confidence in leadership and teaching others to do the same. Archetypes: the actor; the leader; the child; the inspired commander; the sun; the male lion.

## VIRGO

The practical healer. Those with a Soul Potential in Virgo strive to be organized, analytical, logical, and precise. Their mission is to serve humanity, especially on health issues. Efficient and dependable, they can be highly discriminating and are able to prioritize their lives and help others do the same. They should be teaching others about order and service, and they need to learn the true meaning of perfection and order to truly value themselves. Archetypes: the nurse; the accountant; the business planner; harvest time.

## LIBRA

The master negotiator. Cultured, artistically refined, and diplomatic, those with Soul Potential in Libra are interested in cooperation and fairness. They strive for balance, harmony, and justice, and they seek to create compromise through negotiation. Libras need to develop harmony in their relationships and to value other points of view. They also desire to create beauty in the world. Archetypes: the judge; the artist; the relationship counselor; the diplomat; the interior designer; the scales of justice; the spiritual judge.

## SCORPIO

The spiritual investigator—powerful, intense, and passionate. Those with Soul Potential in Scorpio can be captivating, probing, and transformative. They seek to comprehend the mysteries of life. They are highly creative, and they know what they want and pursue it intensely. They must focus on accessing and understanding their inner power and their abilities to control it. They need to investigate the depths of their emotions and how to use them as a means for self-healing and helping others. They yearn to transform darkness into light. Archetypes: the psychiatrist; the detective; the hypnotist; the eagle.

## SAGITTARIUS

The spiritual teacher. Philosophical and expansive, free in mind, body, and spirit, those who have their Soul Potential in Sagittarius gravitate toward travel, which helps them develop their big-picture view of life. They strive to be highly ethical and believe in helping others to see all the rich experiences life has to offer. They are generous and inspirational, teaching by example. Freedom of thought and a devout belief in serendipity (all things happen for good reasons) are the energies they seek. Archetypes: the teacher; the philosopher; the traveler; the wild stallion; the plains.

## CAPRICORN

The spiritual father. Those with Soul Potential in Capricorn are known for being responsible, sagacious, goal-oriented, loyal, committed, disciplined, and reality based. They value precedent as a learning experience and place high value on maturity and wisdom. They help others see the path to their soul mission and continually make adjustments to succeed at the goals they've set. Archetypes: the good father; the corporate leader; the oak tree.

## AQUARIUS

The spiritual individualist. Highly innovative, those with Aquarius as their Soul Potential sign believe in causes that will help them grow spiritually and intellectually. Considered unconventional, they believe in the future and have the alacrity to change what does not work. Open to new ideas and philosophies, they can draw quick insights with their deep understanding of the mind-body-spirit connection. They may also be scientific, with an ability to grasp new technology intuitively. Archetypes: the quantum physicist; the computer tech/software developer; the revolutionary; the astrologer.

## PISCES

The spiritual companion. Sensitive, adapting, imaginative, sympathetic, and holistic, those with their Soul Potential in Pisces are highly emotional and intuitional and are able to express their feelings easily. They can be musically inclined, trusting, devoted, and serene. Through the creative arts, music, and meditation, they are able to connect with their spiritual centers. They have a need to serve others, in order to develop their healing potential. Archetypes: the priest; the dancer; the musician; the swimmer; the ballet; creatures of the ocean.

# CHAPTER 5

# Mercury: Your Orientation to the World

The way we view the world is colored by all the obvious components of our identity: race, religion, economic strata, gender, geography, and culture. For examples, we need look no farther than the deep fissure in the United States between blacks and whites, the tortuous struggle for peace between Israelis and Palestinians, the age-old hatred between Catholics and Protestants in Northern Ireland, the continued savagery between Hutus and Tutsis in Rwanda, and unrest that continues to plague the fractionalized states of the former Yugoslavia. John Gray's *Men Are from Mars, Women Are from Venus* has sold millions of copies predicated on one premise: that men and women are different and perceive things from entirely different vantage points.

But our perceptions are also greatly influenced by a less obvious factor that has nothing to do with our ethnicity, our genitalia, the color of our skin, or our religion. The impact of our personal filter—our Mercury placement—transcends all of the effects manifested in us by our nationality, race, gender, and so on. Mercury is about who we are, how we receive and perceive information, what we do with it, and how we express ourselves once we have it.

Mercury symbolizes the way each of us indigenously comprehends the world at large within the context of our own lives. Children of the same parents, raised in the same home, attending the same school, trained in the same religious and social environment, can be extraordinarily different in how they filter their world.

Mercury helps us understand our intellectual and emotional orientations to life, showing us how we communicate our innate talents and connect with others. It defines how we wish to align ourselves with others by sharing our ideas, thoughts, and ideals. It represents our desire to express our needs, perceptions, and ideas through speech, as well as our need to be understood.

I divide Mercury traits into two categories:

1. Receptive—receiving information
2. Expressive—giving information

One of the first things I tell my new interns is that it is our responsibility to hear, understand, and communicate effectively with our clients. In order to do that, I tell them, they must learn and master the symbols, meanings, and energies of all twelve astrological signs. You can imagine their reaction upon learning that they must master twelve languages! But acknowledging that there are twelve different ways to perceive and process information is the philosophical underpinning on which the study of Mercury is based.

Considering that people's views of the world are influenced by twelve different spiritual filters, compounded by their religious, racial, and ethnic contexts, the enduring conflagrations across the globe become easier to comprehend, if no less distressing. Communicating effectively is one of our highest priorities, paramount to the success of all our relationships, yet few people understand that there are twelve different ways to do it. Learning about your personal filter—your Mercury's traits—and the filters of those people with whom you interact undoubtedly will be one of the most essential lessons you glean from this book.

Mercury differs from the other planets in that it is not a karmic planet. It deals only with issues relating to our personality in this life. Your Mercury filter was chosen for you by your soul, for your personality's intellectual evolution.

*"Since the measuring device has been constructed by the observer . . . we have to remember that what we observe is not nature in itself but nature exposed to our method of questioning."*

Werner Heisenberg

## MERCURY TRAITS: HOW WE PROCESS INFORMATION

Each of us has a sign into which the planet Mercury is located at the time of our birth. The following chart provides you with your personal Mercury placement.

### *Mercury Placements*

| If you were born: | Your Mercury is in the sign of . . . | If you were born: | Your Mercury is in the sign of . . . |
|---|---|---|---|
| Jan. 1–Jan. 9, 1900 | Sagittarius | May 30–June 26, 1902 | Cancer |
| Jan. 10–Jan. 28, 1900 | Capricorn | June 27–July 13, 1902 | Gemini |
| Jan. 29–Feb. 14, 1900 | Aquarius | July 14–Aug. 2, 1902 | Cancer |
| Feb. 15–Mar. 3, 1900 | Pisces | Aug. 3–Aug. 17, 1902 | Leo |
| Mar. 4–Mar. 29, 1900 | Aries | Aug. 18–Sept. 4, 1902 | Virgo |
| Mar. 30–April 17, 1900 | Pisces | Sept. 5–Sept. 28, 1902 | Libra |
| April 18–May 11, 1900 | Aries | Sept. 29–Oct. 15, 1902 | Scorpio |
| May 12–May 26, 1900 | Taurus | Oct. 16–Nov. 10, 1902 | Libra |
| May 27–June 9, 1900 | Gemini | Nov. 11–Nov. 30, 1902 | Scorpio |
| June 10–June 27, 1900 | Cancer | Dec. 1–Dec. 18, 1902 | Sagittarius |
| June 28–Sept. 3, 1900 | Leo | Dec. 19–Jan. 6, 1903 | Capricorn |
| Sept. 4–Sept. 18, 1900 | Virgo | Jan. 7–Mar. 14, 1903 | Aquarius |
| Sept. 19–Oct. 7, 1900 | Libra | Mar. 15–April 2, 1903 | Pisces |
| Oct. 8–Oct. 30, 1900 | Scorpio | April 3–April 16, 1903 | Aries |
| Oct. 31–Nov. 18, 1900 | Sagittarius | April 17–May 2, 1903 | Taurus |
| Nov. 19–Dec. 12, 1900 | Scorpio | May 3–July 10, 1903 | Gemini |
| Dec. 13–Jan. 2, 1901 | Sagittarius | July 11–July 25, 1903 | Cancer |
| Jan. 3–Jan. 21, 1901 | Capricorn | July 26–Aug. 9, 1903 | Leo |
| Jan. 22–Feb. 7, 1901 | Aquarius | Aug. 10–Aug. 29, 1903 | Virgo |
| Feb. 8–April 15, 1901 | Pisces | Aug. 30–Nov. 4, 1903 | Libra |
| April 16–May 3, 1901 | Aries | Nov. 5–Nov. 22, 1903 | Scorpio |
| May 4–May 17, 1901 | Taurus | Nov. 23–Dec. 11, 1903 | Sagittarius |
| May 18–June 1, 1901 | Gemini | Dec. 12–Jan. 2, 1904 | Capricorn |
| June 2–Aug. 10, 1901 | Cancer | Jan. 3–Jan. 14, 1904 | Aquarius |
| Aug. 11–Aug. 25, 1901 | Leo | Jan. 15–Feb. 15, 1904 | Capricorn |
| Aug. 26–Sept. 11, 1901 | Virgo | Feb. 16–Mar. 7, 1904 | Aquarius |
| Sept. 12–Oct. 1, 1901 | Libra | Mar. 8–Mar. 23, 1904 | Pisces |
| Oct. 2–Dec. 6, 1901 | Scorpio | Mar. 24–April 7, 1904 | Aries |
| Dec. 7–Dec. 26, 1901 | Sagittarius | April 8–June 14, 1904 | Taurus |
| Dec. 27–Jan. 13, 1902 | Capricorn | June 15–July 1, 1904 | Gemini |
| Jan. 14–Feb. 1, 1902 | Aquarius | July 2–July 16, 1904 | Cancer |
| Feb. 2–Feb. 18, 1902 | Pisces | July 17–Aug. 1, 1904 | Leo |
| Feb. 19–Mar. 19, 1902 | Aquarius | Aug. 2–Aug. 28, 1904 | Virgo |
| Mar. 20–April 9, 1902 | Pisces | Aug. 29–Sept. 7, 1904 | Libra |
| April 10–April 25, 1902 | Aries | Sept. 8–Oct. 9, 1904 | Virgo |
| April 26–May 9, 1902 | Taurus | Oct. 10–Oct. 26, 1904 | Libra |
| May 10–May 29, 1902 | Gemini | Oct. 27–Nov. 14, 1904 | Scorpio |

| If you were born: | Your Mercury is in the sign of . . . | If you were born: | Your Mercury is in the sign of . . . |
|---|---|---|---|
| Nov. 15–Dec. 4, 1904 | Sagittarius | Feb. 6–April 12, 1908 | Pisces |
| Dec. 5–Feb. 9, 1905 | Capricorn | April 13–April 29, 1908 | Aries |
| Feb. 10–Feb. 27, 1905 | Aquarius | April 30–May 13, 1908 | Taurus |
| Feb. 28–Mar. 15, 1905 | Pisces | May 14–May 30, 1908 | Gemini |
| Mar. 16–April 1, 1905 | Aries | May 31–Aug. 6, 1908 | Cancer |
| April 2–April 28, 1905 | Taurus | Aug. 7–Aug. 22, 1908 | Leo |
| April 29–May 15, 1905 | Aries | Aug. 23–Sept. 7, 1908 | Virgo |
| May 16–June 8, 1905 | Taurus | Sept. 8–Sept. 28, 1908 | Libra |
| June 9–June 23, 1905 | Gemini | Sept. 29–Nov. 1, 1908 | Scorpio |
| June 24–July 7, 1905 | Cancer | Nov. 2–Nov. 11, 1908 | Libra |
| July 8–July 27, 1905 | Leo | Nov. 12–Dec. 3, 1908 | Scorpio |
| July 28–Oct. 1, 1905 | Virgo | Dec. 4–Dec. 22, 1908 | Sagittarius |
| Oct. 2–Oct. 19, 1905 | Libra | Dec. 23–Jan. 10, 1909 | Capricorn |
| Oct. 20–Nov. 7, 1905 | Scorpio | Jan. 11–Mar. 17, 1909 | Aquarius |
| Nov. 8–Dec. 2, 1905 | Sagittarius | Mar. 18–April 6, 1909 | Pisces |
| Dec. 3–Dec. 10, 1905 | Capricorn | April 7–April 21, 1909 | Aries |
| Dec. 11–Jan. 12, 1906 | Sagittarius | April 22–May 5, 1909 | Taurus |
| Jan. 13–Feb. 2, 1906 | Capricorn | May 6–July 13, 1909 | Gemini |
| Feb. 3–Feb. 20, 1906 | Aquarius | July 14–July 30, 1909 | Cancer |
| Feb. 21–Mar. 8, 1906 | Pisces | July 31–Aug. 13, 1909 | Leo |
| Mar. 9–May 15, 1906 | Aries | Aug. 14–Aug. 31, 1909 | Virgo |
| May 16–May 31, 1906 | Taurus | Sept. 1–Nov. 7, 1909 | Libra |
| June 1–June 14, 1906 | Gemini | Nov. 8–Nov. 26, 1909 | Scorpio |
| June 15–June 30, 1906 | Cancer | Nov. 27–Dec. 15, 1909 | Sagittarius |
| July 1–Sept. 7, 1906 | Leo | Dec. 16–Jan. 3, 1910 | Capricorn |
| Sept. 8–Sept. 24, 1906 | Virgo | Jan. 4–Jan. 31, 1910 | Aquarius |
| Sept. 25–Oct. 11, 1906 | Libra | Feb. 1–Feb. 15, 1910 | Capricorn |
| Oct. 12–Nov. 1, 1906 | Scorpio | Feb. 16–Mar. 11, 1910 | Aquarius |
| Nov. 2–Dec. 6, 1906 | Sagittarius | Mar. 12–Mar. 29, 1910 | Pisces |
| Dec. 7–Dec. 12, 1906 | Scorpio | Mar. 30–April 13, 1910 | Aries |
| Dec. 13–Jan. 7, 1907 | Sagittarius | April 14–April 30, 1910 | Taurus |
| Jan. 8–Jan. 26, 1907 | Capricorn | May 1–June 1, 1910 | Gemini |
| Jan. 27–Feb. 12, 1907 | Aquarius | June 2–June 11, 1910 | Taurus |
| Feb. 13–Mar. 3, 1907 | Pisces | June 12–July 7, 1910 | Gemini |
| Mar. 4–Mar. 14, 1907 | Aries | July 8–July 21, 1910 | Cancer |
| Mar. 15–April 18, 1907 | Pisces | July 22–Aug. 6, 1910 | Leo |
| April 19–May 8, 1907 | Aries | Aug. 7–Aug. 27, 1910 | Virgo |
| May 9–May 23, 1907 | Taurus | Aug. 28–Sept. 28, 1910 | Libra |
| May 24–June 6, 1907 | Gemini | Sept. 29–Oct. 12, 1910 | Virgo |
| June 7–June 27, 1907 | Cancer | Oct. 13–Oct. 31, 1910 | Libra |
| June 28–July 26, 1907 | Leo | Nov. 1–Nov. 19, 1910 | Scorpio |
| July 27–Aug. 12, 1907 | Cancer | Nov. 20–Dec. 8, 1910 | Sagittarius |
| Aug. 13–Aug. 31, 1907 | Leo | Dec. 9–Feb. 13, 1911 | Capricorn |
| Sept. 1–Sept. 16, 1907 | Virgo | Feb. 14–Mar. 4, 1911 | Aquarius |
| Sept. 17–Oct. 5, 1907 | Libra | Mar. 5–Mar. 21, 1911 | Pisces |
| Oct. 6–Dec. 11, 1907 | Scorpio | Mar. 22–April 5, 1911 | Aries |
| Dec. 12–Dec. 31, 1907 | Sagittarius | April 6–June 13, 1911 | Taurus |
| Jan. 1–Jan. 18, 1908 | Capricorn | June 14–June 28, 1911 | Gemini |
| Jan. 19–Feb. 5, 1908 | Aquarius | June 29–July 13, 1911 | Cancer |

| If you were born: | Your Mercury is in the sign of . . . | If you were born: | Your Mercury is in the sign of . . . |
|---|---|---|---|
| July 14–July 30, 1911 | Leo | Dec. 28–Jan. 15, 1915 | Capricorn |
| July 31–Oct. 6, 1911 | Virgo | Jan. 16–Feb. 2, 1915 | Aquarius |
| Oct. 7–Oct. 24, 1911 | Libra | Feb. 3–Feb. 23, 1915 | Pisces |
| Oct. 25–Nov. 12, 1911 | Scorpio | Feb. 24–Mar. 19, 1915 | Aquarius |
| Nov. 13–Dec. 3, 1911 | Sagittarius | Mar. 20–April 10, 1915 | Pisces |
| Dec. 4–Dec. 27, 1911 | Capricorn | April 11–April 26, 1915 | Aries |
| Dec. 28–Jan. 15, 1912 | Sagittarius | April 27–May 10, 1915 | Taurus |
| Jan. 16–Feb. 7, 1912 | Capricorn | May 11–May 29, 1915 | Gemini |
| Feb. 8–Feb. 25, 1912 | Aquarius | May 30–Aug. 4, 1915 | Cancer |
| Feb. 26–Mar. 12, 1912 | Pisces | Aug. 5–Aug. 19, 1915 | Leo |
| Mar. 13–May 16, 1912 | Aries | Aug. 20–Sept. 5, 1915 | Virgo |
| May 17–June 5, 1912 | Taurus | Sept. 6–Sept. 28, 1915 | Libra |
| June 6–June 19, 1912 | Gemini | Sept. 29–Oct. 21, 1915 | Scorpio |
| June 20–July 4, 1912 | Cancer | Oct. 22–Nov. 11, 1915 | Libra |
| July 5–July 26, 1912 | Leo | Nov. 12–Dec. 1, 1915 | Scorpio |
| July 27–Aug. 21, 1912 | Virgo | Dec. 2–Dec. 20, 1915 | Sagittarius |
| Aug. 22–Sept. 10, 1912 | Leo | Dec. 21–Jan. 8, 1916 | Capricorn |
| Sept. 11–Sept. 28, 1912 | Virgo | Jan. 9–Mar. 15, 1916 | Aquarius |
| Sept. 29–Oct. 15, 1912 | Libra | Mar. 16–April 2, 1916 | Pisces |
| Oct. 16–Nov. 4, 1912 | Scorpio | April 3–April 17, 1916 | Aries |
| Nov. 5–Jan. 10, 1913 | Sagittarius | April 18–May 2, 1916 | Taurus |
| Jan. 11–Jan. 30, 1913 | Capricorn | May 3–July 10, 1916 | Gemini |
| Jan. 31–Feb. 16, 1913 | Aquarius | July 11–July 26, 1916 | Cancer |
| Feb. 17–Mar. 4, 1913 | Pisces | July 27–Aug. 10, 1916 | Leo |
| Mar. 5–April 7, 1913 | Aries | Aug. 11–Aug. 29, 1916 | Virgo |
| April 8–April 14, 1913 | Pisces | Aug. 30–Nov. 4, 1916 | Libra |
| April 15–May 12, 1913 | Aries | Nov. 5–Nov. 23, 1916 | Scorpio |
| May 13–May 28, 1913 | Taurus | Nov. 24–Dec. 12, 1916 | Sagittarius |
| May 29–June 10, 1913 | Gemini | Dec. 13–Jan. 1, 1917 | Capricorn |
| June 11–June 28, 1913 | Cancer | Jan. 2–Jan. 18, 1917 | Aquarius |
| June 29–Sept. 4, 1913 | Leo | Jan. 19–Feb. 15, 1917 | Capricorn |
| Sept. 5–Sept. 20, 1913 | Virgo | Feb. 16–Mar. 8, 1917 | Aquarius |
| Sept. 21–Oct. 8, 1913 | Libra | Mar. 9–Mar. 25, 1917 | Pisces |
| Oct. 9–Oct. 30, 1913 | Scorpio | Mar. 26–April 9, 1917 | Aries |
| Oct. 31–Nov. 23, 1913 | Sagittarius | April 10–June 14, 1917 | Taurus |
| Nov. 24–Dec. 13, 1913 | Scorpio | June 15–July 3, 1917 | Gemini |
| Dec. 14–Jan. 3, 1914 | Sagittarius | July 4–July 17, 1917 | Cancer |
| Jan. 4–Jan. 22, 1914 | Capricorn | July 18–Aug. 2, 1917 | Leo |
| Jan. 23–Feb. 8, 1914 | Aquarius | Aug. 3–Aug. 26, 1917 | Virgo |
| Feb. 9–April 16, 1914 | Pisces | Aug. 27–Sept. 14, 1917 | Libra |
| April 17–May 5, 1914 | Aries | Sept. 15–Oct. 10, 1917 | Virgo |
| May 6–May 19, 1914 | Taurus | Oct. 11–Oct. 28, 1917 | Libra |
| May 20–June 3, 1914 | Gemini | Oct. 29–Nov. 15, 1917 | Scorpio |
| June 4–Aug. 11, 1914 | Cancer | Nov. 16–Dec. 5, 1917 | Sagittarius |
| Aug. 12–Aug. 27, 1914 | Leo | Dec. 6–Feb. 10, 1918 | Capricorn |
| Aug. 28–Sept. 12, 1914 | Virgo | Feb. 11–Mar. 1, 1918 | Aquarius |
| Sept. 13–Oct. 2, 1914 | Libra | Mar. 2–Mar. 17, 1918 | Pisces |
| Oct. 3–Dec. 8, 1914 | Scorpio | Mar. 18–April 2, 1918 | Aries |
| Dec. 9–Dec. 27, 1914 | Sagittarius | April 3–June 10, 1918 | Taurus |

| If you were born: | Your Mercury is in the sign of . . . | If you were born: | Your Mercury is in the sign of . . . |
|---|---|---|---|
| June 11–June 24, 1918 | Gemini | Sept. 30–Dec. 5, 1921 | Scorpio |
| June 25–July 9, 1918 | Cancer | Dec. 6–Dec. 24, 1921 | Sagittarius |
| July 10–July 28, 1918 | Leo | Dec. 25–Jan. 11, 1922 | Capricorn |
| July 29–Oct. 3, 1918 | Virgo | Jan. 12–Feb. 1, 1922 | Aquarius |
| Oct. 4–Oct. 20, 1918 | Libra | Feb. 2–Feb. 9, 1922 | Pisces |
| Oct. 21–Nov. 8, 1918 | Scorpio | Feb. 10–Mar. 18, 1922 | Aquarius |
| Nov. 9–Dec. 1, 1918 | Sagittarius | Mar. 19–April 7, 1922 | Pisces |
| Dec. 2–Dec. 15, 1918 | Capricorn | April 8–April 22, 1922 | Aries |
| Dec. 16–Jan. 13, 1919 | Sagittarius | April 23–May 7, 1922 | Taurus |
| Jan. 14–Feb. 3, 1919 | Capricorn | May 8–June 1, 1922 | Gemini |
| Feb. 4–Feb. 21, 1919 | Aquarius | June 2–June 10, 1922 | Cancer |
| Feb. 22–Mar. 9, 1919 | Pisces | June 11–July 13, 1922 | Gemini |
| Mar. 10–May 16, 1919 | Aries | July 14–July 31, 1922 | Cancer |
| May 17–June 2, 1919 | Taurus | Aug. 1–Aug. 15, 1922 | Leo |
| June 3–June 16, 1919 | Gemini | Aug. 16–Sept. 2, 1922 | Virgo |
| June 17–July 2, 1919 | Cancer | Sept. 3–Oct. 1, 1922 | Libra |
| July 3–Sept. 9, 1919 | Leo | Oct. 2–Oct. 5, 1922 | Scorpio |
| Sept. 10–Sept. 25, 1919 | Virgo | Oct. 6–Nov. 8, 1922 | Libra |
| Sept. 26–Oct. 13, 1919 | Libra | Nov. 9–Nov. 27, 1922 | Scorpio |
| Oct. 14–Nov. 2, 1919 | Scorpio | Nov. 28–Dec. 17, 1922 | Sagittarius |
| Nov. 3–Jan. 8, 1920 | Sagittarius | Dec. 18–Jan. 4, 1923 | Capricorn |
| Jan. 9–Jan. 27, 1920 | Capricorn | Jan. 5–Feb. 6, 1923 | Aquarius |
| Jan. 28–Feb. 13, 1920 | Aquarius | Feb. 7–Feb. 13, 1923 | Capricorn |
| Feb. 14–Mar. 2, 1920 | Pisces | Feb. 14–Mar. 13, 1923 | Aquarius |
| Mar. 3–Mar. 19, 1920 | Aries | Mar. 14–Mar. 30, 1923 | Pisces |
| Mar. 20–April 17, 1920 | Pisces | Mar. 31–April 14, 1923 | Aries |
| April 18–May 8, 1920 | Aries | April 15–May 1, 1923 | Taurus |
| May 9–May 24, 1920 | Taurus | May 2–July 8, 1923 | Gemini |
| May 25–June 7, 1920 | Gemini | July 9–July 23, 1923 | Cancer |
| June 8–June 26, 1920 | Cancer | July 24–Aug. 7, 1923 | Leo |
| June 27–Aug. 2, 1920 | Leo | Aug. 8–Aug. 27, 1923 | Virgo |
| Aug. 3–Aug. 10, 1920 | Cancer | Aug. 28–Oct. 4, 1923 | Libra |
| Aug. 11–Aug. 31, 1920 | Leo | Oct. 5–Oct. 11, 1923 | Virgo |
| Sept. 1–Sept. 16, 1920 | Virgo | Oct. 12–Nov. 2, 1923 | Libra |
| Sept. 17–Oct. 5, 1920 | Libra | Nov. 3–Nov. 20, 1923 | Scorpio |
| Oct. 6–Oct. 30, 1920 | Scorpio | Nov. 21–Dec. 9, 1923 | Sagittarius |
| Oct. 31–Nov. 10, 1920 | Sagittarius | Dec. 10–Feb. 14, 1924 | Capricorn |
| Nov. 11–Dec. 11, 1920 | Scorpio | Feb. 15–Mar. 5, 1924 | Aquarius |
| Dec. 12–Dec. 31, 1920 | Sagittarius | Mar. 6–Mar. 21, 1924 | Pisces |
| Jan. 1–Jan. 19, 1921 | Capricorn | Mar. 22–April 5, 1924 | Aries |
| Jan. 20–Feb. 5, 1921 | Aquarius | April 6–June 13, 1924 | Taurus |
| Feb. 6–April 14, 1921 | Pisces | June 14–June 29, 1924 | Gemini |
| April 15–May 1, 1921 | Aries | June 30–July 13, 1924 | Cancer |
| May 2–May 15, 1921 | Taurus | July 14–July 30, 1924 | Leo |
| May 16–May 31, 1921 | Gemini | July 31–Oct. 7, 1924 | Virgo |
| June 1–Aug. 8, 1921 | Cancer | Oct. 8–Oct. 24, 1924 | Libra |
| Aug. 9–Aug. 23, 1921 | Leo | Oct. 25–Nov. 12, 1924 | Scorpio |
| Aug. 24–Sept. 9, 1921 | Virgo | Nov. 13–Dec. 2, 1924 | Sagittarius |
| Sept. 10–Sept. 29, 1921 | Libra | Dec. 3–Dec. 31, 1924 | Capricorn |

| If you were born: | Your Mercury is in the sign of . . . | If you were born: | Your Mercury is in the sign of . . . |
|---|---|---|---|
| Jan. 1–Jan. 14, 1925 | Sagittarius | Mar. 19–April 11, 1928 | Pisces |
| Jan. 15–Feb. 7, 1925 | Capricorn | April 12–April 27, 1928 | Aries |
| Feb. 8–Feb. 25, 1925 | Aquarius | April 28–May 11, 1928 | Taurus |
| Feb. 26–Mar. 13, 1925 | Pisces | May 12–May 28, 1928 | Gemini |
| Mar. 14–April 1, 1925 | Aries | May 29–Aug. 4, 1928 | Cancer |
| April 2–April 15, 1925 | Taurus | Aug. 5–Aug. 19, 1928 | Leo |
| April 16–May 17, 1925 | Aries | Aug. 20–Sept. 5, 1928 | Virgo |
| May 18–June 6, 1925 | Taurus | Sept. 6–Sept. 27, 1928 | Libra |
| June 7–June 20, 1925 | Gemini | Sept. 28–Oct. 24, 1928 | Scorpio |
| June 21–July 5, 1925 | Cancer | Oct. 25–Nov. 11, 1928 | Libra |
| July 6–July 26, 1925 | Leo | Nov. 12–Dec. 1, 1928 | Scorpio |
| July 27–Aug. 27, 1925 | Virgo | Dec. 2–Dec. 20, 1928 | Sagittarius |
| Aug. 28–Sept. 11, 1925 | Leo | Dec. 21–Jan. 8, 1929 | Capricorn |
| Sept. 12–Sept. 29, 1925 | Virgo | Jan. 9–Mar. 16, 1929 | Aquarius |
| Sept. 30–Oct. 17, 1925 | Libra | Mar. 17–April 3, 1929 | Pisces |
| Oct. 18–Nov. 5, 1925 | Scorpio | April 4–April 19, 1929 | Aries |
| Nov. 6–Jan. 11, 1926 | Sagittarius | April 20–May 3, 1929 | Taurus |
| Jan. 12–Jan. 31, 1926 | Capricorn | May 4–July 11, 1929 | Gemini |
| Feb. 1–Feb. 17, 1926 | Aquarius | July 12–July 27, 1929 | Cancer |
| Feb. 18–Mar. 6, 1926 | Pisces | July 28–Aug. 11, 1929 | Leo |
| Mar. 7–May 13, 1926 | Aries | Aug. 12–Aug. 30, 1929 | Virgo |
| May 14–May 29, 1926 | Taurus | Sept. 1–Nov. 5, 1929 | Libra |
| May 30–June 12, 1926 | Gemini | Nov. 6–Nov. 24, 1929 | Scorpio |
| June 13–June 29, 1926 | Cancer | Nov. 25–Dec. 13, 1929 | Sagittarius |
| June 30–Sept. 5, 1926 | Leo | Dec. 14–Jan. 2, 1930 | Capricorn |
| Sept. 6–Sept. 21, 1926 | Virgo | Jan. 3–Jan. 23, 1930 | Aquarius |
| Sept. 22–Oct. 9, 1926 | Libra | Jan. 24–Feb. 15, 1930 | Capricorn |
| Oct. 10–Oct. 31, 1926 | Scorpio | Feb. 16–Mar. 9, 1930 | Aquarius |
| Nov. 1–Nov. 28, 1926 | Sagittarius | Mar. 10–Mar. 26, 1930 | Pisces |
| Nov. 29–Dec. 13, 1926 | Scorpio | Mar. 27–April 10, 1930 | Aries |
| Dec. 14–Jan. 5, 1927 | Sagittarius | April 11–May 1, 1930 | Taurus |
| Jan. 6–Jan. 24, 1927 | Capricorn | May 2–May 17, 1930 | Gemini |
| Jan. 25–Feb. 10, 1927 | Aquarius | May 18–June 14, 1930 | Taurus |
| Feb. 11–April 17, 1927 | Pisces | June 15–July 4, 1930 | Gemini |
| April 18–May 6, 1927 | Aries | July 5–July 19, 1930 | Cancer |
| May 7–May 20, 1927 | Taurus | July 20–Aug. 4, 1930 | Leo |
| May 21–June 4, 1927 | Gemini | Aug. 5–Aug. 26, 1930 | Virgo |
| June 5–June 28, 1927 | Cancer | Aug. 27–Sept. 20, 1930 | Libra |
| June 29–July 14, 1927 | Leo | Sept. 21–Oct. 11, 1930 | Virgo |
| July 15–Aug. 12, 1927 | Cancer | Oct. 12–Oct. 29, 1930 | Libra |
| Aug. 13–Aug. 28, 1927 | Leo | Oct. 30–Nov. 17, 1930 | Scorpio |
| Aug. 29–Sept. 14, 1927 | Virgo | Nov. 18–Dec. 6, 1930 | Sagittarius |
| Sept. 15–Oct. 3, 1927 | Libra | Dec. 7–Feb. 11, 1931 | Capricorn |
| Oct. 4–Dec. 9, 1927 | Scorpio | Feb. 12–Mar. 2, 1931 | Aquarius |
| Dec. 10–Dec. 29, 1927 | Sagittarius | Mar. 3–Mar. 18, 1921 | Pisces |
| Dec. 30–Jan. 16, 1928 | Capricorn | Mar. 19–April 3, 1931 | Aries |
| Jan. 17–Feb. 3, 1928 | Aquarius | April 4–June 11, 1931 | Taurus |
| Feb. 4–Feb. 29, 1928 | Pisces | June 12–June 26, 1931 | Gemini |
| Mar. 1–Mar. 18, 1928 | Aquarius | June 27–July 10, 1931 | Cancer |

| If you were born: | Your Mercury is in the sign of . . . | If you were born: | Your Mercury is in the sign of . . . |
|---|---|---|---|
| July 11–July 28, 1931 | Leo | Dec. 26–Jan. 13, 1935 | Capricorn |
| July 29–Oct. 4, 1931 | Virgo | Jan. 14–Feb. 1, 1935 | Aquarius |
| Oct. 5–Oct. 22, 1931 | Libra | Feb. 2–Feb. 15, 1935 | Pisces |
| Oct. 23–Nov. 10, 1931 | Scorpio | Feb. 15–Mar. 18, 1935 | Aquarius |
| Nov. 11–Dec. 1, 1931 | Sagittarius | Mar. 19–April 8, 1935 | Pisces |
| Dec. 2–Dec. 20, 1931 | Capricorn | April 9–April 24, 1935 | Aries |
| Dec. 21–Jan. 14, 1932 | Sagittarius | April 25–May 8, 1935 | Taurus |
| Jan. 15–Feb. 5, 1932 | Capricorn | May 9–May 29, 1935 | Gemini |
| Feb. 6–Feb. 23, 1932 | Aquarius | May 30–June 20, 1935 | Cancer |
| Feb. 24–Mar. 9, 1932 | Pisces | June 21–July 13, 1935 | Gemini |
| Mar. 10–May 15, 1932 | Aries | July 14–Aug. 2, 1935 | Cancer |
| May 16–June 2, 1932 | Taurus | Aug. 3–Aug. 16, 1935 | Leo |
| June 3–June 16, 1932 | Gemini | Aug. 17–Sept. 3, 1935 | Virgo |
| June 17–July 2, 1932 | Cancer | Sept. 4–Sept. 28, 1935 | Libra |
| July 3–July 27, 1932 | Leo | Sept. 29–Oct. 12, 1935 | Scorpio |
| July 28–Aug. 10, 1932 | Virgo | Oct. 13–Nov. 10, 1935 | Libra |
| Aug. 11–Sept. 9, 1932 | Leo | Nov. 11–Nov. 29, 1935 | Scorpio |
| Sept. 10–Sept. 26, 1932 | Virgo | Nov. 30–Dec. 18, 1935 | Sagittarius |
| Sept. 27–Oct. 13, 1932 | Libra | Dec. 19–Jan. 6, 1936 | Capricorn |
| Oct. 14–Nov. 2, 1932 | Scorpio | Jan. 7–Mar. 13, 1936 | Aquarius |
| Nov. 3–Jan. 8, 1933 | Sagittarius | Mar. 14–Mar. 31, 1936 | Pisces |
| Jan. 9–Jan. 27, 1933 | Capricorn | April 1–April 15, 1936 | Aries |
| Jan. 28–Feb. 14, 1933 | Aquarius | April 16–May 1, 1936 | Taurus |
| Feb. 15–Mar. 3, 1933 | Pisces | May 2–July 8, 1936 | Gemini |
| Mar. 4–Mar. 25, 1933 | Aries | July 9–July 23, 1936 | Cancer |
| Mar. 26–April 17, 1933 | Pisces | July 24–Aug. 7, 1936 | Leo |
| April 18–May 10, 1933 | Aries | Aug. 8–Aug. 27, 1936 | Virgo |
| May 11–May 25, 1933 | Taurus | Aug. 28–Nov. 2, 1936 | Libra |
| May 26–June 8, 1933 | Gemini | Nov. 3–Nov. 21, 1936 | Scorpio |
| June 9–June 27, 1933 | Cancer | Nov. 22–Dec. 10, 1936 | Sagittarius |
| June 28–Sept. 2, 1933 | Leo | Dec. 11–Jan. 1, 1937 | Capricorn |
| Sept. 3–Sept. 18, 1933 | Virgo | Jan. 2–Jan. 9, 1937 | Aquarius |
| Sept. 19–Oct. 6, 1933 | Libra | Jan. 10–Feb. 14, 1937 | Capricorn |
| Oct. 7–Oct. 30, 1933 | Scorpio | Feb. 15–Mar. 6, 1937 | Aquarius |
| Oct. 31–Nov. 16, 1933 | Sagittarius | Mar. 7–Mar. 23, 1937 | Pisces |
| Nov. 17–Dec. 12, 1933 | Scorpio | Mar. 24–April 7, 1937 | Aries |
| Dec. 13–Jan. 1, 1934 | Sagittarius | April 8–June 13, 1937 | Taurus |
| Jan. 2–Jan. 20, 1934 | Capricorn | June 14–July 1, 1937 | Gemini |
| Jan. 21–Feb. 6, 1934 | Aquarius | July 2–July 15, 1937 | Cancer |
| Feb. 7–April 15, 1934 | Pisces | July 16–July 31, 1937 | Leo |
| April 16–May 2, 1934 | Aries | Aug. 1–Oct. 8, 1937 | Virgo |
| May 3–May 16, 1934 | Taurus | Oct. 9–Oct. 26, 1937 | Libra |
| May 17–June 1, 1934 | Gemini | Oct. 27–Nov. 13, 1937 | Scorpio |
| June 2–Aug. 9, 1934 | Cancer | Nov. 14–Dec. 3, 1937 | Sagittarius |
| Aug. 10–Aug. 25, 1934 | Leo | Dec. 4–Jan. 6, 1938 | Capricorn |
| Aug. 26–Sept. 10, 1934 | Virgo | Jan. 7–Jan. 12, 1938 | Sagittarius |
| Sept. 11–Sept. 30, 1934 | Libra | Jan. 13–Feb. 8, 1938 | Capricorn |
| Oct. 1–Dec. 6, 1934 | Scorpio | Feb. 9–Feb. 27, 1938 | Aquarius |
| Dec. 7–Dec. 25, 1934 | Sagittarius | Feb. 28–Mar. 14, 1938 | Pisces |

| If you were born: | Your Mercury is in the sign of . . . | If you were born: | Your Mercury is in the sign of . . . |
|---|---|---|---|
| Mar. 15–April 1, 1938 | Aries | April 29–May 13, 1941 | Taurus |
| April 2–April 23, 1938 | Taurus | May 14–May 29, 1941 | Gemini |
| April 24–May 16, 1938 | Aries | May 30–Aug. 6, 1941 | Cancer |
| May 17–June 8, 1938 | Taurus | Aug. 7–Aug. 21, 1941 | Leo |
| June 9–June 22, 1938 | Gemini | Aug. 22–Sept. 6, 1941 | Virgo |
| June 23–July 7, 1938 | Cancer | Sept. 7–Sept. 28, 1941 | Libra |
| July 8–July 26, 1938 | Leo | Sept. 29–Oct. 29, 1941 | Scorpio |
| July 27–Sept. 3, 1938 | Virgo | Oct. 30–Nov. 11, 1941 | Libra |
| Sept. 4–Sept. 10, 1938 | Leo | Nov. 12–Dec. 2, 1941 | Scorpio |
| Sept. 11–Oct. 1, 1938 | Virgo | Dec. 3–Dec. 22, 1941 | Sagittarius |
| Oct. 2–Oct. 18, 1938 | Libra | Dec. 23–Jan. 9, 1942 | Capricorn |
| Oct. 19–Nov. 6, 1938 | Scorpio | Jan. 10–Mar. 16, 1942 | Aquarius |
| Nov. 7–Jan. 12, 1939 | Sagittarius | Mar. 17–April 5, 1942 | Pisces |
| Jan. 13–Feb. 1, 1939 | Capricorn | April 6–April 20, 1942 | Aries |
| Feb. 2–Feb. 19, 1939 | Aquarius | April 21–May 5, 1942 | Taurus |
| Feb. 20–Mar. 7, 1939 | Pisces | May 6–July 12, 1942 | Gemini |
| Mar. 8–May 14, 1939 | Aries | July 13–July 29, 1942 | Cancer |
| May 15–May 31, 1939 | Taurus | July 30–Aug. 13, 1942 | Leo |
| June 1–June 13, 1939 | Gemini | Aug. 14–Aug. 31, 1942 | Virgo |
| June 14–June 30, 1939 | Cancer | Sept. 1–Nov. 7, 1942 | Libra |
| July 1–Sept. 7, 1939 | Leo | Nov. 8–Nov. 25, 1942 | Scorpio |
| Sept. 8–Sept. 23, 1939 | Virgo | Nov. 26–Dec. 14, 1942 | Sagittarius |
| Sept. 24–Oct. 11, 1939 | Libra | Dec. 15–Jan. 3, 1943 | Capricorn |
| Oct. 12–Nov. 1, 1939 | Scorpio | Jan. 4–Jan. 27, 1943 | Aquarius |
| Nov. 2–Dec. 3, 1939 | Sagittarius | Jan. 28–Feb. 15, 1943 | Capricorn |
| Dec. 4–Dec. 13, 1939 | Scorpio | Feb. 16–Mar. 11, 1943 | Aquarius |
| Dec. 14–Jan. 6, 1940 | Sagittarius | Mar. 12–Mar. 28, 1943 | Pisces |
| Jan. 7–Jan. 25, 1940 | Capricorn | Mar. 29–April 12, 1943 | Aries |
| Jan. 26–Feb. 11, 1940 | Aquarius | April 13–April 30, 1943 | Taurus |
| Feb. 12–Mar. 4, 1940 | Pisces | May 1–May 26, 1943 | Gemini |
| Mar. 5–Mar. 8, 1940 | Aries | May 27–June 14, 1943 | Taurus |
| Mar. 9–April 17, 1940 | Pisces | June 15–July 6, 1943 | Gemini |
| April 18–May 6, 1940 | Aries | July 7–July 20, 1943 | Cancer |
| May 7–May 21, 1940 | Taurus | July 21–Aug. 5, 1943 | Leo |
| May 22–June 4, 1940 | Gemini | Aug. 6–Aug. 27, 1943 | Virgo |
| June 5–June 26, 1940 | Cancer | Aug. 28–Sept. 25, 1943 | Libra |
| June 27–July 21, 1940 | Leo | Sept. 26–Oct. 11, 1943 | Virgo |
| July 22–Aug. 11, 1940 | Cancer | Oct. 12–Oct. 30, 1943 | Libra |
| Aug. 12–Aug. 29, 1940 | Leo | Oct. 31–Nov. 18, 1943 | Scorpio |
| Aug. 30–Sept. 14, 1940 | Virgo | Nov. 19–Dec. 8, 1943 | Sagittarius |
| Sept. 15–Oct. 3, 1940 | Libra | Dec. 9–Feb. 12, 1944 | Capricorn |
| Oct. 4–Dec. 9, 1940 | Scorpio | Feb. 13–Mar. 3, 1944 | Aquarius |
| Dec. 10–Dec. 29, 1940 | Sagittarius | Mar. 4–Mar. 19, 1944 | Pisces |
| Dec. 30–Jan. 16, 1941 | Capricorn | Mar. 20–April 3, 1944 | Aries |
| Jan. 17–Feb. 3, 1941 | Aquarius | April 4–June 11, 1944 | Taurus |
| Feb. 4–Mar. 7, 1941 | Pisces | June 12–June 27, 1944 | Gemini |
| Mar. 8–Mar. 16, 1941 | Aquarius | June 28–July 11, 1944 | Cancer |
| Mar. 17–April 12, 1941 | Pisces | July 12–July 28, 1944 | Leo |
| April 13–April 28, 1941 | Aries | July 29–Oct. 5, 1944 | Virgo |

| If you were born: | Your Mercury is in the sign of . . . | If you were born: | Your Mercury is in the sign of . . . |
|---|---|---|---|
| Oct. 6–Oct. 22, 1944 | Libra | Mar. 19–April 9, 1948 | Pisces |
| Oct. 23–Nov. 10, 1944 | Scorpio | April 10–April 25, 1948 | Aries |
| Nov. 11–Dec. 1, 1944 | Sagittarius | April 26–May 9, 1948 | Taurus |
| Dec. 2–Dec. 23, 1944 | Capricorn | May 10–May 28, 1948 | Gemini |
| Dec. 24–Jan. 14, 1945 | Sagittarius | May 29–June 28, 1948 | Cancer |
| Jan. 15–Feb. 5, 1945 | Capricorn | June 29–July 11, 1948 | Gemini |
| Feb. 6–Feb. 23, 1945 | Aquarius | July 12–Aug. 2, 1948 | Cancer |
| Feb. 24–Mar. 11, 1945 | Pisces | Aug. 3–Aug. 17, 1948 | Leo |
| Mar. 12–May 16, 1945 | Aries | Aug. 18–Sept. 3, 1948 | Virgo |
| May 17–June 4, 1945 | Taurus | Sept. 4–Sept. 27, 1948 | Libra |
| June 5–June 18, 1945 | Gemini | Sept. 28–Oct. 17, 1948 | Scorpio |
| June 19–July 3, 1945 | Cancer | Oct. 18–Nov. 10, 1948 | Libra |
| July 4–July 26, 1945 | Leo | Nov. 11–Nov. 29, 1948 | Scorpio |
| July 27–Aug. 17, 1945 | Virgo | Nov. 30–Dec. 18, 1948 | Sagittarius |
| Aug. 18–Sept. 10, 1945 | Leo | Dec. 19–Jan. 6, 1949 | Capricorn |
| Sept. 11–Sept. 27, 1945 | Virgo | Jan. 7–Mar. 14, 1949 | Aquarius |
| Sept. 28–Oct. 14, 1945 | Libra | Mar. 15–April 1, 1949 | Pisces |
| Oct. 15–Nov. 3, 1945 | Scorpio | April 2–April 16, 1949 | Aries |
| Nov. 4–Jan. 9, 1946 | Sagittarius | April 17–May 2, 1949 | Taurus |
| Jan. 10–Jan. 29, 1946 | Capricorn | May 3–July 10, 1949 | Gemini |
| Jan. 30–Feb. 15, 1946 | Aquarius | July 11–July 25, 1949 | Cancer |
| Feb. 16–April 16, 1946 | Pisces | July 26–Aug. 9, 1949 | Leo |
| April 17–May 11, 1946 | Aries | Aug. 10–Aug. 28, 1949 | Virgo |
| May 12–May 27, 1946 | Taurus | Aug. 29–Nov. 3, 1949 | Libra |
| May 28–June 10, 1946 | Gemini | Nov. 4–Nov. 22, 1949 | Scorpio |
| June 11–June 27, 1946 | Cancer | Nov. 23–Dec. 11, 1949 | Sagittarius |
| June 28–Sept. 3, 1946 | Leo | Dec. 12–Jan. 1, 1950 | Capricorn |
| Sept. 4–Sept. 19, 1946 | Virgo | Jan. 2–Jan. 15, 1950 | Aquarius |
| Sept. 20–Oct. 7, 1946 | Libra | Jan. 16–Feb. 14, 1950 | Capricorn |
| Oct. 8–Oct. 30, 1946 | Scorpio | Feb. 15–Mar. 7, 1950 | Aquarius |
| Oct. 31–Nov. 20, 1946 | Sagittarius | Mar. 8–Mar. 24, 1950 | Pisces |
| Nov. 21–Dec. 12, 1946 | Scorpio | Mar. 25–April 8, 1950 | Aries |
| Dec. 13–Jan. 3, 1947 | Sagittarius | April 9–June 14, 1950 | Taurus |
| Jan. 4–Jan. 21, 1947 | Capricorn | June 15–July 2, 1950 | Gemini |
| Jan. 22–Feb. 8, 1947 | Aquarius | July 3–July 16, 1950 | Cancer |
| Feb. 9–April 16, 1947 | Pisces | July 17–Aug. 2, 1950 | Leo |
| April 17–May 4, 1947 | Aries | Aug. 3–Aug. 27, 1950 | Virgo |
| May 5–May 18, 1947 | Taurus | Aug. 28–Sept. 10, 1950 | Libra |
| May 19–June 2, 1947 | Gemini | Sept. 11–Oct. 9, 1950 | Virgo |
| June 3–Aug. 10, 1947 | Cancer | Oct. 10–Oct. 27, 1950 | Libra |
| Aug. 11–Aug. 26, 1947 | Leo | Oct. 28–Nov. 15, 1950 | Scorpio |
| Aug. 27–Sept. 11, 1947 | Virgo | Nov. 16–Dec. 5, 1950 | Sagittarius |
| Sept. 12–Oct. 1, 1947 | Libra | Dec. 6–Feb. 9, 1951 | Capricorn |
| Oct. 2–Dec. 7, 1947 | Scorpio | Feb. 10–Feb. 29, 1951 | Aquarius |
| Dec. 8–Dec. 26, 1947 | Sagittarius | Mar. 1–Mar. 16, 1951 | Pisces |
| Dec. 27–Jan. 14, 1948 | Capricorn | Mar. 17–April 2 , 1951 | Aries |
| Jan. 15–Feb. 2, 1948 | Aquarius | April 3–May 1, 1951 | Taurus |
| Feb. 3–Feb. 20, 1948 | Pisces | May 2–May 15, 1951 | Aries |
| Feb. 21–Mar. 18, 1948 | Aquarius | May 16–June 9, 1951 | Taurus |

| If you were born: | Your Mercury is in the sign of . . . | If you were born: | Your Mercury is in the sign of . . . |
| --- | --- | --- | --- |
| June 10–June 24, 1951 | Gemini | Sept. 30–Nov. 4, 1954 | Scorpio |
| June 25–July 8, 1951 | Cancer | Nov. 5–Nov. 11, 1954 | Libra |
| July 9–July 27, 1951 | Leo | Nov. 12–Dec. 4, 1954 | Scorpio |
| July 28–Oct. 2, 1951 | Virgo | Dec. 5–Dec. 23, 1954 | Sagittarius |
| Oct. 3–Oct. 19, 1951 | Libra | Dec. 24–Jan. 10, 1955 | Capricorn |
| Oct. 20–Nov. 8, 1951 | Scorpio | Jan. 11–Mar. 17, 1955 | Aquarius |
| Nov. 9–Dec. 1, 1951 | Sagittarius | Mar. 18–April 6, 1955 | Pisces |
| Dec. 2–Dec. 12, 1951 | Capricorn | April 7–April 22, 1955 | Aries |
| Dec. 13–Jan. 13, 1952 | Sagittarius | April 23–May 6, 1955 | Taurus |
| Jan. 14–Feb. 3, 1952 | Capricorn | May 7–July 13, 1955 | Gemini |
| Feb. 4–Feb. 20, 1952 | Aquarius | July 14–July 30, 1955 | Cancer |
| Feb. 21–Mar. 7, 1952 | Pisces | July 31–Aug. 14, 1955 | Leo |
| Mar. 8–May 14, 1952 | Aries | Aug. 15–Sept. 30, 1955 | Virgo |
| May 15–May 31, 1952 | Taurus | Oct. 1–Nov. 8, 1955 | Libra |
| June 1–June 14, 1952 | Gemini | Nov. 9–Nov. 27, 1955 | Scorpio |
| June 15–June 30, 1952 | Cancer | Nov. 28–Dec. 16, 1955 | Sagittarius |
| July 1–Sept. 7, 1952 | Leo | Dec. 17–Jan. 4, 1956 | Capricorn |
| Sept. 8–Sept. 23, 1952 | Virgo | Jan. 5–Mar. 11, 1956 | Aquarius |
| Sept. 24–Oct. 11, 1952 | Libra | Mar. 12–Mar. 31, 1956 | Pisces |
| Oct. 12–Nov. 1, 1952 | Scorpio | April 1–April 12, 1956 | Aries |
| Nov. 2–Jan. 6, 1953 | Sagittarius | April 13–April 29, 1956 | Taurus |
| Jan. 7–Jan. 25, 1953 | Capricorn | April 30–July 6, 1956 | Gemini |
| Jan. 26–Feb. 11, 1953 | Aquarius | July 7–July 21, 1956 | Cancer |
| Feb. 12–Mar. 2, 1953 | Pisces | July 22–Aug. 5, 1956 | Leo |
| Mar. 3–Mar. 15, 1953 | Aries | Aug. 6–Aug. 26, 1956 | Virgo |
| Mar. 16–April 17, 1953 | Pisces | Aug. 27–Sept. 30, 1956 | Libra |
| April 18–May 8, 1953 | Aries | Oct. 1–Oct. 11, 1956 | Virgo |
| May 9–May 23, 1953 | Taurus | Oct. 12–Oct. 31, 1956 | Libra |
| May 24–June 6, 1953 | Gemini | Nov. 1–Nov. 18, 1956 | Scorpio |
| June 7–June 26, 1953 | Cancer | Nov. 19–Dec. 8, 1956 | Sagittarius |
| June 27–July 28, 1953 | Leo | Dec. 9–Feb. 12, 1957 | Capricorn |
| July 29–Aug. 11, 1953 | Cancer | Feb. 13–Mar. 4, 1957 | Aquarius |
| Aug. 12–Aug. 30, 1953 | Leo | Mar. 5–Mar. 20, 1957 | Pisces |
| Aug. 31–Sept. 15, 1953 | Virgo | Mar. 21–April 7, 1957 | Aries |
| Sept. 16–Oct. 4, 1953 | Libra | April 5–June 12, 1957 | Taurus |
| Oct. 5–Oct. 31, 1953 | Scorpio | June 13–June 27, 1957 | Gemini |
| Nov. 1–Nov. 6, 1953 | Sagittarius | June 28–July 12, 1957 | Cancer |
| Nov. 7–Dec. 10, 1953 | Scorpio | July 13–July 30, 1957 | Leo |
| Dec. 11–Dec. 30, 1953 | Sagittarius | July 31–Oct. 6, 1957 | Virgo |
| Dec. 31–Jan. 18, 1954 | Capricorn | Oct. 7–Oct. 23, 1957 | Libra |
| Jan. 19–Feb. 4, 1954 | Aquarius | Oct. 24–Nov. 11, 1957 | Scorpio |
| Feb. 5–April 13, 1954 | Pisces | Nov. 12–Jan. 14, 1958 | Sagittarius |
| April 14–April 30, 1954 | Aries | Jan. 15–Feb. 6, 1958 | Capricorn |
| May 1–May 14, 1954 | Taurus | Feb. 7–Feb. 24, 1958 | Aquarius |
| May 15–May 30, 1954 | Gemini | Feb. 25–Mar. 12, 1958 | Pisces |
| May 31–Aug. 7, 1954 | Cancer | Mar. 13–May 17, 1958 | Aries |
| Aug. 8–Aug. 22, 1954 | Leo | May 18–June 5, 1958 | Taurus |
| Aug. 23–Sept. 8, 1954 | Virgo | June 6–June 20, 1958 | Gemini |
| Sept. 9–Sept. 29, 1954 | Libra | June 21–July 4, 1958 | Cancer |

| If you were born: | Your Mercury is in the sign of . . . | If you were born: | Your Mercury is in the sign of . . . |
|---|---|---|---|
| July 5–July 26, 1958 | Leo | Nov. 11–Nov. 30, 1961 | Scorpio |
| July 27–Aug. 23, 1958 | Virgo | Dec. 1–Dec. 20, 1961 | Sagittarius |
| Aug. 24–Sept. 11, 1958 | Leo | Dec. 21–Jan. 7, 1962 | Capricorn |
| Sept. 12–Sept. 28, 1958 | Virgo | Jan. 8–Mar. 15, 1962 | Aquarius |
| Sept. 29–Oct. 16, 1958 | Libra | Mar. 16–April 3, 1962 | Pisces |
| Oct. 17–Nov. 5, 1958 | Scorpio | April 4–April 18, 1962 | Aries |
| Nov. 6–Jan. 10, 1959 | Sagittarius | April 19–May 3, 1962 | Taurus |
| Jan. 11–Jan. 30, 1959 | Capricorn | May 4–July 11, 1962 | Gemini |
| Jan. 31–Feb. 17, 1959 | Aquarius | July 12–July 26, 1962 | Cancer |
| Feb. 18–Mar. 5, 1959 | Pisces | July 27–Aug. 10, 1962 | Leo |
| Mar. 6–May 12, 1959 | Aries | Aug. 11–Aug. 29, 1962 | Virgo |
| May 13–May 28, 1959 | Taurus | Aug. 30–Nov. 5 , 1962 | Libra |
| May 29–June 11, 1959 | Gemini | Nov. 6–Nov. 23, 1962 | Scorpio |
| June 12–June 28, 1959 | Cancer | Nov. 24–Dec. 12, 1962 | Sagittarius |
| June 29–Sept. 5, 1959 | Leo | Dec. 13–Jan. 2, 1963 | Capricorn |
| Sept. 6–Sept. 21, 1959 | Virgo | Jan. 3–Jan. 20, 1963 | Aquarius |
| Sept. 22–Oct. 9, 1959 | Libra | Jan. 21–Feb. 15, 1963 | Capricorn |
| Oct. 10–Oct. 31, 1959 | Scorpio | Feb. 16–Mar. 9, 1963 | Aquarius |
| Nov. 1–Nov. 25, 1959 | Sagittarius | Mar. 10–Mar. 26, 1963 | Pisces |
| Nov. 26–Dec. 13, 1959 | Scorpio | Mar. 27–April 9, 1963 | Aries |
| Dec. 14–Jan. 4, 1960 | Sagittarius | April 10–May 3, 1963 | Taurus |
| Jan. 5–Jan. 23, 1960 | Capricorn | May 4–May 10, 1963 | Gemini |
| Jan. 24–Feb. 9, 1960 | Aquarius | May 11–June 14, 1963 | Taurus |
| Feb. 10–April 16, 1960 | Pisces | June 15–July 4, 1963 | Gemini |
| April 17–May 4, 1960 | Aries | July 5–July 18, 1963 | Cancer |
| May 5–May 19, 1960 | Taurus | July 19–Aug. 3, 1963 | Leo |
| May 20–June 2, 1960 | Gemini | Aug. 4–Aug. 26, 1963 | Virgo |
| June 3–June 30, 1960 | Cancer | Aug. 27–Sept. 16, 1963 | Libra |
| July 1–July 6, 1960 | Leo | Sept. 17–Oct. 10, 1963 | Virgo |
| July 7–Aug. 10, 1960 | Cancer | Oct. 11–Oct. 28, 1963 | Libra |
| Aug. 11–Aug. 27, 1960 | Leo | Oct. 29–Nov. 16, 1963 | Scorpio |
| Aug. 28–Sept. 12, 1960 | Virgo | Nov. 17–Dec. 6, 1963 | Sagittarius |
| Sept. 13–Oct. 1, 1960 | Libra | Dec. 7–Feb. 10, 1964 | Capricorn |
| Oct. 2–Dec. 7, 1960 | Scorpio | Feb. 11–Feb. 29, 1964 | Aquarius |
| Dec. 8–Dec. 27, 1960 | Sagittarius | Mar. 1–Mar. 16, 1964 | Pisces |
| Dec. 28–Jan. 14, 1961 | Capricorn | Mar. 17–April 2, 1964 | Aries |
| Jan. 15–Feb. 1, 1961 | Aquarius | April 3–June 9, 1964 | Taurus |
| Feb. 2–Feb. 24, 1961 | Pisces | June 10–June 24, 1964 | Gemini |
| Feb. 25–Mar. 18, 1961 | Aquarius | June 25–July 9, 1964 | Cancer |
| Mar. 19–April 10, 1961 | Pisces | July 10–July 27, 1964 | Leo |
| April 11–April 26, 1961 | Aries | July 28–Oct. 2, 1964 | Virgo |
| April 27–May 10, 1961 | Taurus | Oct. 3–Oct. 20, 1964 | Libra |
| May 11–May 28, 1961 | Gemini | Oct. 21–Nov. 8, 1964 | Scorpio |
| May 28–Aug. 4, 1961 | Cancer | Nov. 9–Nov. 30, 1964 | Sagittarius |
| Aug. 5–Aug. 18, 1961 | Leo | Dec. 1–Dec. 16, 1964 | Capricorn |
| Aug. 19–Sept. 4, 1961 | Virgo | Dec. 17–Jan. 13, 1965 | Sagittarius |
| Sept. 5–Sept. 27, 1961 | Libra | Jan. 14–Feb. 3, 1965 | Capricorn |
| Sept. 28–Oct. 22, 1961 | Scorpio | Feb. 4–Feb. 21, 1965 | Aquarius |
| Oct. 23–Nov. 10, 1961 | Libra | Feb. 22–Mar. 9, 1965 | Pisces |

| If you were born: | Your Mercury is in the sign of . . . | If you were born: | Your Mercury is in the sign of . . . |
| --- | --- | --- | --- |
| Mar. 10–May 15, 1965 | Aries | July 14–July 31, 1968 | Cancer |
| May 16–June 2, 1965 | Taurus | Aug. 1–Aug. 15, 1968 | Leo |
| June 3–June 16, 1965 | Gemini | Aug. 16–Sept. 1, 1968 | Virgo |
| June 17–July 1, 1965 | Cancer | Sept. 2–Sept. 28, 1968 | Libra |
| July 2–July 31, 1965 | Leo | Sept. 29–Oct. 7, 1968 | Scorpio |
| Aug. 1–Aug. 3, 1965 | Virgo | Oct. 8–Nov. 8, 1968 | Libra |
| Aug. 4–Sept. 8, 1965 | Leo | Nov. 9–Nov. 27, 1968 | Scorpio |
| Sept. 9–Sept. 25, 1965 | Virgo | Nov. 28–Dec. 16, 1968 | Sagittarius |
| Sept. 26–Oct. 12, 1965 | Libra | Dec. 17–Jan. 4, 1969 | Capricorn |
| Oct. 13–Nov. 2, 1965 | Scorpio | Jan. 5–Mar. 12, 1969 | Aquarius |
| Nov. 3–Jan. 7, 1966 | Sagittarius | Mar. 13–Mar. 30, 1969 | Pisces |
| Jan. 8–Jan. 27, 1966 | Capricorn | Mar. 31–April 14, 1969 | Aries |
| Jan. 28–Feb. 13, 1966 | Aquarius | April 15–April 30, 1969 | Taurus |
| Feb. 14–Mar. 3, 1966 | Pisces | May 1–July 8, 1969 | Gemini |
| Mar. 4–Mar. 22, 1966 | Aries | July 9–July 22, 1969 | Cancer |
| Mar. 23–April 17, 1966 | Pisces | July 23–Aug. 7, 1969 | Leo |
| April 18–May 9, 1966 | Aries | Aug. 8–Aug. 27, 1969 | Virgo |
| May 10–May 24, 1966 | Taurus | Aug. 28–Oct. 7, 1969 | Libra |
| May 25–June 7, 1966 | Gemini | Oct. 8–Oct. 9, 1969 | Virgo |
| June 8–June 26, 1966 | Cancer | Oct. 10–Nov. 1, 1969 | Libra |
| June 27–Sept. 1, 1966 | Leo | Nov. 2–Nov. 20, 1969 | Scorpio |
| Sept. 2–Sept. 17, 1966 | Virgo | Nov. 21–Dec. 9, 1969 | Sagittarius |
| Sept. 18–Oct. 5, 1966 | Libra | Dec. 10–Feb. 13, 1970 | Capricorn |
| Oct. 6–Oct. 30, 1966 | Scorpio | Feb. 14–Mar. 5, 1970 | Aquarius |
| Oct. 31–Nov. 13, 1966 | Sagittarius | Mar. 6–Mar. 22, 1970 | Pisces |
| Nov. 14–Dec. 11, 1966 | Scorpio | Mar. 23–April 6, 1970 | Aries |
| Dec. 12–Jan. 1, 1967 | Sagittarius | April 7–June 13, 1970 | Taurus |
| Jan. 2–Jan. 19, 1967 | Capricorn | June 14–June 30, 1970 | Gemini |
| Jan. 20–Feb. 6, 1967 | Aquarius | July 1–July 14, 1970 | Cancer |
| Feb. 7–April 14, 1967 | Pisces | July 15–July 31, 1970 | Leo |
| April 15–May 1, 1967 | Aries | Aug. 1–Oct. 7, 1970 | Virgo |
| May 2–May 16, 1967 | Taurus | Oct. 8–Oct. 25, 1970 | Libra |
| May 17–May 31, 1967 | Gemini | Oct. 26–Nov. 13, 1970 | Scorpio |
| June 1–Aug. 8, 1967 | Cancer | Nov. 14–Dec. 3, 1970 | Sagittarius |
| Aug. 9–Aug. 24, 1967 | Leo | Dec. 4–Jan. 2, 1971 | Capricorn |
| Aug. 25–Sept. 9, 1967 | Virgo | Jan. 3–Jan. 14, 1971 | Sagittarius |
| Sept. 10–Sept. 30, 1967 | Libra | Jan. 15–Feb. 7, 1971 | Capricorn |
| Oct. 1–Dec. 5, 1967 | Scorpio | Feb. 8–Feb. 26, 1971 | Aquarius |
| Dec. 6–Dec. 24, 1967 | Sagittarius | Feb. 27–Mar. 14, 1971 | Pisces |
| Dec. 25–Jan. 12, 1968 | Capricorn | Mar. 15–April 1, 1971 | Aries |
| Jan. 13–Feb. 1, 1968 | Aquarius | April 2–April 18, 1971 | Taurus |
| Feb. 2–Feb. 11, 1968 | Pisces | April 19–May 17, 1971 | Aries |
| Feb. 12–Mar. 17, 1968 | Aquarius | May 18–June 7, 1971 | Taurus |
| Mar. 18–April 7, 1968 | Pisces | June 8–June 21, 1971 | Gemini |
| April 8–April 22, 1968 | Aries | June 22–July 6, 1971 | Cancer |
| April 23–May 6, 1968 | Taurus | July 7–July 26, 1971 | Leo |
| May 7–May 29, 1968 | Gemini | July 27–Aug. 29, 1971 | Virgo |
| May 30–June 13, 1968 | Cancer | Aug. 30–Sept. 11, 1971 | Leo |
| June 14–July 13, 1968 | Gemini | Sept. 12–Sept. 30, 1971 | Virgo |

| If you were born: | Your Mercury is in the sign of . . . | If you were born: | Your Mercury is in the sign of . . . |
|---|---|---|---|
| Oct. 1–Oct. 17, 1971 | Libra | Mar. 17–April 4, 1975 | Pisces |
| Oct. 18–Nov. 6, 1971 | Scorpio | April 5–April 19, 1975 | Aries |
| Nov. 7–Jan. 11, 1972 | Sagittarius | April 20–May 4, 1975 | Taurus |
| Jan. 12–Jan. 31, 1972 | Capricorn | May 5–July 12, 1975 | Gemini |
| Feb. 1–Feb. 18, 1972 | Aquarius | July 13–July 28, 1975 | Cancer |
| Feb. 19–Mar. 5, 1972 | Pisces | July 29–Aug. 12, 1975 | Leo |
| Mar. 6–May 12, 1972 | Aries | Aug. 13–Aug. 30, 1975 | Virgo |
| May 13–May 30, 1972 | Taurus | Aug. 31–Nov. 6, 1975 | Libra |
| May 31–June 12, 1972 | Gemini | Nov. 7–Nov. 25, 1975 | Scorpio |
| June 13–June 28, 1972 | Cancer | Nov. 26–Dec. 14, 1975 | Sagittarius |
| June 29–Sept. 5, 1972 | Leo | Dec. 15–Jan. 2, 1976 | Capricorn |
| Sept. 6–Sept. 21, 1972 | Virgo | Jan. 3–Jan. 25, 1976 | Aquarius |
| Sept. 22–Oct. 9, 1972 | Libra | Jan. 26–Feb. 15, 1976 | Capricorn |
| Oct. 10–Oct. 30, 1972 | Scorpio | Feb. 16–Mar. 9, 1976 | Aquarius |
| Oct. 31–Nov. 29, 1972 | Sagittarius | Mar. 10–Mar. 26, 1976 | Pisces |
| Nov. 30–Dec. 12, 1972 | Scorpio | Mar. 27–April 10, 1976 | Aries |
| Dec. 13–Jan. 4, 1973 | Sagittarius | April 11–April 29, 1976 | Taurus |
| Jan. 5–Jan. 23, 1973 | Capricorn | April 30–May 19, 1976 | Gemini |
| Jan. 24–Feb. 9, 1973 | Aquarius | May 20–June 13, 1976 | Taurus |
| Feb. 10–April 16, 1973 | Pisces | June 14–July 4, 1976 | Gemini |
| April 17–May 6 , 1973 | Aries | July 5–July 18, 1976 | Cancer |
| May 7–May 20, 1973 | Taurus | July 19–Aug. 3, 1976 | Leo |
| May 21–June 4, 1973 | Gemini | Aug. 4–Aug. 25, 1976 | Virgo |
| June 5–June 27, 1973 | Cancer | Aug. 26–Sept. 21, 1976 | Libra |
| June 28–July 16, 1973 | Leo | Sept. 22–Oct. 10, 1976 | Virgo |
| July 17–Aug. 11, 1973 | Cancer | Oct. 11–Oct. 29, 1976 | Libra |
| Aug. 12–Aug. 28, 1973 | Leo | Oct. 30–Nov. 16, 1976 | Scorpio |
| Aug. 29–Sept. 13, 1973 | Virgo | Nov. 17–Dec. 6, 1976 | Sagittarius |
| Sept. 14–Oct. 2, 1973 | Libra | Dec. 7–Feb. 10, 1976 | Capricorn |
| Oct. 3–Dec. 8, 1973 | Scorpio | Feb. 11–Mar. 2, 1977 | Aquarius |
| Dec. 9–Dec. 28, 1973 | Sagittarius | Mar. 3–Mar. 18, 1977 | Pisces |
| Dec. 29–Jan. 16, 1974 | Capricorn | Mar. 19–April 3, 1977 | Aries |
| Jan. 17–Feb. 2, 1974 | Aquarius | April 4–June 10, 1977 | Taurus |
| Feb. 3–Mar. 2, 1974 | Pisces | June 11–June 26, 1977 | Gemini |
| Mar. 3–Mar. 17, 1974 | Aquarius | June 27–July 10, 1977 | Cancer |
| Mar. 18–April 11, 1974 | Pisces | July 11–July 28, 1977 | Leo |
| April 12–April 28, 1974 | Aries | July 29–Oct. 4, 1977 | Virgo |
| April 29–May 12, 1974 | Taurus | Oct. 5–Oct. 21, 1977 | Libra |
| May 13–May 29, 1974 | Gemini | Oct. 22–Nov. 9, 1977 | Scorpio |
| May 30–Aug. 5, 1974 | Cancer | Nov. 10–Dec. 1, 1977 | Sagittarius |
| Aug. 6–Aug. 20, 1974 | Leo | Dec. 2–Dec. 21, 1977 | Capricorn |
| Aug. 21–Sept. 6, 1974 | Virgo | Dec. 22–Jan. 13, 1978 | Sagittarius |
| Sept. 7–Sept. 28, 1974 | Libra | Jan. 14–Feb. 4, 1978 | Capricorn |
| Sept. 29–Oct. 26, 1974 | Scorpio | Feb. 5–Feb. 22, 1978 | Aquarius |
| Oct. 27–Nov. 11, 1974 | Libra | Feb. 23–Mar. 10, 1978 | Pisces |
| Nov. 12–Dec. 2, 1974 | Scorpio | Mar. 11–May 16, 1978 | Aries |
| Dec. 3–Dec. 21, 1974 | Sagittarius | May 17–June 3, 1978 | Taurus |
| Dec. 22–Jan. 8, 1975 | Capricorn | June 4–June 17, 1978 | Gemini |
| Jan. 9–Mar. 16, 1975 | Aquarius | June 18–July 2, 1978 | Cancer |

| If you were born: | Your Mercury is in the sign of . . . | If you were born: | Your Mercury is in the sign of . . . |
|---|---|---|---|
| July 3–July 27, 1978 | Leo | Sept. 28–Oct. 13, 1981 | Scorpio |
| July 28–Aug. 13, 1978 | Virgo | Oct. 14–Nov. 9, 1981 | Libra |
| Aug. 14–Sept. 9, 1978 | Leo | Nov. 10–Nov. 28, 1981 | Scorpio |
| Sept. 10–Sept. 26, 1978 | Virgo | Nov. 29–Dec. 17, 1981 | Sagittarius |
| Sept. 27–Oct. 14, 1978 | Libra | Dec. 18–Jan. 5, 1982 | Capricorn |
| Oct. 15–Nov. 3, 1978 | Scorpio | Jan. 6–Mar. 13, 1982 | Aquarius |
| Nov. 4–Jan. 8, 1979 | Sagittarius | Mar. 14–Mar. 31, 1982 | Pisces |
| Jan. 9–Jan. 28, 1979 | Capricorn | April 1–April 15, 1982 | Aries |
| Jan. 29–Feb. 14, 1979 | Aquarius | April 16–May 1, 1982 | Taurus |
| Feb. 15–Mar. 3, 1979 | Pisces | May 2–July 9, 1982 | Gemini |
| Mar. 4–Mar. 28, 1979 | Aries | July 10–July 24, 1982 | Cancer |
| Mar. 29–April 17, 1979 | Pisces | July 25–Aug. 8, 1982 | Leo |
| April 18–May 10, 1979 | Aries | Aug. 9–Aug. 27, 1982 | Virgo |
| May 11–May 26, 1979 | Taurus | Aug. 28–Nov. 2, 1982 | Libra |
| May 27–June 9, 1979 | Gemini | Nov. 3–Nov. 21, 1982 | Scorpio |
| June 10–June 27, 1979 | Cancer | Nov. 22–Dec. 10, 1982 | Sagittarius |
| June 28–Sept. 2, 1979 | Leo | Dec. 11–Jan. 1, 1983 | Capricorn |
| Sept. 3–Sept. 18, 1979 | Virgo | Jan. 2–Jan. 12, 1983 | Aquarius |
| Sept. 19–Oct. 7, 1979 | Libra | Jan. 13–Feb. 14, 1983 | Capricorn |
| Oct. 8–Oct. 30, 1979 | Scorpio | Feb. 15–Mar. 6, 1983 | Aquarius |
| Oct. 31–Nov. 18, 1979 | Sagittarius | Mar. 7–Mar. 23, 1983 | Pisces |
| Nov. 19–Dec. 12, 1979 | Scorpio | Mar. 24–April 7, 1983 | Aries |
| Dec. 13–Jan. 2, 1980 | Sagittarius | April 8–June 14, 1983 | Taurus |
| Jan. 3–Jan. 21, 1980 | Capricorn | June 15–July 1, 1983 | Gemini |
| Jan. 22–Feb. 7, 1980 | Aquarius | July 2–July 15, 1983 | Cancer |
| Feb. 8–April 14, 1980 | Pisces | July 16–Aug. 1, 1983 | Leo |
| April 15–May 2, 1980 | Aries | Aug. 2–Aug. 29, 1983 | Virgo |
| May 3–May 16, 1980 | Taurus | Aug. 30–Sept. 5, 1983 | Libra |
| May 17–May 31, 1980 | Gemini | Sept. 6–Oct. 8, 1983 | Virgo |
| June 1–Aug. 8, 1980 | Cancer | Oct. 9–Oct. 26, 1983 | Libra |
| Aug. 9–Aug. 24, 1980 | Leo | Oct. 27–Nov. 14, 1983 | Scorpio |
| Aug. 25–Sept. 9, 1980 | Virgo | Nov. 15–Dec. 4, 1983 | Sagittarius |
| Sept. 10–Sept. 29, 1980 | Libra | Dec. 5–Feb. 9, 1984 | Capricorn |
| Sept. 30–Dec. 5, 1980 | Scorpio | Feb. 10–Feb. 27, 1984 | Aquarius |
| Dec. 6–Dec. 24, 1980 | Sagittarius | Feb. 28–Mar. 14, 1984 | Pisces |
| Dec. 25–Jan. 12, 1981 | Capricorn | Mar. 15–Mar. 31, 1984 | Aries |
| Jan. 13–Jan. 31, 1981 | Aquarius | April 1–April 25, 1984 | Taurus |
| Feb. 1–Feb. 16, 1981 | Pisces | April 26–May 15, 1984 | Aries |
| Feb. 17–Mar. 17, 1981 | Aquarius | May 16–June 7, 1984 | Taurus |
| Mar. 18–April 8, 1981 | Pisces | June 8–June 22, 1984 | Gemini |
| April 9–April 24, 1981 | Aries | June 23–July 6, 1984 | Cancer |
| April 25–May 8, 1981 | Taurus | July 7–July 26, 1984 | Leo |
| May 9–May 28, 1981 | Gemini | July 27–Sept. 30, 1984 | Virgo |
| May 29–June 22, 1981 | Cancer | Oct. 1–Oct. 17, 1984 | Libra |
| June 23–July 12, 1981 | Gemini | Oct. 18–Nov. 6, 1984 | Scorpio |
| July 13–Aug. 1, 1981 | Cancer | Nov. 7–Dec. 1, 1984 | Sagittarius |
| Aug. 2–Aug. 16, 1981 | Leo | Dec. 2–Dec. 7, 1984 | Capricorn |
| Aug. 17–Sept. 2, 1981 | Virgo | Dec. 8–Jan. 11, 1985 | Sagittarius |
| Sept. 3–Sept. 27, 1981 | Libra | Jan. 12–Feb. 1, 1985 | Capricorn |

| If you were born: | Your Mercury is in the sign of . . . | If you were born: | Your Mercury is in the sign of . . . |
|---|---|---|---|
| Feb. 2–Feb. 18, 1985 | Aquarius | July 13–July 28, 1988 | Cancer |
| Feb. 19–Mar. 6, 1985 | Pisces | July 29–Aug. 12, 1988 | Leo |
| Mar. 7–May 13, 1985 | Aries | Aug. 13–Aug. 30, 1988 | Virgo |
| May 14–May 30, 1985 | Taurus | Aug. 31–Nov. 6, 1988 | Libra |
| May 31–June 13, 1985 | Gemini | Nov. 7–Nov. 25, 1988 | Scorpio |
| June 14–June 29, 1985 | Cancer | Nov. 26–Dec. 14, 1988 | Sagittarius |
| June 30–Sept. 6, 1985 | Leo | Dec. 15–Jan. 2, 1989 | Capricorn |
| Sept. 7–Sept. 22, 1985 | Virgo | Jan. 3–Jan. 28, 1989 | Aquarius |
| Sept. 23–Oct. 10 1985 | Libra | Jan. 29–Feb. 14, 1989 | Capricorn |
| Oct. 11–Oct. 31, 1985 | Scorpio | Feb. 15–Mar. 10, 1989 | Aquarius |
| Nov. 1–Dec. 4, 1985 | Sagittarius | Mar. 11–Mar. 27, 1989 | Pisces |
| Dec. 5–Dec. 12, 1985 | Scorpio | Mar. 28–April 11, 1989 | Aries |
| Dec. 13–Jan. 5, 1986 | Sagittarius | April 12–April 29, 1989 | Taurus |
| Jan. 6–Jan. 24, 1986 | Capricorn | April 30–May 28, 1989 | Gemini |
| Jan. 25–Feb. 11, 1986 | Aquarius | May 29–June 12, 1989 | Taurus |
| Feb. 12–April 17, 1986 | Pisces | June 13–July 5, 1989 | Gemini |
| April 18–May 7, 1986 | Aries | July 6–July 20, 1989 | Cancer |
| May 8–May 22, 1986 | Taurus | July 21–Aug. 4, 1989 | Leo |
| May 23–June 5, 1986 | Gemini | Aug. 5–Aug. 26, 1989 | Virgo |
| June 6–June 26, 1986 | Cancer | Aug. 27–Sept. 26, 1989 | Libra |
| June 27–July 23, 1986 | Leo | Sept. 27–Oct. 11, 1989 | Virgo |
| July 24–Aug. 11, 1986 | Cancer | Oct. 12–Oct. 30, 1989 | Libra |
| Aug. 12–Aug. 29, 1986 | Leo | Oct. 31–Nov. 17, 1989 | Scorpio |
| Aug. 30–Sept. 14, 1986 | Virgo | Nov. 18–Dec. 7, 1989 | Sagittarius |
| Sept. 15–Oct. 3, 1986 | Libra | Dec. 8–Feb. 12, 1990 | Capricorn |
| Oct. 4–Dec. 9, 1986 | Scorpio | Feb. 13–Mar. 3, 1990 | Aquarius |
| Dec. 10–Dec. 29, 1986 | Sagittarius | Mar. 4–Mar. 19, 1990 | Pisces |
| Dec. 30–Jan. 17, 1987 | Capricorn | Mar. 20–April 4, 1990 | Aries |
| Jan. 18–Feb. 4, 1987 | Aquarius | April 5–June 12, 1990 | Taurus |
| Feb. 5–Mar. 11, 1987 | Pisces | June 13–June 27, 1990 | Gemini |
| Mar. 12–Mar. 13, 1987 | Aquarius | June 28–July 11, 1990 | Cancer |
| Mar. 14–April 12, 1987 | Pisces | July 12–July 29, 1990 | Leo |
| April 13–April 29, 1987 | Aries | July 30–Oct. 5, 1990 | Virgo |
| April 30–May 13, 1987 | Taurus | Oct. 6–Oct. 23, 1990 | Libra |
| May 14–May 29, 1987 | Gemini | Oct. 24–Nov. 10, 1990 | Scorpio |
| May 30–Aug. 6, 1987 | Cancer | Nov. 11–Dec. 1, 1990 | Sagittarius |
| Aug. 7–Aug. 21, 1987 | Leo | Dec. 2–Dec. 25, 1990 | Capricorn |
| Aug. 22–Sept. 7, 1987 | Virgo | Dec. 26–Jan. 14, 1991 | Sagittarius |
| Sept. 8–Sept. 28, 1987 | Libra | Jan. 15–Feb. 5, 1991 | Capricorn |
| Sept. 29–Oct. 31, 1987 | Scorpio | Feb. 6–Feb. 24, 1991 | Aquarius |
| Nov. 1–Nov. 11, 1987 | Libra | Feb. 25–Mar. 11, 1991 | Pisces |
| Nov. 12–Dec. 3, 1987 | Scorpio | Mar. 12–May 16, 1991 | Aries |
| Dec. 4–Dec. 22, 1987 | Sagittarius | May 17–June 5, 1991 | Taurus |
| Dec. 23–Jan. 10, 1988 | Capricorn | June 6–June 19, 1991 | Gemini |
| Jan. 11–Mar. 16, 1988 | Aquarius | June 20–July 4, 1991 | Cancer |
| Mar. 17–April 4, 1988 | Pisces | July 5–July 26, 1991 | Leo |
| April 5–April 20, 1988 | Aries | July 27–Aug. 19, 1991 | Virgo |
| April 21–May 4, 1988 | Taurus | Aug. 20–Sept. 10, 1991 | Leo |
| May 5–July 12, 1988 | Gemini | Sept. 11–Sept. 28, 1991 | Virgo |

| If you were born: | Your Mercury is in the sign of . . . | If you were born: | Your Mercury is in the sign of . . . |
|---|---|---|---|
| Sept. 29–Oct. 15, 1991 | Libra | April 3–April 17, 1995 | Aries |
| Oct. 16–Nov. 4, 1991 | Scorpio | April 18–May 2, 1995 | Taurus |
| Nov. 5–Jan. 10, 1992 | Sagittarius | May 3–July 10, 1995 | Gemini |
| Jan. 11–Jan. 29, 1992 | Capricorn | July 11–July 25, 1995 | Cancer |
| Jan. 30–Feb. 16, 1992 | Aquarius | July 26–Aug. 10, 1995 | Leo |
| Feb. 17–Mar. 3, 1992 | Pisces | Aug. 11–Aug. 29, 1995 | Virgo |
| Mar. 4–April 14, 1992 | Aries | Aug. 30–Nov. 4, 1995 | Libra |
| April 15–May 11, 1992 | Aries | Nov. 5–Nov. 22, 1995 | Scorpio |
| May 12–May 26, 1992 | Taurus | Nov. 23–Dec. 12, 1995 | Sagittarius |
| May 27–June 9, 1992 | Gemini | Dec. 13–Jan. 1, 1996 | Capricorn |
| June 10–June 27, 1992 | Cancer | Jan. 2–Jan. 17, 1996 | Aquarius |
| June 28–Sept. 3, 1992 | Leo | Jan. 18–Feb. 15, 1996 | Capricorn |
| Sept. 4–Sept. 19, 1992 | Virgo | Feb. 16–Mar. 7, 1996 | Aquarius |
| Sept. 20–Oct. 7, 1992 | Libra | Mar. 8–Mar. 24, 1996 | Pisces |
| Oct. 8–Oct. 29, 1992 | Scorpio | Mar. 25–April 8, 1996 | Aries |
| Oct. 30–Nov. 21, 1992 | Sagittarius | April 9–June 13, 1996 | Taurus |
| Nov. 22–Dec. 12, 1992 | Scorpio | June 14–July 2, 1996 | Gemini |
| Dec. 13–Jan. 2, 1993 | Sagittarius | July 3–July 16, 1996 | Cancer |
| Jan. 3–Jan. 21, 1993 | Capricorn | July 17–Aug. 1, 1996 | Leo |
| Jan. 22–Feb. 7, 1993 | Aquarius | Aug. 2–Aug. 26, 1996 | Virgo |
| Feb. 8–April 15, 1993 | Pisces | Aug. 27–Sept. 12, 1996 | Libra |
| April 16–May 3, 1993 | Aries | Sept. 13–Oct. 9, 1996 | Virgo |
| May 4–May 18, 1993 | Taurus | Oct. 10–Oct. 27, 1996 | Libra |
| May 19–June 2, 1993 | Gemini | Oct. 28–Nov. 14, 1996 | Scorpio |
| June 3–Aug. 10, 1993 | Cancer | Nov. 15–Dec. 4, 1996 | Sagittarius |
| Aug. 11–Aug. 26, 1993 | Leo | Dec. 5–Feb. 9, 1997 | Capricorn |
| Aug. 27–Sept. 11, 1993 | Virgo | Feb. 10–Feb. 28, 1997 | Aquarius |
| Sept. 12–Oct. 1, 1993 | Libra | Mar. 1–Mar. 16, 1997 | Pisces |
| Oct. 2–Dec. 7, 1993 | Scorpio | Mar. 17–April 1, 1997 | Aries |
| Dec. 8–Dec. 26, 1993 | Sagittarius | April 2–May 5, 1997 | Taurus |
| Dec. 27–Jan. 14, 1994 | Capricorn | May 6–May 12, 1997 | Aries |
| Jan. 15–Feb. 1, 1994 | Aquarius | May 13–June 8, 1997 | Taurus |
| Feb. 2–Feb. 21, 1994 | Pisces | June 9–June 23, 1997 | Gemini |
| Feb. 22–Mar. 18, 1994 | Aquarius | June 24–July 8, 1997 | Cancer |
| Mar. 19–April 9, 1994 | Pisces | July 9–July 27, 1997 | Leo |
| April 10–April 25, 1994 | Aries | July 28–Oct. 2, 1997 | Virgo |
| April 26–May 9, 1994 | Taurus | Oct. 3–Oct. 19, 1997 | Libra |
| May 10–May 28, 1994 | Gemini | Oct. 20–Nov. 7, 1997 | Scorpio |
| May 29–Aug. 3, 1994 | Cancer | Nov. 8–Nov. 30, 1997 | Sagittarius |
| Aug. 4–Aug. 18, 1994 | Leo | Dec. 1–Dec. 13, 1997 | Capricorn |
| Aug. 19–Sept. 4, 1994 | Virgo | Dec. 14–Jan. 12, 1998 | Sagittarius |
| Sept. 5–Sept. 27, 1994 | Libra | Jan. 13–Feb. 2, 1998 | Capricorn |
| Sept. 28–Oct. 19, 1994 | Scorpio | Feb. 3–Feb. 20, 1998 | Aquarius |
| Oct. 20–Nov. 10, 1994 | Libra | Feb. 21–Mar. 8, 1998 | Pisces |
| Nov. 11–Nov. 30, 1994 | Scorpio | Mar. 9–May 15, 1998 | Aries |
| Dec. 1–Dec. 19, 1994 | Sagittarius | May 16–June 1, 1998 | Taurus |
| Dec. 20–Jan. 6, 1995 | Capricorn | June 2–June 15, 1998 | Gemini |
| Jan. 7–Mar. 14, 1995 | Aquarius | June 16–June 30, 1998 | Cancer |
| Mar. 15–April 2, 1995 | Pisces | July 1–Sept. 8, 1998 | Leo |

| If you were born: | Your Mercury is in the sign of . . . | If you were born: | Your Mercury is in the sign of . . . |
|---|---|---|---|
| Sept. 9–Sept. 24, 1998 | Virgo | May 24–June 7, 1999 | Gemini |
| Sept. 25–Oct. 12, 1998 | Libra | June 8–June 26, 1999 | Cancer |
| Oct. 13–Nov. 1, 1998 | Scorpio | June 27–July 31, 1999 | Leo |
| Nov. 2–Jan. 7, 1999 | Sagittarius | Aug. 1–Aug. 11, 1999 | Cancer |
| Jan. 8–Jan. 26, 1999 | Capricorn | Aug. 12–Aug. 31, 1999 | Leo |
| Jan. 27–Feb. 12, 1999 | Aquarius | Sept. 1–Sept. 16, 1999 | Virgo |
| Feb. 13–Mar. 2, 1999 | Pisces | Sept. 17–Oct. 5, 1999 | Libra |
| Mar. 3–Mar. 18, 1999 | Aries | Oct. 6–Oct. 31, 1999 | Scorpio |
| Mar. 19–April 17, 1999 | Pisces | Nov. 1–Nov. 9, 1999 | Sagittarius |
| April 18–May 8, 1999 | Aries | Nov. 10–Dec. 11, 1999 | Scorpio |
| May 9–May 23, 1999 | Taurus | Dec. 12–Dec. 31, 1999 | Sagittarius |

Although the characteristics of the twelve signs are widely disparate, they can be classified into four general groups based on some shared similarities: Earth, Fire, Air, and Water. Since the four elements are the foundations of the natural, they manifest in the heavens through the astrological signs. For example, the Earth element reflects Earth energy in the heavens through the constellations of Taurus, Virgo, and Capricorn; Water reflects Cancer, Scorpio, and Pisces; Air reflects Gemini, Libra, and Aquarius; and Fire reflects Aries, Leo, and Sagittarius. Each of the elements symbolizes a general temperament. For instance, Earth signs are concrete, practical, material, and sensation-oriented. Water signs are emotional, intuitional, sensitive, and creative. Air signs are intellectual, communicative, and relational. Fire signs are action-oriented, willful, inspirational, and spontaneous. The totality of the four groups is the human personality. Mercury takes on the basic temperament of the element in which it is placed.

Once you've looked up the sign of your Mercury placement, consult the elements chart below to determine the type of filter you possess and how it influences the way you receive, process, and express information.

## The Elements
*Mercury in Earth: Taurus, Virgo, Capricorn*
- Ideas and thoughts are practical, determined, visual, and concrete.

- Learning is best accomplished through the five senses: visual, auditory, tactile, kinesthetic, and olfactory.
- Filter is earthy and sensational, focused on the senses.
- Communication is persistent, specific, cautious, and patient.
- Thought processes are shaped by practical realities and traditional material concerns.

*Mercury in Water: Cancer, Scorpio, Pisces*
- Ideas and thoughts are influenced by deeply felt emotions.
- Learning is best accomplished by being creative, intuitional, and sensitive.
- Filter is the feeling and desire for emotional connectedness.
- Communication is emotional, empathic, intuitional, sometimes psychic, and withheld and evasive if strong emotions are present.
- Thought processes are shaped by emotional and intuitional concerns.

*Mercury in Air: Gemini, Libra, Aquarius*
- Ideas and thoughts are important in and of themselves.
- Learning is best accomplished by gathering information about many different ideals, and social and environmental situations.
- Filter is based on curiosity and versatility.
- Communication is versatile, socially adept, articulate, innovative, and objective.
- Thought processes are shaped by a love of sharing ideas.

*Mercury in Fire: Aries, Leo, Sagittarius*
- Ideas and thoughts are influenced by future visions, philosophy, beliefs, and hopes.
- Learning is best accomplished through understanding abstract concepts or the bigger picture, as well as by taking action assertively.
- Filter is the need to have insight, to understand the gestalts of life.

- Communication is powerful, inspirational, assertive, quick, spontaneous, and enthusiastic.
- Thought processes are shaped by sharing inspired philosophical beliefs.

## AWARENESS OF FILTERS

As a former administrator in education, I remain fascinated with the way children communicate. I strongly believe that if we would approach teaching by trying to reach children based on their respective orientations to the world, they would learn more quickly and encounter less frustration. More recently, I was very fortunate to be introduced to the teachers and administrators of two fine private schools. One teacher invited me to come to her third-grade class for Career Day. I used it as an opportunity to introduce the children to their Mercury placements. It was the first time that I had grouped children by Mercuries. I divided them into groups according to the four elements. Soon they began to develop relationships between themselves and their elemental filter. They talked about "their" element as if it were their best friend. They laughed and discussed how the members of their own group were so alike. Then I did some role-playing, using a stuffed dog as a prop. I had a child with Mercury in Air discuss the dog with a child who had Mercury in Water. The Air child, because of her orientation toward wanting to share ideas, told the Water child she wanted to name the dog. The Water child, with her filter skewed toward emotion, wanted to love the dog, hug the dog, and pet it. The Air child became a little annoyed and started listing possible names. The Water child shrugged and continued to hug the stuffed animal. There was virtually no communication between the two children.

What happened? The Air child's filter to the world was to think about it and label it. That's what Air Mercuries do: they're interested in words, in labeling, articulating, and classifying things by description. Naming the dog was important to her, but expressing her opinion to the Water child was equally important. She wanted an intellectual exchange to find the right name. By contrast, the Water child's filter was to perceive the world through feelings and to express herself emotionally. She wanted to connect with the stuffed animal and did. She was unable to identify with the Air child on an emotional level, so she put her feelings where she could: on the dog.

I then had two more children do the same role-playing with the dog, except this time one little girl had a Fire Mercury, the other an Earth Mercury. The Fire child took the dog from me, put it on the floor, and pretended to walk it. She wanted the Earth Mercury to walk it with her. The Earth child did not respond. Getting bored, the Fire child began to play catch with it. Consistent with the characteristics of Fire in Mercury, the Fire child's first two impulses upon seeing the dog were to take action in some way. The Earth child reached down and took the dog and began to pet it. She needed to have the dog in her possession. She was interested in the dog's coat and its texture. She told the Fire child how soft the dog's fur was. The Fire child took the dog and again played catch with it. This bothered the Earth child, who wanted to pet it. Once again, there was no communication between the children.

Before resuming the role-playing, I talked to all four girls about their experience and their inherent differences. Then I coached them to help them create alignment in their interaction. I reminded the Air child that her friend, "Water," was more interested in feelings than thoughts. I asked her to think about and share her emotions about the dog, even though that wasn't her first reaction. I told the Air child that if she wanted to talk to her friend, she would have to use words her friend could understand. So "Air" told "Water" she "felt happy" when she held the dog and then asked "Water" how she felt. "Water" responded by agreeing that she also felt happy when she held the dog. Then I asked the Water child to pay attention to her feelings after talking with "Air." She told me she was happy because "Air" was "interested" in her feelings. After I reminded her, the Water child was able to cooperate with the Air child about what she needed.

I used the same coaching technique to reach the Fire and Earth children. All I had to do was to remind each one of the other's needs. I told the Fire child how important touching was to the Earth child, and she suggested that the Earth child "hold the dog." In turn, I reminded the Earth child that doing something was important to "Fire." Because the Earth child was secure with having the dog in her possession, she was able to participate in "Fire's" game. In turn, the Fire child was happy because she was able to create some new action—an imaginary three-way game of catch—for both of them to enjoy. "Earth" happily complied. "Fire" threw a make-believe ball to the dog, and "Earth" caught the "ball" from the dog and threw it back to "Fire."

## YOUR PERSONAL FILTER TO THE WORLD

This section chronicles the twelve filters, the communication style associated with each, the challenges inherent in each, and ways to overcome those challenges. To maximize this information, research the Mercuries of the most important people in your life in addition to consulting your own Mercury filter. Having an awareness of your own filter is significant, but ultimately you can create harmony with the people closest to you only by grasping the philosophical underpinnings of the way they see the world.

Remember, your Mercury sign represents your orientation, some of which may be embedded in your unconscious. Thus, some of the qualities listed here may seem more familiar to you than others. Karmic astrology embodies symmetry and balance. For additional guidance in how to overcome the challenges inherent in each filter, consult the sign of the Mercury filter that opposes yours: Taurus/Scorpio, Gemini/Sagittarius, Aries/Libra, Pisces/Virgo, Aquarius/Leo, and Capricorn/Cancer.

### MERCURY IN ARIES

You see the world through the eyes of an explorer, always seeking to discover uncharted territory. The world is an exciting reality to be explored and conquered. You are confident that you can impact any situation by being strong, assertive, and independent. You believe that through your self-awareness and creativity, you can make anything happen. You welcome physical challenges and usually rise to the top because of your physical strength, will, and agility.

**The way you communicate** You are a dynamic, fiery, optimistic, and talkative communicator. You will fight for your ideals. You can be enthusiastic in your eagerness to share new ideas. You are willing to take risks with your communication style and can be quite creative and pioneering. Albert Einstein is a wonderful example of this energy. You can sometimes be sarcastic, combative, and brusque when angry. Others may be afraid of your impulsive and aggressive style. You can be self-absorbed, and your insistence on making yourself the center of your communication may turn off others.

**Challenges to your filter** You can be impatient if things go too slowly. You want life to be a series of new beginnings and can be easily distracted and bored if it is not.

**Overcoming your challenges** When you are bored, remember how creative you are and that you are in charge of creating new beginnings. Then take an action. Curb your impulsiveness by choosing to think before you speak. Deal with anger as a self process; don't use it against someone else. Transform aggression into physical challenges. Constantly be cognizant of ways to mediate and be diplomatic. Practice seeing both sides of a conflict and listening.

### MERCURY IN TAURUS

You see the world through the eyes of a creative gardener to be seeded and tended. You desire material security and creating physical bonds with the earth on many different levels. Because you value consistency, you build your earthy life cautiously, carefully, and conservatively. You seed your garden one step at a time so that it will flourish forever. You are patient and determined to finish the projects you begin. Quality and practical value are vital in all things you create and possess. You seek serenity and calm in your responses to the world. You are ultimately interested in the integration of earthly and spiritual concerns. The Buddha is a wonderful example of this energy.

**The way you communicate**   You speak in a slow, methodical fashion to make sure that your ideas will be understood. You tend to create pictures with your words because of your desire to use all the physical senses in your communication. Many of you are singers who do exactly that. The communication of your ideas and thoughts is practical and conservative in orientation. You do not waste words. When challenged, you can be argumentative and fixed in your opinions. Your tendency toward indolence keeps you from communicating effectively.

**Challenges to your filter**   You can be stubborn and fixed in your beliefs. You are resistant to change. You can be indulgent and lazy.

**Overcoming your challenges**   When you are fixed and stubborn in communicating your beliefs, work on being probing and curious about someone else's beliefs. Agree to disagree when you're feeling argumentative, and find your comfort zone of serenity. Think about being passionate and intense when you have an inclination to be lazy.

### MERCURY IN GEMINI

You see the world through the eyes of an information gatherer. Life is a library filled with new ideas, thoughts, and experiences to satisfy your insatiable curiosity. Because you are mentally alert, you are quick to grasp a new idea. You love words and language, and you are an avid reader and writer. You respond to the world with mental agility, brightness, and cleverness.

**The way you communicate**   You are a messenger: Gemini is always about talking, sharing, and communicating. You speak eloquently with flair and excitement. You cleverly put different words together and are known for your creative use of language. President Harry Truman's colloquial, down-home communication style is an excellent example of this Mercury. You often do more than one thing at a time: watching TV, reading a book, and talking on the phone. You make an excellent reporter because you wish to share ideas as quickly as you can. Sometimes you become distracted and speak in vague and confusing patterns. Being gossipy and deceptive are potential problems for you. You are more interested in the trees than the forest.

**Challenges to your filter** You can become too intellectually stimulated and confused. You may be restless and distracted.

**Overcoming your challenges** When you are too intellectually stimulated, go to a favorite spot outdoors. Ground yourself by hugging a tree or sitting on the grass. Allow your mind energy to connect to the earth. Write down goals instead of keeping everything in your mind. Transmute your restlessness into philosophic exploration. Choose inspirational, broader concept words instead of mundane, gossipy ones. This will help you include the forest (abstraction) as well as the trees (specific details) in your communication.

#### MERCURY IN CANCER

You see the world through the eyes of an emotionally sensitive cosmic nurturer and mother. You would like the world to be an extended home to provide you with emotional foundations, support, and security. You are a sensitive listener, always paying close attention to your emotional environment. If the words you hear don't mesh with your emotions, you often ignore them. Emotions color all your perceptions and thoughts. There are moments when you may lose your emotional identity because of your highly developed empathy to others. Princess Diana is a poignant example of this Mercury.

**The way you communicate** Your speech is emotional, caring, and nurturing. You are sympathetic and supportive in your relationships. You frequently refer to your love of home, family, children, and the past. Much of your communication is not through words but through actions, like cooking, finding a sentimental greeting card, or being emotionally present when someone is in pain. You are emotionally expressive by being affectionate and physical. You are highly creative, especially in the area of the home. Because of your gentle nature, you can be intimidated easily by others and feel a need to close down emotionally for protection, at which time communicating with you becomes very difficult.

**Challenges to your filter**   You can lack objectivity because you are so sensitive. You can be moody and too self-pitying. You continually bring past memories into the present.

**Overcoming your challenges**   You need to learn how to protect yourself from your own emotional sensitivity. Learning personal boundaries, like when to say no, or when not to need being needed, will help. When you're too caught up in your emotions, looking at situations from a practical and earthy perspective will also help. Being organized and structured will keep you more centered in reality and less emotional. Be realistic and discriminating about how much you need to bring past experiences into the present.

### MERCURY IN LEO

You see the world through the eyes of an actor. The world then becomes a stage on which you dramatically perform your life. You watch for opportunities to be on center stage and obtain the applause you feel is necessary for your happiness. You perceive the world from your heart, needing relationships that will enhance your sense of dignity and acknowledgment. You find fun, excitement, and childlike wonder in the world. You love luxuries and have a strong sense of style. Jacqueline Kennedy Onassis exemplifies this Mercury.

**The way you communicate**   Your speech has a strong dramatic, self-confident flair. You are commanding and self-assured in your communication. You have pride and dignity, and much of your speech resonates with the power of royalty. Much of your need for powerful expression comes from your heart's desire to explore fun, childlike wonder, and heart-to-heart connection. Much of what you say is calculated to receive admiration, praise, and approval, making your words appear to some as boastful, insincere, and theatrical.

**Challenges to your filter** You can be self-indulgent and too self-absorbed. Because you may believe you are the ruler of your domain, you can be dominating and overbearing. Vulnerable to others' approval, you can be too vulnerable to needing their love and respect.

**Overcoming your challenges** Being able to refocus your authoritarian tendencies into leadership qualities will help when you are feeling too self-centered. Think about how you can inspire and become more attuned to humanitarian concerns. Learning how to become benignly detached and more objective will help you when you are feeling susceptible to your own internal demands. Learning to love, honor, and approve of yourself will keep you from communicating this vulnerability to others.

### MERCURY IN VIRGO

You perceive the world through the eyes of an organizer. The world, then, is a complex system of thought, work, and service needing structure and order. Because you consider yourself the right person to create this systematic environment, you become its efficient, concerned promoter. You believe in its intrinsic, earthly perfection. You want to maintain high standards through your methodical, logical, analytical style. You look for ways to create healthy physical systems for yourself and others. You use your powers of discrimination to find ways to be of service to those who request it. You are exacting, and you seek to bring coherence to the world. Labor leader Walter Reuther embodies this Mercury filter.

**The way you communicate** Your speech is clear, analytical, discriminating, and exact. You are devoted to organizing your speech to be practical, efficient, and precise. Your propensity for inductive reasoning shows through your words and expressed thoughts. Much of your language involves health issues, work habits and environment, and a need for order. You are interested in fixing situations you consider broken. You can be judgmental, critical, and extreme in your speech. Because your standards are so high, you can appear as a worried, anxious communicator.

**Challenges to your filter**  You can be obsessed with very small details, putting your life in boxes. You can be too analytical and perfectionistic.

**Overcoming your challenges**  Changing your orientation to perfection is critical to overcoming your challenges. Realizing the intrinsic perfection of your deep self will keep you from worrying about external perfection. Strive for excellence, not perfection. Be gentle and compassionate with yourself when you are inclined to be anxious about doing things right. Be cognizant of your extreme expectations, and be more creative.

### MERCURY IN LIBRA

You see the world through the eyes of a benevolent judge with the world as your cosmic courtroom. You abhor injustice and unfairness. You seek refinement, beauty, balance, and harmony in the world. Your world is a web of social relationships that need mediation and arbitration, through your skills of cooperation and need for justice. You perceive both sides of all arguments and endeavor to find the balanced center and middle ground. You want to see a socially refined and charming world. President Dwight Eisenhower is a good example of this Mercury.

**The way you communicate**  Your speech is diplomatic, cultured, and socially oriented. You can be charming, affectionate, and persuasive in your words. You express thoughts that produce compromise and negotiation in social situations. Your actions, as much a part of your communication as words, seek to please, to avoid conflict, and to create beautiful surroundings. You can be too flattering of others because you do not wish to hurt anyone's feelings. You compromise so much that at times you compromise yourself and are more interested in others' needs than your own.

**Challenges to your filter**  You can be superficial and too interested in what other people think of you. Your desperate need for finding balance and harmony can mire you in indecision and ambivalence. You care about pleasing others, at the expense of yourself.

**Overcoming your challenges** Learning to think about yourself as an important relationship in addition to all your external relationships is vital. Create the same level of compromise for you as you do for them. Learn how to say no on occasion. Learn how to be present to a conflict, if it is important to you. An assertiveness training course would help. Take an action on an issue on which you would otherwise straddle the fence.

## MERCURY IN SCORPIO

You perceive the world through the eyes of the phoenix, seeing the transformational potential in all things. You are an emotional investigator seeking intensity and passion—even emotional chaos—in order to find the deep understanding you desire. Your thoughts and ideas are colored by your emotional needs to probe the human psyche. You seek the transformation of material desires into spiritual values. You respect and attract all forms of courage. You see the world as exciting, intriguing, and somewhat dangerous. You seek to understand the darker side of the human condition. Gandhi is a wonderful example of this Mercury.

**The way you communicate** Your speech is tinged with emotional intensity and a need for internal power. You are extreme; your all-or-nothing attitude is evident in your words as well as your expressed ideas and thoughts. You are passionate about your beliefs and are not afraid to articulate them to others. Your speech can be intimidating and frightening to those less intense than you. You can be relentless in your quest to sort out the mysteries of life—especially death and sexuality—and you seek to communicate your ideas frequently. Because you can be extreme, you can also withhold communication and appear to be cold and emotionally withdrawn.

**Challenges to your filter** You can be controlling, wanting power for its own sake. You can be relentless and judgmental. You may never know how much is enough.

**Overcoming your challenges** Learn patience and serenity. Gardening can help because it will modulate your intensity. Read

*Desiderata,* and observe how its words resonate with you. Use your deep understanding of emotions to read others' feelings, and act accordingly. Find creative outlets for your passion. Be aware of your tendency toward extremes; find third options and discover how being creative relieves your need to withdraw.

### Mercury in Sagittarius

You perceive the world through the eyes of a philosopher. Your environment is a giant cornucopia of boundless opportunities and knowledge. Nature becomes the symbol for freedom, expansion, the natural order, and experience. You learn, through the explicate order of nature, how things work. Through it you see and learn about serendipity, prosperity, joy, and survival. You learn best by experiencing life, not just thinking or talking about it. You see the highest potential in all people through your filter of faith, hope, and optimism. You perceive the world as something to be experienced, without boundary or restriction. All things are possible as long as you have enough faith. You wish to discover the truth so you can share it and teach it to others. You are the spiritual visionary and teacher, creating goals that are idealistic and devotional. Anthropologist Margaret Mead is a vivid example of this Mercury.

**The way you communicate** You express your thoughts and ideas with optimism and enthusiasm. You are continually searching for the truth in all of life's situations. You speak as a teacher and a philosopher exploring abstract ideas. You are more interested in the forest than the trees. Honesty and openness are vital to your communication style. You are an enthusiastic traveler searching for enlightenment with every step you take. You easily communicate with nature and animals. Teaching others is your way of learning more. Sometimes you can be too honest and too direct, hurting others. You can be so involved with your philosophy that you speak it dogmatically.

**Challenges to your filter** Your truth is the only truth. You can be pedantic and preachy and too brutally honest. Your bias is to philosophize and not listen to others' communication.

**Overcoming your challenges** Paying attention to the trees as well as the forest is essential. Gathering more information to support your philosophies will help you be less dogmatic. Learning to listen as well as talk will help you be better understood by those with whom you wish to communicate. Thinking before you speak is vital to curbing the directness that can get you in trouble.

## MERCURY IN CAPRICORN

You perceive the world through the eyes of the wise man. You want the world to be a place of practical, traditional wisdom. You seek reality in thought and action and are methodical in how you view the world. You are disciplined and reserved, careful and cautious in your judgment of how things work. You want to impose your responsible organizational nature on life's inconsistencies. You look at the ladder of life and want to climb to the top. You value the world's material bounty and want to claim it. Ronald Reagan is a good example of this Mercury placement.

**The way you communicate** Your speech is conservative and reserved. You think long and hard before you speak. Your words are practical, realistic, and mature. You have excellent common sense. You incorporate your respect for history and traditions into your thoughts and words. You prepare for any verbal presentation thoroughly, because you take your communication seriously. You have an avuncular way, and you tend to speak about self-reliance, honor, and respect. You are an excellent disciplinarian and leader. However, you may be inflexible and intolerant of views that seem too far-fetched for you. Your rigidity may make you judgmental of others' views.

**Challenges to your filter** You can be stern and rigid. You can be pessimistic and see life's failures rather than its successes.

**Overcoming your challenges** Work on accessing your emotions as well as your beliefs. Work on becoming more relaxed and optimistic. Be cognizant of your tendency toward rigidity; figure out what it represents and alter it. Try to be more whimsical, carefree, and enthusiastic. Make an effort to do something fun when you feel pressured to do something more weighty.

## MERCURY IN AQUARIUS

You perceive the world through the eyes of a reformer. For you, the world is a place filled with innovation and invention, with a rational divine order to the universe. You think that all things that occur in life have a reason, although you may not always understand them. Accepting others' differences, you value individuals for their innovation and uniqueness. You search for global tolerance, cooperation, and humanitarianism. You see future possibilities and invent new technologies to improve the human condition. With a broad philosophical outlook, you understand the New Age triangle of mind, body, and soul. You seek equality and gravitate toward like-minded groups that share your reformer's vision. Inventor Thomas Edison is a wonderful example of this Mercury placement.

**The way you communicate** You are a highly innovative thinker and communicator. You are intuitional in what you say and how you say it. You value and speak about equality. Wishing to share your ideas with the world, you are a progressive, cause-oriented thinker. You have a predilection toward high tech, computers, science, and New Age philosophy, and you express your ideas unabashedly. You are humanistic and talk about how one person can make a difference. However, you can be erratic and eccentric at times, occasionally losing your audience. Your speech hints at your rebellious and radical side.

**Challenges to your filter** You can be so detached that you appear as if your mind is somewhere else. You can be very internal and impersonal.

**Overcoming your challenges** Learning to connect with other people is important. This will help you get into the game of life, instead of being so emotionally unavailable. Find activities that will help you appreciate more practical, mundane realities. Be aware of your radical tendencies; work on being inspirational instead.

## MERCURY IN PISCES

You perceive the world through the eyes of a spiritual romantic. You want the world to be beautiful, sensitive, and loving. You seek the creative, the poetic, the lyrical. Your psychic, intuitive self seeks ways to make the world a more spiritual place. Your thoughts and ideas are colored by your deep emotional desire for compassion and love. You are sensitive to the emotional pain of the world. You absorb environmental energies because you are so empathetic. Mystic Edgar Cayce is a good example of this Mercury.

**The way you communicate** You are a sensitive, intuitional communicator. Your language is gentle, loving, spiritual, and creative. You express your ideas and thoughts carefully, so as not to hurt anyone's feelings. And because you are so perceptive and intuitional, you know what to say and how to say it. However, this may mean that you're not entirely honest in how you express your own wants and needs. You express your poetic and romantic feelings when you feel safe. Otherwise you can be very quiet and shy. Because you are so sensitive to others' feelings, you can alter your own emotions very quickly to match theirs and therefore appear moody and inconsistent.

**Challenges to your filter** You sometimes sacrifice your own needs in order to satisfy the needs of others. You have set no boundaries between yourself and the rest of the world. You are so sensitive that sometimes you have trouble dealing with harsh realities.

**Overcoming your challenges** Because you are so intuitional and empathetic, you need to learn how to create personal boundaries so you know where you and your emotions stop and someone else's begin. Learn to be as gentle and compassionate with yourself as you are with others. Be more assertive: say no occasionally. Express what you want. You'll become more comfortable expressing your creative self by working on feeling more secure within yourself.

### Exercise: Mercury Filter

This brief exercise will help you confirm and better understand your Mercury filter:

My Mercury is in:
My Mercury is ruled by the element of:

My filter to the world is:

I am most comfortable expressing myself in the following ways:

I learn best by (consult the "Elements" chart and your personal Mercury filter):

## MERCURY IN RELATIONSHIPS

The notion that men are strong and silent and tend to eschew communication while women are emotional and needful of interaction is a parochial attempt to oversimplify the way we relate to one another. Our societal expectations require that a man communicate like a man, a woman like a woman, further perpetuating these rules and the myths they embody. When we cross the line and express ourselves in a way considered gender atypical, we're criticized and discouraged.

Despite their obvious flaws, on some level we feel we need the reinforcement of our predictable, age-old concepts. They make our lives simpler and easier to understand. Still, this narrow, all-or-nothing approach has limited us by producing expectations that are unrealistic and damaging to our relatedness. With twelve different orientations and four elemental categories, a person's sex makes little difference.

Let's take a look at the importance of Mercury in relationships. Mercury can be further divided into masculine and feminine energy, but clearly the distinction is energetic rather than sexual. Masculine energy represents focused externalized action or expressed energy. Female energy, conversely, represents enveloping, internal reaction or receptive energy. Masculine Mercuries are Aries, Leo, Scorpio, Sagittarius, and Capricorn; those classified as feminine are Taurus, Cancer, Virgo, Libra, and Pisces. Two signs, Gemini and Aquarius, represent the integration of male and female energy and are therefore androgynous.

We need to be clear: men can have Mercuries that have feminine energy and women can have Mercuries that are masculine. Thus a man's filter to the world can be emotional, intuitional, sensitive, and receptive, and his expressive communication style can be emotional, shy, and intuitional. A woman's filter can be assertive, aggressive, action oriented, and dynamic, and her expressive communication style can be strong, powerful, and dominating. This incongruence complicates relationships quite a bit, because we often feel uncomfortable with it.

Mark and Denise's relationship embodies this basic role reversal. Both in their late twenties, they were having serious communication problems and sought me out based on a relative's recommendation. Mark explained that he felt shell-shocked when trying to talk to Denise. He described her communication style as too aggressive, too direct, too hostile, and too impulsive. Her Mercury was in the sign of Aries, a masculine sign. Whenever they had a confrontation or a disagreement, he would become intimidated and defensive; he would feel himself "closing down" emotionally, unable to speak. His Mercury was in the sign of Pisces, a female sign, which he understood to mean that he was highly intuitive, emotional, spiritual, creative, and compassionate. Denise's complaint about Mark was that he was too sensitive, too insecure, too vulnerable and weak. These judgments devastated him, a reaction that further perpetuated her beliefs about him. She said that she basically agreed with his assessment of her communication style, although she would have described herself as assertive rather than aggressive; honest instead of direct; healthily angry, not hostile; and spontaneous, not impulsive.

This couple is a classic example of how a man can have a strong feminine orientation in thinking and speaking and a woman can express herself with a more masculine energy. Until Mark and Denise met me and learned about their particular Mercury placements, all they had were judgments about each other. Mark also shared his confusion and fear that he was "weird" because he knew how sensitive he was and felt that it wasn't "manly." He had been teased as a child for crying a lot and being emotional. Denise, on the other hand, had always been proud of her powerful and aggressive communication abilities.

For this couple, understanding each other's differences was the first step in untangling their communication conflicts. The second step was to ask each of them to honor and respect each other's individuality and to curb their judgments and criticisms of one another. They wanted to, and they did. Step three was to convince them to respect their soul contract and to learn from each other. For example, Mark needed to learn how to be more assertive instead of closing down and being quiet. Denise needed to learn how to become less self-oriented and more sensitive to her partner's needs.

Mark and Denise are happily married and continue to work on their relationship. Their opposite-sex Mercuries are now a gift, not a problem, because they understand what each of them has to learn from the other. This philosophical shift has enhanced the lives of both of them. They now have a child, whose Mercury is in the sign of Aquarius. Mark and Denise both know the potential challenges they will have with their son, since he is different from both of them. They are becoming experts in understanding how Aquarians communicate, so they will be better able to align with him.

Marcy's marriage was fine; it was her son she had had trouble connecting with, almost since he was born. But once she learned more about his filter, she was able to improve her relationship with him.

*I have a child named Billy, who is now ten years old. Almost from the moment Billy could talk, we had terrible conflicts, the source of which was inexplicable. I was either angry at him, or feeling guilty because I was angry at him. It didn't take long before I had become very jealous of my husband's relationship with him. They never argued, always had fun together, and laughed a lot. I know this sounds terribly selfish, but it broke my heart every time I heard them giggling. I would walk into the room, say something to my son, and immediately sparks would fly. I never could say anything to him that worked. Mostly he wouldn't listen to me.*

*So when a friend told me about a workshop that she had attended that had helped her understand her child, I knew that I had to do it too. The workshop changed everything for me. I dis-*

*covered that my Mercury is in Leo (Fire) and my son's is in Scorpio (Water). I learned that my communication style was a little over-bearing and that I could be dominating. I also learned how truly vulnerable I was to other people's approval and appreciation. My pride would get wounded if I was ignored or not listened to. Before we had Billy, my vision of having a child had been that he would show me constant love and adoration. But Billy never did. My heart ached each time he would look at me as if I were the child and he the adult. Because Billy's Mercury is in Scorpio, part of the Water element, he could read my insecurity, fear, and vulnerability, because of his sensitivity to emotions. He didn't even hear my words most of the time, and when he did they seemed not to make sense to him. My words were powerful, but my feelings were child-like. His Mercury in Scorpio was probing, intense, and controlling. He intimidated me, and I didn't know it. The bottom line was that my little boy was inherently more self-possessed than I was, and I hated him for that. I took that workshop three years ago. Billy and I have made great strides in our communication. I have learned to be okay with his intense style and share my feelings with him openly. He responds to that and is less intimidating to me. I have learned not to expect his adoration. He has learned to be less intense and to communicate with me gently and with compassion, because I have shared my vulnerability with him. I also learned that my husband has Mercury in Scorpio too. That could explain why he and Billy understood each other's communication styles so well. That made me feel a lot better.*

## MERCURY AND YOUR SOUL MISSION

How is understanding our filter through Mercury connected to obtaining and living our soul mission? If we are aware of our own orientation toward life's experiences, then we can see that our filter is either congruent or in conflict with the way we *need* to see life in order to achieve our soul mission. Just by being cognizant that the way you *actually* see things may diverge widely from the way you *need* to see things, you are beginning to alter your prevailing filter for the approach embodied by your Soul Potential sign.

The only way to understand and distinguish between your actual orientation and the orientation you need to undertake is to learn about your personal filter, as well as the filter represented by your Soul Potential sign in Mercury. As mentioned earlier, some of us have trouble contemplating living our soul mission, or the type of life articulated by our Soul Potential. The reason is that we are viewing that soul mission through the same Mercury filter, rather than through the Mercury filter of our Soul Potential.

Only when we are able to envision life through the filter represented by our Soul Potential will we be able to overcome the challenges inherent in reaching our Soul Potential. For example, if I have a client whose Mercury is in Taurus, she will have a Taurean outlook on life, meaning she will desire material security and may create physical bonds with the earth on many different levels. She will value consistency, building her life with caution and care. She may be argumentative and fixed in her opinions. According to the Energetics Model in Chapter 4, her Soul Potential is in Cancer. She needs to access Mercury in her Soul Potential sign—Cancer—to see things from that vantage point and achieve and live her soul mission. Having an outlook influenced by Cancer means seeing life through the eyes of a nurturer, wanting to be supportive and an influence in all one's relationships. She would have to explore how that felt, and continue to think about what life would be like from that vantage point.

Some people's Mercury is located in the same sign as their Soul Potential, making it easier for them to grasp the traits, characteristics, and energy of their Soul Potential; since their filter already aligns with their soul mission, less reframing is needed. Conversely, those whose Mercuries are located in the same sign as their Soul Pattern face a more difficult challenge in gaining the perspective needed to achieve their soul mission. For example, if both your Mercury and your Soul Pattern are in Cancer, then your filter to the world is emotional and you will have a propensity to be emotional. Conversely, your Soul Potential sign is in Capricorn, requiring more practical, realistic, and rational behavior from you. You have a great challenge in altering your orientation before you can make that leap of faith to your spiritual mission.

Regardless of what sign your Mercury is in, the filter through which you perceive the world will affect how you perceive your spiritual mission. It will also add a specific flavor to your spiritual experience, which could either support or detract from it. An example of how it can support: suppose you have Mercury in Sagittarius and your Soul Potential is in Leo (both Fire signs). The inspirational leader quality of Leo will be expressed and manifested through the philosophy, optimism, and teaching talents of Sagittarius. An example of how the filter can detract: suppose your Mercury filter is in Capricorn and your Soul Potential is in Pisces. Your filter makes you earthy, structured, reality-based, and practical, while your Soul Potential sign requires you to work on being intuitional, faith-based, spiritual, and adaptive. You can see the potential difficulties with these two energies. Yet in all situations, whether supportive or not, there is an important reason why our souls would create these challenges. Refer to your Soul Potential and your Mercury placement, and see how they could support or detract from achieving your spiritual mission. Being consciously aware of the relationship between your Mercury filter and your Soul Potential could help you reframe your orientation and communication style, which would assist you in achieving your soul mission.

### Exercise: Linking Your Mercury Filter to Your Soul Mission

Below is an example of the correlation between someone's Mercury filter and Soul Potential.

Sample Worksheet

My Soul Potential is in the sign of: *Leo*
My Mercury is the sign of: *Sagittarius*

| Soul Potential Characteristics | Mercury Characteristics |
|---|---|
| (Leo) | (Sagittarius) |
| charismatic, inspired leader | teacher, philosopher |
| self-confident, powerful | expansive, experiential |
| fun-loving, dramatic | seeker of truth, too honest |
| connected to others, joyful | preachy, insatiable |
| freedom, understanding | |

Here's how you might use this information, to answer the following questions:

### HOW CAN MY MERCURY AID ME IN ACHIEVING MY SOUL POTENTIAL?

My Sagittarius Mercury can provide me with philosophical truths so that I can fulfill my Leo potential to teach and inspire others. It can seek the personal experiences I need so that I gain Leo's confidence. It helps me teach others in an expansive manner so that I can be powerful and charismatic.

### HOW CAN MY MERCURY CHALLENGE ME IN ACHIEVING MY SOUL POTENTIAL?

My Sagittarius Mercury can be too preachy, which would turn people off and interfere with my leadership. Its need for so much freedom would keep me from being commited to the people who need me. Speaking before I think and being too brutally honest could keep me from connecting on a heart-centered level to the people I teach.

### HOW CAN I TRANSFORM MY MERCURY CHALLENGES SO THAT THEY WILL AID ME IN THE ACHIEVEMENT OF MY SOUL POTENTIAL?

I can transform my preachiness into speaking about my truth as only *my* truth, not someone else's. I can understand freedom as an internal experience so that I don't need so much on an external level. I can commit to relationships, and I can learn how to think before I talk, to make sure I don't hurt someone with words that I can't take back.

Your Worksheet

My Soul Potential is in the sign of: _____
My Mercury filter is in the sign of: _____

List your Soul Potential characteristics:

List your Mercury characteristics:

Using this information, answer the following questions in your journal.

**HOW CAN MY MERCURY AID ME IN PURSUING MY SOUL POTENTIAL?**

**HOW CAN MY MERCURY CHALLENGE ME IN PURSUING MY SOUL POTENTIAL?**

**HOW CAN I TRANSFORM MY MERCURY CHALLENGES SO THAT THEY WILL AID ME IN MY PURSUIT OF MY SOUL POTENTIAL?**

# CHAPTER 6

# Symbolism and the Unconscious

Through the unconscious mind, the soul provides us with answers to all of life's questions, by deluging us with hundreds of symbols. Jung defines the unconscious, in *The Structure and Dynamics of the Psyche,* as: "Everything of which I know, but of which I am not at the moment thinking; everything of which I was once conscious, but have now forgotten; everything perceived by my senses, but not noted by my conscious mind; everything which, involuntarily and without paying attention to it, I feel, think, remember, want and do; all the future things that are taking shape in me and will sometime come to consciousness; all this is the content of the unconscious." To Jung's definition I would add that the unconscious contains memories not only from this life but from other lives as well. Our unconscious minds project all of the wisdom gleaned from previous incarnations through the language of symbology.

The unconscious part of our personality, which I refer to as the shadow, contains many of the undesirable traits and characteristics we consciously reject and therefore repress. Afraid of the dark, unseemly memories we might unearth and the havoc they might wreak, many of us fear our unconscious mind. However, it is the converse that is true: what we don't know *can* hurt us.

Your unconscious mind can be your best friend, a warehouse of information that you want to bring to consciousness. The challenge is how to access that information. The source of the difficulty is that our unconscious mind has no direct communication with our conscious mind, which means we can explore its knowledge only indirectly. Moreover, while our conscious mind provides us with information more literally, the language of our unconscious mind is largely symbolic. Thus to pursue our unconscious mind's vast information, we must use processes that include astrology, dream interpretation, and various forms of symbology.

## CULLING PERSONAL DATA THROUGH DREAMS

> *"The dream is the small hidden door in the deepest and most intimate sanctum of the soul, which opens into that primeval cosmic night that was soul long before there was conscious ego and will be soul far beyond what a conscious ego could ever reach."*
>
> Carl Jung

Analyzing our dreams can be an illuminating and insightful experience, as long as we know how to interpret the symbols provided by our unconscious mind. Numerous theories and books on the subject of dream analysis abound, but my view is simple: like Jung, I believe that everything in your dream is a reflection of you. I also believe that there is a correlation between your dream symbology and your astrological symbols. Using both provides an enormous amount of relevant data. Before I show you how it works, let's consider a few symbolic structures.

### Sex

What role does sex play in a dream? Usually, whichever sex you dream about is the part of you that you need to explore. If you're female and have a dream about a man, then he is a manifestation of your male side. If you're male dreaming about a woman, the converse is true. If the man in your dream is angry, it could mean that you need to look at the anger that you've been hiding from yourself. This approach can be somewhat unsettling since our dreams can portray the players as nightmarish. You may find it difficult to believe that that garish person could represent any part of yourself. If, however, you are experiencing the same types of conflicts in your waking life, you need to be able to claim those behaviors and take responsibility for them.

Suppose, for example, that you're a man and have been having periodic dreams about your Aunt Bianca. Aunt Bianca is now a representation of your female side. You wish to discover more about that hidden side, so you analyze Aunt Bianca's behaviors in your dreams. In your list of her characteristics, you notice that one in particular causes you some discomfort: her tendency to be somewhat clingy and dependent. Perhaps the hidden female in you has a tendency to be clingy and dependent. And maybe in your waking life, you attract women who are clingy and dependent, a tendency that you find deplorable but unalterable. Dreaming about Aunt Bianca has given you a phenomenal gift: you are now aware of the female part of you that you can explore and change, to help create a resolution.

Houses are a common dream symbol. They are separated into floors: the basement can represent what is not known to us—our unconscious; the first floor can be our ego or personality; and the attic, our spiritual side. Houses also can be seen as an opportunity to put the dream in the context of time: old houses often symbolize past life memories, as do houses that we perceive as ours in our dream but in actuality aren't. Various parts of a house and its surroundings are also significant and correspond to specific astrological characteristics. The following list will give you an idea of the correspondence between the parts of a house and the astrological signs:

**Aries:** doorway, any entrance like an anteroom, reception rooms
**Taurus:** garden, furniture
**Gemini:** hallway, telephone, garage
**Cancer:** kitchen, family room, water faucet
**Leo:** children's room, game room, television room
**Virgo:** bathroom, shower, laundry
**Libra:** art and decorations, living room
**Scorpio:** septic system, toilet
**Sagittarius:** balcony, deck, library, attic

**Capricorn:** formal dining room, roof, home office
**Aquarius:** electrical wiring and appliances, computers
**Pisces:** drainage system

Many of my clients have difficulty remembering their dreams. Here are a few tips that can help. First and foremost, make a commitment to recalling your dreams by keeping a dream journal. Have it available by your bed. As soon as you wake up, jot down any remembrance, no matter how small. If you dislike writing in a journal, have a tape recorder there and record yourself describing the dream. Give yourself time in the morning to remember. Before you go to sleep each night, ask your soul to aid you in remembering your dreams. Let it know that you are ready to know what memories are stored in your unconscious mind—that you are not afraid.

Another helpful hint is to spend a few minutes thinking about your day before you sleep. This way your dreams will be more than just a mundane review of your day. People who have difficulty remembering their dreams usually are reluctant to deal with their unconscious on other levels. They may be afraid of the information stored there, preferring the "what-I-don't-know-won't-hurt-me" approach. But by having the courage to listen to their unconscious, they would live happier, more fulfilling lives. Thomas Edison, just one of a score of notable personalities who believed that answers could be mined from our unconscious, would "sleep" on a problem involving one of his inventions. Below are some examples of the type of information we can glean from our dreams:

- skills we've had in past lives
- details about our shadow self
- information on past life personalities
- karmic events that have shaped us
- explanations about our present fears and phobias
- aspects of our soul mission
- ways to communicate with our soul
- how we've been victimized

- how we've abused others
- past life relationships
- the meaning of our soul contracts

Nightmares are also important because of the potential insights they represent. We've all had them; some of us have had the same ones repeatedly. I often ask my clients to tell me about their bad dreams, especially the recurring ones. The clues to past life conflicts may manifest through the terrifying imagery of a nightmare. Singling out those symbols and pairing them with karmic astrological symbology is an effective way to find their meaning.

For instance, suppose you dream you are running. It is night and very foggy. You know that you are being followed. You find yourself at the top of a cliff, trapped. You panic. A noise, and then a large man is in front of you. He has flaming red hair and is wearing a dark cape. He's angry. He shouts words that you cannot understand. He draws a knife and lunges at you. You wake up, physically shaken and scared. You've had this dream before. But this time you decide you're going to interpret the dream as a manifestation of yourself. You have Saturn in Aries (see Chapter 7), which you know is a symbol of yourself in a past life. The man in your dream has red hair (an Aries symbol), he is angry (another Aries symbol), and he is lunging at you with a knife (a major Aries symbol). If you have fears of knives and blood in this life, you may have found the source of those fears in the nightmare—not as a victim, but as an aggressor. In a past life you were a large angry man who probably injured someone. Your unconscious mind has given you these nightmares so that you can become aware of this life, get rid of your guilt, and be free. Chances are very good that you will not have this nightmare again. Once we figure out what our dreams symbolize, they need not return.

*"The major task of the twentieth century will be to explore the unconscious, to investigate the subsoil of the mind."*

Henri Bergson

Let's interpret the meaning of a fairly typical dream, by combining what we now know about astrology, house symbology, and colors. You dream that you are in an old house that is yours but does not look like your current home. Walking into a red kitchen that is located in the basement of that house, you are very upset. This dream is telling you that an unconscious memory (the basement) involving something from the past (the old house), involving nurturing and emotions (the kitchen as an astrological Cancer symbol), has made you angry (red). Your unconscious mind has allowed an old memory from the past to resurface in this dream. Now that you are conscious of it, you can explore it further.

Dreams can provide us with unifying cultural themes. In the 1970s and 1980s many people were having tidal wave dreams, which, I believe, were symbolic of the coming of the Age of Aquarius. One cold, wintry January evening in 1983, I had a tidal wave dream that has proven to be one of the most important transformational experiences of my life.

In this dream a white, expansive beach was filled with hundreds of people. Telephone lines crisscrossed the beach, with men dangling from the telephone poles. People were milling about in small groups, with a view of a very calm ocean. Yet there was an ominous sense of foreboding. Children were even caught up in the anxiety. No one was in the water; no one was playing in the sand. I was standing apart, on a higher dune of sand. I could see the entire beach and the men perched high on the telephone poles. I was terrified! My husband Michael appeared and took my hand to calm me, but to no avail. I was sure something terrible was going to happen. But what? My attention was drawn to the telephone wires. Somehow they had the answer. A voice said: "You will have a warning from the wires. It will tell you when it will begin. The wave is coming. You will soon know how many will survive. What you have done is all that you had time to do. Wait and relax. It is soon to come." I ran down to the beach, leaving Michael. I was now the leader of the group. I had a moment of panic that Michael and I would be lost to each other. The people gathered around me in a circle. I shared the voice's message. We sat on the sand and waited for the wires to hum. Holding hands, we passed blue energy around the circle. I began to relax and then felt incredible peace within me. I looked at the people and knew that they were feeling the same energy. I was relieved when Michael appeared in the circle, sitting directly across from me. Seconds later, the wires vibrated. The men got the message, scurried down the poles, and joined the circle. "Five minutes!" they shouted. The minutes crept by, giving way to a deafeningly thunderous sound unrivaled by anything I had ever heard before. As we looked out to sea, a mountain of water began to rise higher and higher, until the whole scene in front of us was filled with this crushing sight. The wave moved in closer and closer. And then it was on the beach—and then I woke up.

This dream was an enigma to me for several weeks. However, the fact that several other people in my life were having a similar dream gave me the clue I needed. I concluded that this dream was my unconscious mind's way, by dint of my soul, of providing me with information about my role in the transition from the Age of Pisces to the Age of Aquarius.

Synchronicity, according to Jung, is the coincidence in time of two or more causally unrelated events that have the same or similar meaning. Suppose you haven't seen your best friend from college in ten years. One day you come across a picture of her, while cleaning your attic. You remember a conflict that was left unresolved between the two of you, and you feel regret. A few hours later she calls. Most of us would call that a coincidence. Jung would call it synchronicity, citing the relationship between the two events. He distinguishes synchronicity from coincidence according to whether the situation has inherent meaning. The situation with the college friend has that meaning. Jung said that meaningful coincidences are unthinkable as pure chance; they have to be thought of as meaningful arrangements. And meaning is what we are looking for in the symbols we create each day.

One client, Faye, who had just turned 40, had seen me a few times intermittently, dropped out, then returned a year later. In her

first session after her hiatus, we talked about her problematic relationship with her mother. Faye was actively working on healing
some of her conflicts with her mother and had visited her in
Florida. While visiting, she noticed that her mother had begun col-
lecting elephants: mainly pictures and a few statues. Shortly after
she returned home, she came across an unusual necklace with elephants on it and sent it to her mother. Her mother loved it. Faye
was amazed: it was the first gift she had given her mother that she
had really appreciated. Mother's Day was approaching, and Faye,
who could paint, decided to do a watercolor of a mother elephant
and its baby for her mother.

During one of our sessions, I asked Faye to pick a card from a
deck portraying different nature scenes. I asked her to ask a question and pick a card. The question she asked was whether she and
her mother would continue to reconcile their differences. The card
she picked was an elephant and its baby—just the picture that she
was planning to paint for her mother. I asked Faye what the card
symbolized to her. "Elephants represent home, tradition, and loyalty. This card is clearly about a mother's love for its child." In that
moment of synchronicity, Faye knew that something beyond her
own personality was at work.

## THE SYMBOLISM OF THE BODY

Our physical body represents one of the most ample means
through which our unconscious mind expresses itself. Our physi-
ology serves as a clear barometer of how we are faring, emotionally and physically. More than twenty years ago, when I began my
practice, few people understood the mind/body/spirit connection.
Physical problems were just that, physical. We ignored what was
happening on an emotional and spiritual plane. Today a holistic
approach is widely accepted. In order to understand basic body
symbology, imagine each body part has a connection to an astrological sign. The following chart will give you an idea of how it
works.

## Astrological Energy of the Physical Body

| | |
|---|---|
| Aries | Head, brain, eyes, face |
| Taurus | Neck, throat, ears |
| Gemini | Hands, arms, shoulders, lungs, nervous system |
| Cancer | Breast, stomach |
| Leo | Heart, upper back, sides |
| Virgo | Gall bladder, liver, intestines, pancreas |
| Libra | Kidneys, lower back |
| Scorpio | Reproductive organs, genitals, rectum, bladder |
| Sagittarius | Upper leg, thigh, hips |
| Capricorn | Knees and lower leg |
| Aquarius | Ankles, circulatory system |
| Pisces | Feet |

The right side of the body symbolizes the masculine principle: external, directed, action-oriented, assertive, and conscious. As an agent of time, it represents the present and the future. The left side of the body symbolizes the feminine principle: receptive, emotional, intuitional, passive, and unconscious. In time it represents the past and can help us understand karmic illnesses or accidents. The left side of the body can also be a valuable asset in helping us understand past life memories.

Let's say that while running up a stairway to catch a train, you trip and hurt your left knee. Knees are a Capricorn symbol, and Capricorn is about rules, responsibility, structure, discipline, commitment, reality, caution, rigidity, arrogance, inflexibility, and more. You now know that your unconscious has created your painful knee to take a look at these symbols. Maybe you've been carrying the burden of too much responsibility at work lately and need to rest. Maybe you've been too inflexible with your husband and need to change your behavior. Or maybe you need to become more committed or disciplined in a particular area of your life. Using Capricorn words can help you ferret out your unconscious mind's symbolic communication.

Now let's add to the equation the fact that it was your left knee. That ties the injury to emotions of the past, maybe even a past life.

Use your imagination, and seek out a possible past life using Capricorn words. As with every other story that you have written from exercises in this book, use the astrological words as a guide, relax, and have fun with it. Writing is another conduit from which your unconscious mind and soul can ply you with information. Use the astrological words as catalysts to discover past life possibilities. Pay attention to how you feel when the possibilities take form. You'll know when it feels "right."

Bradley, 45, a house painter, suffered from the worst psoriasis I have ever seen. Both of his hands would become dry, then crack and bleed when he used them. He tried everything—creams, ointments, herbs—and nothing worked. In an act of desperation, he made an appointment with me. Hands are ruled by Gemini, which gave me a place to start.

I asked him if he had any difficulty with communication. "Y-Yes," he stammered. Bradley had begun to stutter when he was 10 years old, although since then he had learned to control it. Prior to that, he been a very fast talker, but he had gotten himself in trouble with his acerbic tongue. Stuttering had slowed him down and taught him to listen more to what other people were saying. He still had moments when he would stutter under stress.

But that did not explain the psoriasis. I asked him if communication or the inability to communicate was causing him any pain in his life now. He hesitated for a moment, then answered, "People are always saying that I talk over them. They feel intimidated by what I say and feel that I am too powerful in how I speak. I cuss a lot and will admit that I can be pretty intense. I love to have deep conversations with people, and sometimes I feel that they shy away from me. It makes me angry when I see that and it hurts my feelings."

"Has it occurred to you that your hands might be trying to tell you something about this conflict?" I asked.

"Well, not until you told me that hands can symbolize communication," he answered ruefully. "So what should I do?"

"Remember how you learned to slow down and listen after you started to stutter? Do you think that would work now? Gemini, at its best, is a great listener and knows the best way to articulate its message so that others will understand. Maybe if you work on that your hands will get better."

Bradley said he'd give it a try. A few sessions later he reported that he was, in fact, more conscious of his communication style and had seen a marked improvement in his dialogue with others. His psoriasis, however, was no better.

A short while later Bradley mentioned offhandedly an occasional conversation that he would have with himself while he was doing physical work. He said that was also when the outbreaks happened.

"What are you saying to yourself when you're doing this physical work?" I asked.

"I say to myself how much I hate doing it. I don't like working on house stuff. I feel it's beneath me. I guess I'm angry that I have to do it," said Bradley, visibly annoyed.

"Well, Bradley, I think we've uncovered your problem. Your hands are an obvious manifestation of the anger that you have in working with them. I would like you to spend a month honoring the physical work you do, and not railing against it. Will you pledge to do that?" I asked.

Bradley said that he would, but clearly he was not happy. It took months to reframe his aversion to what he referred to as "menial work."

Six months ago, Bradley came to his session bragging that he was repainting his old Victorian home, and the great news was that he was *loving* the work. His hands, although not without some cracks, were much improved.

### Exercise: Body Parts

Take a moment, and try to recall an illness or injury that you've had recently. After isolating the part of the body involved, find the corresponding astrological sign. Then check the challenging qualities of the sign found in the Soul Pattern Energetics Model (Chart 2 in Chapter 4). Ask yourself about the sign's most challenging characteristics.

Now factor in the side of the body. If your left side was involved in the problem, put your imagination to work, use the appropriate astrological words, and create a possible past life scenario. By conjuring that scenario, you are learning about a past issue that your soul wants you to resolve. If the illness or injury was on the right side of your body, there is a current action you need to perform.

My illness or injury was:

The part of my body affected was:

It corresponds to the astrological sign of:

Keywords of that sign that could be appropriate to this issue are:

Reasons for this illness or injury are:

The illness or injury was on the ___ side of my body.

The timing that this illness or injury symbolizes is:

Betty is a very committed client. At 47, she has seen me almost every week for more than three years, during which time she's learned a great deal about her soul mission and her Soul Potential. A very cautious, shy woman, Betty still talks about a river of darkness that lurks deeply within her. It terrifies her. She feels that if she is not totally "vigilant" and very careful, this dark side will "become a tidal wave" that will destroy her. If she lives her life within certain tight parameters, takes no risks, does not draw attention to herself, and stays in the shadows, maybe it won't "get" her. After years of work she knew that this darkness had nothing to do with this life; it was a karmic memory. Yet she was still reluctant to explore it. "It is bigger than I am," she said, and if she acknowledged it, it would take control of her and she would cease to "exist." Nothing I said could convince her otherwise. She could not bring herself to put a halt to this dark obsession.

But shortly after her mother had major surgery and was put on a respirator, Betty experienced a turning point. She could not stay in her mother's hospital room without panicking: her throat constricted and she felt as though she needed to scream. The next day her mother was taken off the respirator, and Betty was able to visit her and was fine. She related this incident to me in our next session. She knew it was important but didn't know why. We spent most of the session investigating other issues surrounding her throat. We found two very significant experiences. The first one had happened as a child, after a tonsillectomy. Betty had awakened from the surgery to another child's screams. For an instant, disoriented, she thought that the child was "having his skin ripped off," and she believed that she was in a torture chamber. It made her so sick that she threw up. The second incident occurred when she worked in a hospital X-ray unit during her college years. A young man had broken his neck and was brought into radiology for X-rays. Betty became unnerved and had to call on someone to complete the X-rays.

We set about correlating Betty's traumatic experiences centering on her throat and neck, with her obsessive fear of her dark side. The throat symbolizes creativity and the power of communication. Ruled by the sign of Taurus, it is the vehicle through which we express ourselves creatively and communicate what is true to ourselves and others. We encounter problems with our throat and neck when we are unduly reticent. When we are not living up to our creative potential, our throat center closes to remind us that we are not being creatively expressive—a point that made perfect sense to Betty. She admitted always being hesitant to speak her mind, ever mindful of what she said and how she said it. Through these experiences Betty's unconscious was trying to get her attention in a powerful way. Her body wanted to help her see that she needed to open up and investigate this darkness, to find the truth, express it, and be free. At that point she would be able to fully express her creativity and begin to love her life.

## THE MEANING OF COLORS

Our universe comprises energy that emits a brilliant spectrum of color. Each color vibrates at a level that corresponds to a part of the body and the emotion that dwells there, and thus to an astrological sign. Colors can effect a change in our emotions, provide us with peace and serenity, warm our soul, or jolt us into action. Colors stimulate, galvanize, relax, relieve, and even heal us. Given our own subjective associations, colors can shape our experience. In meditation color is a powerful vehicle to enhance and heal our internal world, while in our external environment it helps us create surroundings that feel energetically correct to us.

The following colors have specific emotional potential as well as symbolic importance. This chart lists their corresponding astrological signs and emotional properties.

Red: Aries
    Symbolizes: will, assertiveness, power, anger
    Characteristics:
        stimulates, warms, excites, and cheers
        provides quick energy
        counteracts feeling depressed
        encourages constructive anger
        increases physical strength

Green: Taurus
    Symbolizes: growth, springtime, love, prosperity
    Characteristics:
        promotes serenity
        enhances desire to evolve
        provides inner balance and harmony
        encourages prosperity
        increases fertility

Yellow: Gemini
    Symbolizes: intellectual stimulation, clarity
    Characteristics:
        stimulates creative potential
        encourages a cerebral approach
        promotes communication
        advances understanding
        fosters educational enrichment
        enhances ability to be open-minded

Silver Blue: Cancer
  Symbolizes: deep feeling, calm, serenity
  Characteristics:
    promotes relaxation
    encourages creative expression
    aids in accessing emotion
    calms anger and agitation
    shields against negative emotional influences

Gold: Leo
  Symbolizes: authentic connections from the heart
  Characteristics:
    creates self-confidence
    builds self-love and self-respect
    provides warm connections to others
    promotes courage

Orange: Virgo
  Symbolizes: healing, energizing
  Characteristics:
    manifests feeling of well-being
    decreases depression
    decreases fears
    increases physical healing when emotions have created pain
    creates self-confidence

Rose Pink: Libra
  Symbolizes: balance, harmony, and cooperation
  Characteristics:
    encourages cooperation
    enhances understanding in relationships
    promotes creativity
    creates air of refinement
    increases harmony and balance

Dark Red: Scorpio
  Symbolizes: power, sexuality, and passion
  Characteristics:
    releases old karmic anger
    encourages intensity
    enhances sexual passion
    increases determination and drive
    provides an increase in enduring energy

Purple: Sagittarius
  Symbolizes: transcendental experience
  Characteristics:
    increases philosophical expansion
    enhances spiritual awareness
    promotes enhanced intuition
    advances communication with the soul
    encourages optimism

Brown: Capricorn
  Symbolizes: being earthy, reliable
  Characteristics:
    concentrates on reality
    encourages discipline and responsibility
    maintains focus on goals
    promotes connection to body for all healing to occur

Electric Blue: Aquarius
  Symbolizes: individuality and originality
  Characteristics:
    encourages uniqueness
    stimulates need for humanism
    creates innovation
    enhances ability to be open-minded
    promotes being rational

Lavender: Pisces
  Symbolizes: spirit, connection to God
  Characteristics:
    increases spiritual awareness
    promotes attunement with higher consciousness
    cleanses psychic channels
    encourages self-forgiveness
    promotes communication with the soul
    creates meditative states that encourage rest and healing

Color can provide us with symbols that we can then correlate to our astrological energy. Madeline, who was in her early fifties, called me in a panic because she had almost been run over by a very large red truck. It was the latest in a series of encounters with red vehicles that she had had in the last few weeks. According to Madeline, "Red cars were coming out of the woodwork." She called me because she was afraid that she would get into an accident.

Red symbolizes anger and assertion; Madeline had a history of avoiding confrontations and anger. We had already talked repeatedly about her need to deal with anger on a more realistic level. It terrified her, and she had avoided the work, but the red truck was the last straw. She decided to start working on anger. She knew the color red symbolized her problems with Aries energy. Her soul had created that near-miss with the red truck to push her to making that decision. She can now work to transform red to gain the courage, confidence, and energy to use her anger constructively.

Bill, while he was in the middle of a session with me, mentioned that he had decided to change his image and buy some new clothes. "Any special color?" I asked. "You know I've always hated the color brown, but now it's all that I seem to be attracted to. Does that mean anything?" I smiled. "Bill, you know me better than that. Of course it means something." Brown symbolizes Capricorn, which is practical, earthy, goal-directed, reliable, stable, and success-oriented. Bill, at 42, was in the running for a promotion at work, and his attraction to brown began soon after he found out about it. This casual aside from Bill about a color turned into several sessions of learning more about his Capricorn energy. His soul had drawn the color brown to him so that he could have this transformational experience.

Colors are all around us; their symbols abound. Pay attention to what colors attract you, and tinker with what each one means to you. See if you can find a pattern. Look at your wardrobe. What colors do you prefer? What color makes you feel powerful? What color makes you feel sexy? Intellectual? Spiritual? Keep the color chart available to check the corresponding meanings. Are you getting ready to redecorate your home? Choose colors that are not only visually pleasing but symbolically evocative. For instance, if you need to experience more self-confidence at work, try adding a bit of orange to your office decor. Every day spend a moment meditating on the color to increase your sense of inner power. Do you have an important presentation to give at a meeting? You need to be sharp and clear to communicate your ideas effectively. Take a few minutes beforehand to channel the color yellow into your body. It will stimulate your intellectual creativity. Wear a yellow tie or scarf to remind you of the color's power. Do you need to create more money in your life? Buy a green plant; then watch it grow and expand. Your affirmation is that as the plant grows, so does your financial picture.

Pay close attention to the color that relates to your Soul Potential. Many of my clients, when I tell them their soul color, say that it is the one color they truly dislike. I remember my chagrin when I learned that the soul color that symbolized my Soul Potential sign, Leo, was gold. I hated gold. I had a beautiful jewelry wardrobe of silver—and a whole series of judgments against gold. I found it ostentatious, gaudy, and flashy. In essence, I made the same judgments about Leo people: that they were pretentious, self-centered, and melodramatic. The truth was, I didn't want my Soul Potential sign in Leo because I didn't like what I couldn't emulate. My aversion to gold was a poignant symbol in helping me understand that. Needless to say, I now have a wonderful collection of gold jewelry. Wearing gold now reminds me of the highest attributes of Leo. I even wear a little gold lion ring that symbolizes my commitment to my soul mission: to be courageous, inspirational, commanding, and confident.

Your soul color vibrates to the same level as your Soul Potential and will help you connect to your soul's energy. When you want to connect and communicate with your soul, imagine your soul color gently flowing through your body, warming you, loving you, and giving you peace. You will be amazed at how easy it is to talk to your soul when you are at its vibrational level. When you wish to live in your soul's love, wear its color and feel its love every minute of the day. Make sure that you have your soul color in your home, car, and office.

## SYMBOLS IN YOUR EVERYDAY LIFE

So far in this chapter, we have discussed the symbols that our soul and unconscious mind give us to interpret. But we can also choose symbols that have conscious meaning to us. For example, I have chosen a symbol that I use for serendipity. As you know from previous chapters, I am a devout believer in serendipity, in understanding and appreciating that unexpected outcomes are just as viable to our evolution and happiness as expected ones. This philosophy is very important to my serenity and optimism, but I've had moments when I forgot about the power and peace of serendipity. I wanted to have an external symbol to remind me of it, so I chose a symbol: a red cardinal. Since then, I've found that this beautiful bird crosses my path at all the right moments. When I catch a glimpse of it, I know my soul is saying, "Serendipity is alive, Linda. Remember." And no matter what is going on, regardless of how painful the moment, it reminds me that a wonderful, unexpected surprise is waiting to be discovered.

All of my students have serendipity symbols, and I would like you to have one too. But I can't tell you which one to choose. Open your mind to finding one that is pleasing to you, that will bring out your innate optimism, hope, and faith. One of my friends chose a golden crown; another, a rose; another, a pearl. My students have chosen blue jays, windmills, diamonds, oak trees, archways, wheat fields, oriental rugs, waterfalls, willow trees, pinafores, and baby grand pianos. After you've chosen your serendipity symbol, your unconscious mind will attract you to it when you need to be reminded of serendipity. It will lighten your heart and spark your mind to see the positive surprises awaiting you by expecting the unexpected.

Everyday symbols can also answer specific routine questions. I often ask my soul to provide me with symbolic answers to current problems. I ask a question—perhaps why I'm feeling sad today—and pay attention to the symbols that my soul creates for me. How do I know which object out of hundreds I encounter represents the answer? I know by how I feel about the things I see. Suppose a blue car is parked outside my house. It is parked there often, but on the particular day that I've queried my soul, perhaps about my sullenness, I not only notice it, but I really hone in on it. I see a dent in the left fender. I have an emotional reaction to the bumper sticker that reads "One Day at a Time." This car is a symbol to help me with my question. For me, cars symbolize movement in the world, while blue represents the ability to access emotion. A dent in the left side represents something in the past that is "dented" or maybe damaged. And the bumper sticker is self-explanatory. Based on this information, I have my answer: I am remembering something painful from my past that is interfering with my ability to move on, and my soul wants me to understand that living today's experiences is more important than reveling in yesterday's memories.

Paying attention to your emotional reactions to normal, everyday symbols will tell you that your soul has given you these clues to help answer a question. You then can interpret the symbols based on your experience with them. A car represents movement to me, but may not symbolize the same thing to you. Find your own personal symbolic language, and practice it. Not only will it help you answer questions, it will help you become more aware of the abundance of information awaiting you from your unconscious mind.

Astrology is a language, and as such it has many words. The following chart lists a few common objects that you may encounter in the course of your day or in your dreams, and the astrological sign that symbolizes them. I am sure you will see the correlation as you review them. As you look at your world through this astrological filter, you will find an increasing number of symbols. When you find a symbol, find its related astrological sign here; then refer to the Energetics Models (Charts 2 and 3 in Chapter 4) to see which characteristics your soul wants you to confront.

## Astrological Signs and the Common Objects They Symbolize

| | |
|---|---|
| Aries | Knives and other sharp objects, the desert, the ram, firemen, soldiers, daybreak, battles, Moses, fire, matches, lighters, karate and other martial arts, the direction east, spring, the number 1 |
| Taurus | Gardens, the Buddha, the bull, sculptors, bankers, money, earth, leaves, singers, songwriters, investments, a wallet, bank deposits, easy chairs, any soft material like velvet or silk, the number 2 |
| Gemini | The wind, cars, newspapers, journalists, books, birds, traffic signs, twins, watches, writing materials, libraries, con men, respiratory therapists, speech therapists, writers, the number 3 |
| Cancer | Lakes, mothers, containers that hold liquid, home, milk products, boats, cooks, food, historians, sailors, restaurants, farmers, the direction north, pools, summer, the number 4 |
| Leo | Actors, theaters, crowns, television, games, children, sun, vacations, parties, movies, kings, a throne, gifts, fun, the lottery, all things glamorous, holidays, the number 5 |
| Virgo | Health foods, doctors, nurses, nutritionists, lists, any program that creates order, organized labor, soap, virgins, wheat, cleaning supplies, prescriptions, small animals, homework, chores, tests, the number 6 |

| Libra | Judges, court, the direction west, partners, contracts, fall fashion designers, color, harmony, scales, stylish clothes, art dealers, weddings, all things beautiful and refined, mediation and mediators, objects that are in balance, the number 7 |
| --- | --- |
| Scorpio | Hidden things, dark places, secrets, researchers, tornadoes, death, funerals, insurance, nuclear weapons, ice, Niagara Falls, psychiatrists, loans, investigators, garbage, sexual affairs, the Mafia, pathologists, dark alleys, occult matters, the number 8 |
| Sagittarius | Horses, gambling, mountains, travel, travel agents, sports, college professors, clergy, law, lawyers, legal affairs, colleges, publications, arrows, religious rituals, space, anything that deals with expansion, luck, the future, the number 9 |
| Capricorn | Father, authority figures, elders, wise people, grandfather clocks, the direction south, winter, licenses, government and government officials, CEOs, calendars, boundaries, foundations, big business, the rewards of recognition, antiques, the number 10 |
| Aquarius | Airplanes, computers, astrology, politics, volunteerism, the Internet, causes, revolutionary ideas, new technology, genius, inventors, rebellion, a team approach, gay population, like-minded groups, holistic practitioners, space technology, the number 11 |
| Pisces | Oceans, whales and dolphins, anesthesia, alcohol, drugs, dreams, psychics, psychic experiences, prisons, hospitals, martyrs, musicians, the ballet and ballet dancers, alcoholics and drug addicts, places of retreat, illusions, secret enemies, the number 12 |

My role as a karmic astrologer and teacher is to listen. Most of my new clients arrive expecting me to "read" their chart, which would mean that I would talk to them for most of the hour while they listen. Imagine their surprise when the session becomes a conversation in which they talk more than I do. While they talk, I listen for the symbols their souls provide as answers to their important life issues. These symbols lead me to specific areas of their astrological information.

Mindy, 36, walked into her first session very upset. But she was able, with my help, to transform her trauma into a symbol that helped her realize her soul mission.

*I was actually crying when Linda answered the door. Concerned, she asked me what was wrong. I told her that a deer had just been killed by a car directly in front of me. Once I sat down in her office and she made me some herbal tea, I felt a little better. I could tell that my story had had an effect on Linda too. I told her I had never seen anything like it before and that it wouldn't have happened if I hadn't been coming to see her, because I never traveled that road.*

*Linda asked me what deer symbolize to me. I didn't know what she meant; I didn't think of life symbolically. But when I thought about it, it occurred to me that deer had always been special to me. My parents had a summer home in New Hampshire when I was a little girl. Deer were everywhere. The feeling that I had when I saw them was happiness. They were symbolic of nature and freedom.*

*When I told Linda that, she nodded. "That's what they are for me, too," she said. Linda also told me that death represents transformation and change. She then looked at my astrological chart and smiled. "Nature and freedom are symbols of Sagittarius. And your Soul Potential sign is Sagittarius! It's important for you to become more involved in nature, the country, freedom, and expansion," she added. I was amazed. I am a loyal city dweller, and except for occasional trips to New Hampshire, I had never considered moving to the country. Yet the reason I had come to see her in the first place was to discuss a possible job move to Northern California. Linda told me that the deer had given me the answer twenty minutes before I got to her office. "You could have saved yourself some money," she laughed, "if you'd known how to read the deer's symbol." She told me that I needed to transform my attitude about moving to the country as a symbol of doing more of my soul's mission. She told me to thank the deer for what it had given me. I moved to Northern California three months later. That deer had answered so many questions. After the move, Linda and I talked regularly, so when she explained about the necessity of a serendipity symbol, I of course chose a deer! It is the symbol of my soul mission.*

We must listen to ourselves when we talk to others. We often use essential words that our soul has given us to answer our own questions, especially in important conversations with the people who mean the most to us. How often do you say something to someone else that is exactly what you need to hear yourself? For me, quite often. When I hear myself providing specific advice to a client that rings especially true to me, I file it away to mull over later, to ask, "Is my soul saying this to me too?" Think about the words that you tend to use to talk to friends, family, and children. Write them down. We all have favorite truisms or sayings that we tend to use over and over. They mean something! They are words your soul wishes you to understand.

# PART III

# Karmic Truth: The Key to Fulfilling Your Soul Mission

# CHAPTER 7

# Saturn: Your Journey to Personal Truth

I n his book *Revelations: The Birth of a New Age,* David Spangler outlines seven laws detailing how we can enhance our spiritual energy and use it more creatively. Two of those laws—one involving love, the other truth—are essential to helping us learn more about ourselves.

> **The Law of Love** "Through love we expand our vision beyond our own seeming limitations and live in awareness of the whole of which we are a part. Hence, we must love ourselves as well, not as a private, selfish entity, but as a unique and meaningful expression and part of the whole."
>
> **The Law of Truth** "Truth does not accept all things to itself: it accepts only what is right and true for that time and place, but it does this without needing to judge the ultimate rightness or wrongness of the person, thing or concept under its discrimination."

Love and truth must be expressed together, writes Spangler. Love enables truth to grow and expand its discriminatory powers without allowing them to settle into a crystallized pattern of judgment and organization. "Truth protects love and gives the power of appropriateness to the energy of love," he explains. "Truth tempers love's acceptance with a keen perception of what is right in the moment and prevents the energy of love from being dissipated over too wide a field or from being taken advantage of."

*"Truth is one forever absolute, but opinion is truth fil-*
*tered through the moods, the blood, the disposition of the*
*spectator."*
                                        Wendell Phillips

How many of us can really say that we are "in love" with ourselves, much less "in truth" with ourselves? Although being "in
truth" with oneself sounds misplaced, it is just as important as loving oneself. When we are deceiving ourselves and perpetuating
illusions, we are limiting our reality, which saps our ability to be
happy. Living with illusions requires us to maintain a misshapen
belief system to support the falsehoods. Often these mispercep-
tions are based on guilt. Thus we don't create happiness or prosperity, because we don't believe we deserve it. Without inner truth,
we create distorted images not only of ourselves but of those
around us, because we have a "need" to see them in a certain light
in order to feed our illusion. Understanding the truth about ourselves, past and present, and having the courage to delve into the
vast recesses of our unconscious to confront our karmic demons,
will lead to personal awareness and freedom.

*"No one is such a liar as the indignant man."*
                                        Friedrich Nietzsche

After centuries of a culture in which we deny who we are and
what we've done and why, we head into the next millennium with a
deep desire to undertake a personal journey where truth is the final
destination. As evidenced by the proliferation of self-help and
inspirational offerings now available in every medium, we want to
do it better, as well as to learn more about who we are as individuals. What we're really doing is expressing a pent-up need to transform our deepest blind spots into awareness, understanding, and
empowerment. We've all repressed into our unconscious issues
that are too terrible to bear on a conscious level. I describe these
deeply guarded secrets we are hesitant to confront as karmic memories. Until we become conscious of them, they feel foreboding,

foreign, and unexplainable, to be feared and tucked away more safely.

Repressing feelings of fear, shame, and anger constricts the way we live and prevents us from expanding our creative abilities. Ironically, the more determined we are to repress our deepest fears and weaknesses, the more they will emerge in our relationships and experiences. Shining the light of understanding on our karmic memories will help us discriminate the truth about ourselves from all of our old, predictable beliefs and feelings.

Gwenn, 50, used to be "stuck, very uncertain about what to do," and was "unclear" about her choices. However, "things began clicking" for her, she says, when she learned the truth about herself and made a conscious effort not to view her experiences through the filters of her past.

*For the first time in a long time, I'm really showing up for myself in creative and unexpected ways. I have clarity and direction and new life goals. I have a newfound appreciation for my relationships and how I express myself within them. I'm letting go of old patterns that never made sense to me anyway, but I felt stuck with them. I'm getting more and more free to live this life in the way that my true self—my soul—longs for.*

*I chose to see the possibility in this work. I suspended disbelief and judgment about astrology, karma, past lives, and the idea of a soul mission. I chose to act as if it all held potential for me, even truth. By opening myself to the possibility and experience of this approach, I am being rewarded with the richness of my own discoveries.*

*I found it particularly wrenching to explore and accept my own darkness—the shadow part, the stuff I secretly "knew" and hated about myself. Linda suggested I start watching the sun rise, to become an observer of the new dawn each day. "Okay," I thought, "I'll give it a try," even though the winter sky seemed so unwelcoming.*

*The first morning, I noticed how chilly and still it was, and how long it actually took the sun to rise above the horizon.*

*The second day, I noticed how beautiful the light was as it came into being, how long a "warning" the sun gives us before showing up.*

*By the third day, I had a deep appreciation for the subleties of the whole thing: how the edges of darkness keep giving way to the pinky glow in a slow and sensuous unfolding.*

*By the fourth and fifth days, it started to make sense for me: the darkness is a natural part of the cycle of life. As I pondered that, I found it increasingly easy to acknowledge my own darkness, as a natural part of my being, just like the light.*

*Each day I looked forward to the coming of the light more and more, especially the gentle way it "took over" the darkness, and its power once the sun emerged. And day by day I became more comfortable with the idea of darkness—the night's and my own—as I watched the power and beauty and triumph of light.*

*As I accepted my darkness, I found it increasingly easy to accept and embrace my light. I became more peaceful with the totality of my being—a wonderful gift. I've been able to discover my own metaphors and recapture my own passion, vision, power, voice—my own life.*

## YOUR KARMIC CONDUCTOR

Saturn is our karmic teacher. It teaches us the truth about ourselves and helps us create order and structure in our lives. Without it, we could not accomplish our soul mission. Saturn presents to us the personal karmic reality each of us needs to face in order to progress toward our soul mission. Saturn tells us the truth about what we need to do rather than what we want to hear.

Imagine that the North Node, your Soul Potential, is the final destination on a train's route. Let's say you board the train at its first stop, which happens to be your South Node, or Soul Pattern. The train signifies the journey to achieving your soul mission. And Saturn is the symbolic conductor of the train. His job is to keep the train and us on the track to ensure we reach our destination. Consult the "Saturn Placements" chart to find the astrological sign your individual Saturn is in. Then use its information to help structure and organize your life to achieve your soul mission.

### Saturn Placements

| If you were born: | Your Saturn is in: | If you were born: | Your Saturn is in: |
|---|---|---|---|
| Jan. 22, 1900–July 18, 1900 | Capricorn | May 30, 1949–Nov. 20, 1950 | Virgo |
| July 19, 1900–Oct. 17, 1900 | Sagittarius | Nov. 21, 1950–Mar. 7, 1951 | Libra |
| Oct. 18, 1900–Jan. 19, 1903 | Capricorn | Mar. 8, 1951–Aug. 13, 1951 | Virgo |
| Jan. 20, 1903–April 13, 1905 | Aquarius | Aug. 14, 1951–Oct. 22, 1953 | Libra |
| April 14, 1905–Aug. 17, 1905 | Pisces | Oct. 23, 1953–Jan. 12, 1956 | Scorpio |
| Aug. 18, 1905–Jan. 8, 1906 | Aquarius | Jan. 13, 1956–May 14, 1956 | Sagittarius |
| Jan. 9, 1906–Mar. 19, 1908 | Pisces | May 15, 1956–Oct. 10, 1956 | Scorpio |
| Mar. 20, 1908–May 17, 1910 | Aries | Oct. 11, 1956–Jan. 5, 1959 | Sagittarius |
| May 18, 1910–Dec. 15, 1910 | Taurus | Jan. 6, 1959–Jan. 3, 1962 | Capricorn |
| Dec. 16, 1910–Jan. 19, 1911 | Aries | Jan. 4, 1962–Mar. 24, 1964 | Aquarius |
| Jan. 20, 1911–July 7, 1912 | Taurus | Mar. 25, 1964–Sept. 17, 1964 | Pisces |
| July 8, 1912–Nov. 30, 1912 | Gemini | Sept. 18, 1964–Dec. 16, 1964 | Aquarius |
| Dec. 1, 1912–Mar. 26, 1913 | Taurus | Dec. 17, 1964–Mar. 3, 1967 | Pisces |
| Mar. 27, 1913–Aug. 24, 1914 | Gemini | Mar. 4, 1967–April 29, 1969 | Aries |
| Aug. 25, 1914–Dec. 7, 1914 | Cancer | April 30, 1969–June 18, 1971 | Taurus |
| Dec. 8, 1914–May 11, 1915 | Gemini | June 19, 1971–Jan. 10, 1972 | Gemini |
| May 12, 1915–Oct. 17, 1916 | Cancer | Jan. 11, 1972–Feb. 21, 1972 | Taurus |
| Oct. 18, 1916–Dec. 7, 1916 | Leo | Feb. 22, 1972–Aug. 1, 1973 | Gemini |
| Dec. 8, 1916–June 24, 1917 | Cancer | Aug. 2, 1973–Jan. 7, 1974 | Cancer |
| June 25, 1917–Aug. 12, 1919 | Leo | Jan. 8, 1974–April 18, 1974 | Gemini |
| Aug. 13, 1919–Oct. 7, 1921 | Virgo | April 19, 1974–June 5, 1976 | Cancer |
| Oct. 8, 1921–Dec. 20, 1923 | Libra | June 6, 1976–Nov. 16, 1977 | Leo |
| Dec. 21, 1923–April 6, 1924 | Scorpio | Nov. 17, 1977–Jan. 5, 1978 | Virgo |
| April 7, 1924–Sept. 13, 1924 | Libra | Jan. 6, 1978–July 26, 1978 | Leo |
| Sept. 14, 1924–Dec. 2, 1926 | Scorpio | July 27, 1978–Sept. 21, 1980 | Virgo |
| Dec. 3, 1926–Mar. 15, 1929 | Sagittarius | Sept. 22, 1980–Nov. 29, 1982 | Libra |
| Mar. 16, 1929–May 5, 1929 | Capricorn | Nov. 30, 1982–May 6, 1983 | Scorpio |
| May 6, 1929–Nov. 30, 1929 | Sagittarius | May 7, 1983–Aug. 24, 1983 | Libra |
| Dec. 1, 1929–Feb. 24, 1932 | Capricorn | Aug. 25, 1983–Nov. 16, 1985 | Scorpio |
| Feb. 25, 1932–Aug. 13, 1932 | Aquarius | Nov. 17, 1985–Feb. 13, 1988 | Sagittarius |
| Aug. 14, 1932–Nov. 19, 1932 | Capricorn | Feb. 14, 1988–June 10, 1988 | Capricorn |
| Nov. 20, 1932–Feb. 14, 1935 | Aquarius | June 11, 1988–Nov. 12, 1988 | Sagittarius |
| Feb. 15, 1935–April 25, 1937 | Pisces | Nov. 13, 1988–Feb. 6, 1991 | Capricorn |
| April 26, 1937–Oct. 18, 1937 | Aries | Feb. 7, 1991–May 20, 1993 | Aquarius |
| Oct. 19, 1937–Jan. 14, 1938 | Pisces | May 21, 1993–June 30, 1993 | Pisces |
| Jan. 15, 1938–Mar. 20, 1940 | Aries | July 1, 1993–Jan. 28, 1994 | Aquarius |
| Mar. 21, 1940–May 9, 1942 | Taurus | Jan. 29, 1994–April 7, 1996 | Pisces |
| May 10, 1942–June 20, 1944 | Gemini | April 8, 1996–June 9, 1998 | Aries |
| June 21, 1944–Aug. 2, 1946 | Cancer | June 10, 1998–Oct. 25, 1998 | Taurus |
| Aug. 3, 1946–Sept. 19, 1948 | Leo | Oct. 26, 1998–Feb. 28, 1999 | Aries |
| Sept. 20, 1948–April 3, 1949 | Virgo | Mar. 1, 1999–Aug. 10, 2000 | Taurus |
| April 4, 1949–May 29, 1949 | Leo | | |

When faced with the unknowns of how to go about achieving our soul mission, we all ask a number of practical questions: How do I reorganize my life to do what I have not done before? How do I set priorities? What specific commitments do I make to achieve success? To what areas should I apply repeated efforts to make my soul mission happen? What responsibilities do I need to claim to realize my Soul Potential? The answers to all these questions may be found in the astrological sign in which your Saturn, your personal conductor, falls. Suppose you have Saturn in Aquarius and your Soul Potential lies in Cancer. Your soul mission is to develop your feminine nature, explore your emotions, and develop a home base for yourself and your family. You would look to your Saturn in Aquarius to provide guidance. What follows is a brief summary of how Saturn in Aquarius, as well as in the eleven other signs, can help us achieve our soul mission.

## SATURN IN THE ASTROLOGICAL SIGNS

### SATURN IN ARIES
You have possible past life experiences as a warrior, a pioneer, an adventurer, or a Native American. Your possible karmic fears are of being alone, taking risks and/or actions, being independent, violence, and anger. You need to take considered risks and spring into action when necessary. Create the strength of will to become more self-assertive in order to take the initiative. You have a strong karmic need to discover true independence on all levels. Committed to having physical energy and to being physically strong and fit, you have a need to be personally competitive and a desire to win for yourself. Know when to forge a new beginning. The path to your soul mission is to become self-aware, self-assured, and self-motivated. Take personal stands when necessary.

### SATURN IN TAURUS
You have possible past lives as a farmer, a banker, and a builder. Your possible karmic fears are of poverty, possessions being taken

away, change, and insecurity. Learn how to integrate material and spiritual values, and to create a practical reality in order to increase your self-esteem and self-value. Your need to foster security within yourself and in your environment is strong. Committed to exploring and manifesting your creative talents, you have the wisdom to create a firm "earthy" foundation and build on it with patience and determination. Building a home, honoring the land, and having comfort and happiness there are important to you. The path to your soul mission is to have a strong sense of personal values that create comfort, security, and serenity.

## SATURN IN GEMINI

You have possible past lives as a writer, a lecturer, and a salesperson. Your possible karmic fears are of being talked about, lied to, and manipulated with words. You must structure and organize a practical and secure intellectual foundation. Constantly needing to gather information and share it, you must become a strong, trustful, and versatile communicator to share your ideas, thoughts, and philosophies. Become a communication chameleon, with the ability to talk to a variety of people with different needs. Commit yourself to being present in the moment and to exploring the possibilities of that moment to their fullest. The path to your soul mission is to intellectually create wise, challenging, and productive thoughts and communicate them with all people.

## SATURN IN CANCER

You have possible past lives as a mother, a cook, an abandoned child, an emotional woman. Your possible karmic fears are of being too emotional and vulnerable, not feeling love, losing a child, having not been nurtured, and failing to assess someone's emotions. Learn to understand and express emotions, and to have the strength to be vulnerable and sensitive to others' emotional needs. You need to become nurturing and mothering and female. At the same time you must break out of a gloomy frame of mind and become more youthful and childlike. Commit yourself to creating and building an emotionally secure and happy home environment for family. The path to your soul mission is to become more female, more emotional, and more connected to nurturing others by understanding their feelings.

## SATURN IN LEO

You have possible past lives as a king, an actor, a perennial child, a gambler. Your possible karmic fears are of assassination, not being applauded, getting old, having fun, and being disregarded. You need to learn about inspired leadership instead of rulership: about being a role model of power and love. Learn to love, honor, and respect yourself instead of requiring it from others. Become an inspired teacher. Find the strength of heart and will to take risks that will ultimately lead to self-confidence and self-empowerment. Try to understand the joyful, spontaneous child within: be creative with fun and activity. Commit yourself to connecting with people heart to heart. The path to your soul mission is to become a self-confident, courageous, inspired leader to those who seek it from you.

## SATURN IN VIRGO

You have possible past lives as a doctor, a nurse, a labor leader, a servant, an animal activist. Your possible karmic fears are of doctors and nurses who cause injury to patients, making mistakes, not being perfect, being too organized, not being organized enough, not understanding, getting ill. You are responsible for understanding the true meaning of perfection (internal, not external). Commit yourself to being of service to others, especially in physical and emotional health. Be organized and efficient, but do not be obsessed with the extremes of what is right or wrong, good or bad. Learn to be highly discriminating by using your analytical and logical strengths. Instead of being overwhelmed by details, incorporate them into a system that encourages productivity. The path to your soul mission is to be a voice of discernment and logic, to encourage health and congruence in yourself and others.

## SATURN IN LIBRA

You have possible past lives as a judge, an interior designer, a mediator, a social climber, an artist, and a relationship junkie. Your possible karmic fears are of imbalance, disharmony, confrontation, loss of relationship, loss of identity (being merged with another), injustice, and unfairness. You are responsible for finding the true balance and harmony between yourself and others. Consider sharing ideas that will create negotiation and mediation. Put yourself in another's shoes to foster understanding and communication. Search for fairness and justice, and share these attitudes with others. Be creative in your use of color and symmetry to produce beauty and peace in your environment. The path to your soul mission is to be a calm, mediating force to create more understanding between people.

## SATURN IN SCORPIO

You have possible past lives as an investigator, a CEO, a psychiatrist, a magician, a financial consultant, a mortician. Your possible karmic fears are of loss of power, too much power, loss of control, being controlled, death, sex, rage, secrets, betrayal, and loss of money. You are responsible for turning chaos into intensity, and fear into drive. Pursue success with great determination and vigor. Reframe your anger and resentment into a passion for more creative pursuits such as philosophy or emotional and sexual intimacy. Commit yourself to probing the mysteries of life and finding personal answers to significant questions. The path to your soul mission is to use your desire and will to understand and connect with another's values.

## SATURN IN SAGITTARIUS

You have possible past lives as a teacher, a philosopher, a lawyer, a cowboy, a wandering minister, and a traveler. Your possible karmic fears are of commitment, loss of freedom and open spaces, traveling, loss of independence, not being believed, and being controlled by religion. You are responsible for structuring your philosophy so it can be shared and taught to others without preachiness. Travel and explore other cultures and religions. Commit yourself to learning how to organize your life based on optimism, truth, and personal freedom. Use your penetrating mind to search for depth and meaning in life. The path to your soul mission is to honestly and enthusiastically share your life experiences to help others find their life's purpose.

## Saturn in Capricorn

You have possible past lives as a business manager, an architect, a strict father, a land baron, and an industry leader. Your possible karmic fears are of financial success or failure, emotions, lack of structure, and controlling men in authority. You are responsible for finding your road to success, organizing and following it with persistence and determination. Claim your authority and ambition and patiently climb your personal mountain to achievement. Commit yourself to self-discipline, self-responsibility, and self-actualization by deliberately ordering your internal and external life. Hone your wisdom and love through your protection of and loyalty to your family and friends. The path to your soul mission is to create an ordered, structured, responsible approach to appropriate goals that will manifest as a mature and wise life.

## Saturn in Aquarius

You have possible past lives as an astrologer, an inventor, a rebel, a revolutionary, a humanitarian, and an astronomer. Your possible karmic fears are of being misunderstood, becoming too emotionally involved, being ostracized, being radical, and mistrust of friends. You have the responsibility to claim your originality and individuality. Find your humanity and translate it into a political and spiritual cause; then join with others who feel the same way. Understand your rational, logical, and observing nature, but also the holistic model (mind, body, and spirit), and integrate it into your approach to life. Maintain an equal, humanistic view in the groups you join and the friends you keep. The path to your soul mission requires that you be avant-garde, visionary, and uniquely different in your objectives.

## SATURN IN PISCES

You have possible past lives as a psychic healer, a dancer, a musician, a martyr, and an addict. Your possible karmic fears are of addiction, sacrificing yourself, being subservient, being used, escapism, and being emotionally obsessed. You have a responsibility for understanding your feelings and expressing them through a strong sense of self. Commit yourself to using your psychic and intuitional gifts to help others claim their spiritual and creative talents and to experience life as an imaginative, magical, and spiritual adventure. Provide gentle service to self and others. Be compassionate and sensitive to others without giving yourself away. The path to your soul mission is to be emotionally and creatively strong, to experience a life of spiritual awareness and interaction with others.

## LEARNING MORE ABOUT YOUR SATURN TRAITS

In order to make sense of the continuum of our existence over lifetimes, we must understand who we have been in the past, and how we were trained and programmed by the beliefs and value systems of the past. Since we often make the mistake of assigning today's values and social mores to previous incarnations, we are left with the residue of guilt. Guilt left unresolved (which we will discuss in Chapter 9) can play a major role in undermining our ability to discover and achieve our soul mission.

The exercises that follow will help you uncover which karmic experiences—critical issues from the past—you've been afraid to confront and have been hiding from yourself. Dealing with a higher level of truth will imbue you with more positive energy and give your relationships more conscious meaning. Although each of you will find different experiences based on your karmic journey, many of us have several recurring themes or life issues in common. We all tend to abhor the misuse of power, greed, disregard of others, selfishness, abuse, dogmatism, ignorance, and self-serving manipulation, to name a few. All of us, in our journey in this lifetime, have experienced all that we abhor. It has been an intrinsic part of the human condition.

Putting your past life experiences into a historical context will help you distinguish the truth about yourself from what you want to believe. Have you ever wondered why so many of the males you draw into your life are so similar in character and temperament? Our souls choose our Saturn placement—the astrological constellation that Saturn was moving through on the day we were born—to remind us of important past lives as men.

Your soul is interested in you having the full panoply of life's experiences from every vantage point imaginable: both genders, all races, all religions, all cultures, and all economic strata. Besides helping you learn more about your male qualities, this exercise will help you understand why you created your father to be the way he is. Learning more about your "Saturn energy" or your "male energy" will also help you focus on the areas in your life where you need to improve by committing yourself to being more responsible, as well as on what you need to do in order to be successful in your endeavors and fulfill your soul mission.

First, consult the "Saturn Placements" chart in order to learn what sign your Saturn was in when you were born. Use your sign and the traits associated with it to complete the exercise below.

### Saturn Exercise

Refer to the Energetics Models (Charts 2 and 3 in Chapter 4) to determine the behavioral characteristics of your particular Saturn. For instance, I was born on December 13, 1942. My Saturn is in the sign of Gemini. Looking at the Soul Pattern Energetics Model (Chart 2 in Chapter 4), I find the characteristics that are more challenging; from the Soul Potential Energetics Model in Chart 3, I find the traits associated with Gemini that are more positive.

Using these traits, I can determine what kind of personality I had in a past life. I was bright, versatile, and articulate. I was probably a writer or speaker who used words to manipulate people to get what I wanted. I quite possibly told the truth when it suited me and lied when it suited me. I was inconsistent and had problems committing to one person. I could have had difficulty with emotions and been unable to express them. This exercise will guide you to complete your own karmic story as well as to glean some personal information meaningful to you.

## STEP 1

My Saturn is in the sign of: _____

(refer to the "Saturn Placements" table).

Positive traits of this sign (refer to Chart 3 in Chapter 4) are:

Challenging traits of this sign (refer to Chart 2 in Chapter 4) are:

## STEP 2

In order to better understand the type of male relationships you've created in this life, write a short story in your journal using the above words. The story should focus on problematic as well as positive aspects of a previous existence as a man. Each word could represent a career, an experience or event, or a possible conflict. Use your imagination to produce a story. Have fun with it. Even if you don't consider yourself a writer, or even a devout believer in past lives, many stories lie within you. Let your unconscious mind provide you with interesting ideas. Don't overanalyze: let the story flow, using the words as your guide.

For example, your "challenging" list might contain the word *aggressive* or perhaps *possessive* or *selfish*. For the purpose of this exercise, let's focus on *aggression*. Let your mind create a story in which being aggressive is the centerpiece. Create a character whose life was imbued with aggressive behavior. What aggressive act might he have done? What were the ramifications of that aggression? Who could he have hurt? Now work in the positive characteristics that refer to this man's personality strengths and depth of character. By making use of all the words, you will develop a powerful story about a male past life.

This exercise will help you build emotional, spiritual, and educational foundations. It is a means to an end: to yield a better understanding of yourself as well as those around you. Try not to get bogged down in deciding whether you have a definitive belief in past lives. Keep an open mind, complete the exercise, and after you've finished, ask yourself whether you have a more insightful view of yourself as well those closest to you.

## STEP 3

How does this story affect your life today? Think about the experience you've just created. Could it have influenced relationships and situations in this life, particularly those that involve men? Using the aggression example (or whatever meaningful word you chose): Have you created soul contracts with men who are aggressive toward you? What are they trying to show you about yourself? Do you hate aggression? Why? Could it be that it is something that you hate about yourself from that old life? Is there an old conflict surrounding aggression that you need to resolve? An obligation that has to be met? Your story is filled with possibilities that you need to resolve in this life.

## STEP 4

Once we are aware of our past, we can alter our present reality. We can resolve our old conflicts and pay back our old obligations. Utilizing our aggression example: Suppose you have a soul contract with a man who has been aggressive toward you. This person signed a soul contract with you to be aggressive, to show you a side of yourself you never knew you had. Realizing that you have an unresolved aggressive pattern in yourself will help you take responsibility for it and do something to change it. Most importantly, you will no longer be a victim to this soul contract's aggression. Perhaps one day you will learn so much about yourself from this relationship that you will actually feel gratitude to this person. You may even find yourself thanking him for this valuable soul reminder. Learning about our past actions, and accepting responsibility for them, enables us to put all of our current relationships in a healthier, more constructive context, rather than being imprisoned by them, providing us with the opportunity to create freedom.

For instance, whenever my stepfather Doug was angry with me, he would always scream part of a biblical reference at me: "You are a liar, and the truth is not in you." On a personality level, that sounds like an abusive thing to say to somone. But on a soul level, he was reminding me of a life where I had been very cavalier with the truth. Doug was a circle-one karmic relationship for me. My soul created the soul contract with him to learn about that past life of lying to get what I wanted. In this life telling the truth is almost a compulsion with me—an interesting symmetry.

For years I found myself falling in love with men who looked physically very similar. They were dark-haired men with beards. I wouldn't even look at a man who did not fit that description. Years later after a great deal of research into my past life as a Civil War soldier, I found a photograph of him. He was dark-haired with a beard. All of my lovers looked remarkably like this soldier. My soul was showing me a fairly accurate picture of what I had looked like.

# CHAPTER 8

# Mars: Handling Anger Wisely

*"Anger is a short madness."*
Horace

*"Anger is a weed; hate is the tree."*
Augustine

*"A wrathful man stirreth up strife: but he that is slow to anger appeaseth strife."*
Proverbs

Anger is as much a part of the vast spectrum of human emotion as any other feeling, yet no emotion has been more maligned and misunderstood. Our most enduring social mores perpetuate the belief that anger is ugly. We've been conditioned to equate its expression with being reckless, abusive, and dangerous. Although holding back our emotions can lead to stress and its concomitant maladies—from heart disease to depression to unmitigated violence—we are still expected to neatly tuck away our rancor deep within the recesses of our psyche. It's acceptable to express ourselves, as long as we don't lose our temper.

Growing up, I was told that anger was unrefined, socially unacceptable, and certainly not ladylike—not to mention immature, childish, and irrational. Many of my students and clients were taught the same thing. Yet contrary to this childhood lesson, expressing anger is healthy—in fact, it is necessary to our health—as long as we do it in an appropriate manner. To deny ourselves any expression of anger would be an impossibility, just as it would be for sadness, happiness, fear, or shame.

Anger motivates us, helps us sustain our determination and drive, and sometimes works as a healing agent. Anger helps us defend ourselves, keeping us from being weak and vulnerable. Anger is the internal fire that gives us the impetus to take action in tense or emotionally challenging situations.

Anger becomes problematic and justifies its traditionally negative connotations when we don't express it in a healthy way, or when we don't express it, period, or when we seethe until we can't hold our anger anymore and then we explode, directing our fury at someone in the form of a verbal barrage or, worse, a physical attack. Abusing people with anger is wrong, so we need to distinguish between telling someone that we are angry with them and actually venting on them. One is done with sheer hostility; the other is done with thought, emotion, and understanding. We can use our anger to be strong and assertive. However, projecting your anger onto someone else implies that someone else's actions have made you angry, or that you have relinquished to that person your responsibility for your own emotions.

## Expressing Anger

| *Healthy* | *Unhealthy* |
|---|---|
| 1. Shout the word *no* repeatedly. | 1. Scream judgments at someone. |
| 2. Hit a whiffle bat on a pillow. | 2. Blame someone for your anger. |
| 3. Take a fast walk around the block. | 3. Hit something alive. |
| 4. Vigorously dig in the dirt. | 4. Be sarcastic to someone. |
| 5. Make a loud noise. | 5. Drive your car too fast. |
| 6. Rip something up. | 6. Drive recklessly. |
| 7. Throw a tennis ball against a wall. | 7. Give someone the finger for cutting you off on the highway. |
| 8. Exercise. | 8. Run a red light. |
| 9. Write an angry letter and burn it. | 9. Plot revenge. |

Mars is about taking responsibility for our anger, laying claim to it, saying, "My anger is my anger, and no one can make me angry." Many clients come to me claiming they're depressed. My first question to them is, "What are you so angry about?" Although they are initially surprised by my question, when we talk about their repressed anger, their depression begins to abate. They are now able to do something about their anger and its related depression.

Most people don't honestly believe that their anger is self-perpetuated. Most of us believe that someone else's behavior, or an exasperating event, is what triggers our anger. I'm challenging you to accept that no one can make you angry without your acquiescence. Have you ever become furious when your 2-year-old threw his dinner on the floor, following a day at work you'd rather forget? And yet at a different time in a different context, when perhaps you were more relaxed—maybe you had just returned from a fun family day at the beach—you handled his dinnertime antics with a laugh. Have you ever become irate while sitting in a traffic tie-up that will make you late for work, while that same traffic jam, on the way to a vacation in the mountains, would elicit a grimace at worst? We have not been taught to believe that *we* are responsible for our emotions.

## HANDLING YOUR ANGER

Anger is a palpable and visceral energy that we would be hard-pressed to release without doing something physical. Some therapists prescribe writing an angry letter and burning it. That's better than doing nothing, but not nearly as effective as physical means.

So go buy a plastic bat, and scream and yell and bat things that are inanimate. Imagine the face of the person with whom you are angry on a pillow, and go to work on it with a plastic bat. Have a temper tantrum! Maybe you were forbidden to do that as a child. What's stopping you now? Perhaps you fear losing control, or that once you begin, you'll never stop. I always tell clients to time their anger work using a loud buzzer, to prove to themselves that they are in control of their angry outburst.

Another powerful exercise involves the use of the word *no. No* has a negative connotation in our culture. It means you're not in alignment with someone or something—be it a plan, a strategy, or a policy—and that you're not going to do what is expected of you. Shouting "No!" can catalyze change within us. I have a lot of clients screaming "No!" in their cars to bleed off their anger.

In fact, the late psychiatrist Milton H. Erickson developed two "indirection" exercises that I've found helpful in this context. One is called a Yes Set, the other a No Set. The purpose of the Yes Set exercise is to help someone create alignment by asking them questions to which they will have to answer *yes*. Let's say you have a friend who is in a terrible frame of mind: she is moody, pessimistic, and negative about all the aspects of her life. By eliciting *yes* responses and creating a more positive energy, you are helping her migrate to a more encouraging mindset.

On the other hand, you may have an extremely passive friend who is being taken advantage of repeatedly by a man she is seeing, but can't muster the energy to draw the line. In order to help her access and confront her anger, you would help her with a No Set exercise. If you ask her questions to which she will have to answer *no,* her anger will build. The more she answers *no,* the angrier she will get.

Think about when and why you say *no:* perhaps you don't want to do something, or you want to protect your own best interests. Most of us were reared by parents who ordained that *no* was an unacceptable response, so *no* becomes one of the most difficult things for us to say as adults. By the same token, developing the ability to say it is a sign of assertiveness and independence.

### Exercise: Mature and Responsible Handling of Anger

When you're in a conflict with another person and begin to get angry:

Step 1: Be present to the feeling and aware of the intensity of it.

Step 2: File the content material—the specific cause of the anger—away somewhere in your conscience so you can look at it later, when you are more reflective, to help you understand some hidden part of yourself.

Step 3: Instead of reacting automatically in anger, give yourself and the other person a time-out. Leave the room for a few minutes, telling the other person that you will return shortly.

Step 4: Do some anger work. Release the toxic, emotional physical energy that belongs to you.

Step 5: Return to the person and the conversation. Begin with an "I" statement: "I was angry when you (fill in the blank). I would like to discuss that with you." You've already released a good deal of the physicality of your anger in step 4. Now you're able to discuss the situation calmly and rationally.

I know what you must be thinking: *What's the other person doing, while I'm being so measured and rational?* It doesn't matter. You are only responsible for your own reactions. It's my experience, personally and through my clients, that if you don't escalate the conflict, the other person will calm down also.

## MARS'S ROLE IN ANGER

Mars, the planet that ruled the Age of Aries, Moses, and most of the Old Testament, represents physical energy, assertion, aggression, war, power, initiation, and will. It is the energy that embodies action, forward motion, and risk taking. It represents independence, boldness, and self-reliance. Our Mars energy is a selfish energy; it wants to win for itself and compete with itself. At its best, Mars represents focused determination and self-motivation.

At its worst, it can be impulsive, reckless, impatient, short-sighted, destructive, and accident-prone.

Mars represents the way we understand and express anger. At its most organic level, it symbolizes the savage in us, the impulsive part that is about action and reaction: no thought, no social consequence or rules. Mars also reveals how we make others angry at us. Karmically, in an astrological chart, Mars tells us about the conflicts and the wars that we have experienced in other lifetimes. The placement of the planet Mars on the day you were born indicates the kinds of conflicts you've initiated, and the havoc you've wrought in the past.

One of the most prominent ways our Mars energy affects us is in our ability or inability to take aggressive action. In past lifetimes we've taken actions that hurt ourselves or others. Now in this life, we're very reluctant to take an aggressive action again, fearing the same injurious result as before. So before we can be free to be more assertive in this life, we have to confront and resolve those previous experiences. If you are afraid of discovering and resolving your Mars conflicts, you've created a new conflict right there. This conflict can be resolved only by uncovering the life where a Mars conflict had an extremely adverse effect on you. Without resolving the conflict, you may be depressed without knowing why.

Thus Mars is extremely important in helping us find out how past life conflicts can cause vague feelings of depression. A powerful clue is anger that we feel in this life that seems to have no immediate cause. To learn more about the issues from which you may be sourcing your anger, consult the "Mars Placements" chart, which will tell you your Mars sign. (See "Mars Placements," pp. 185–192.) Each sign possesses a different residue of karmic anger.

Marilyn, who lives in Seattle, was plagued by a deep despondency that she couldn't entirely overcome, until she discovered and confronted her anger, sourced from a traumatic event from her past.

*I spent the first forty years of my life proud of my ability to control my emotions, especially anger. As a young child, I would have temper tantrums, but they were gone by the time I made it to middle school. I hadn't experienced any type of anger since then. Upon turning forty-one, I entered the most depressing time of my life: I gained weight, I could not socialize with my friends, I got my first mediocre job evaluation, and I cried a lot. All of my old intellectual skills failed me. At first I thought I was going through early menopause. My doctor discounted that possibility and suggested a therapist. I took her advice, and a year later I was almost back to being my old self. Yet I still felt a vague sense of discomfort that wouldn't go away.*

*I saw Linda when she made one of her trips to Seattle, because I was interested in my spiritual mission. One of my friends had suggested that my dissatisfaction might be due to my lack of a spiritual path. Linda told me that my spiritual mission was to learn to be Arian and that Aries was ruled by Mars. She asked me how easily I assessed and dealt with my anger. I told her my story.*

*"Would you be willing to change your mind about controlling your anger?" she asked.*

*"No," I said emphatically, "I will not go back to being an out-of-control child having tantrums."*

*"There are other ways," Linda said softly.*

*I have to say that at this point of the session, I was not happy. I had come to Linda to understand my spiritual mission, and here we were talking about anger. It made no sense to me. I'm not sure what she did or said that kept me in her office that day. But I'm extremely grateful that I did stay. I learned that my Mars in Aries was about more than anger, but to be able to accept its gifts, I would need to value anger as part of my experience.*

*We did a meditation. She asked me to remember what had made me so angry as a child. I couldn't think of anything. I was able to remember my reactions but not what caused them. Then she asked me to visualize a bright fire-engine red. The color came immediately. It had been my favorite color as a child. At her request I allowed the color to locate in my lower back.*

*"Just be with the color. Let it turn into a picture," she said in her soothing voice.*

*I saw the color swirl, then slow down. It was like a kaleidoscope, and then there was a scene. The red was now blood on the hands of what looked like a young man. He was running, very scared, and breathing very heavily. Behind him was the body of a young woman, lying in a pool of blood.*

*Linda's voice was coaching me to speak. Somehow I knew that the young man in the scene was me. I told her what the scene was.*

*"Where did the blood come from?" Linda asked.*

*"A knife. I killed her with a knife," I reported, aghast at what I was saying, because it felt so true.*

*"Why?" Linda asked.*

*"She didn't love me. She was going to marry someone else. I got so angry, I couldn't control it. I killed her because I loved her so much."*

*Tears flowed down my face. Then I opened my eyes and looked at Linda, who was smiling. It seemed so contradictory to me that she would be smiling. I had just remembered killing someone.*

*"Remember that vague discomfort that's been torturing you for the last year? You just found the source of it. Congratulations!" Linda said. "You also just figured out why you're so afraid of anger. You think it's not only dangerous but murderous."*

*I knew it was true. I felt strangely relieved and so very tired. I saw Linda twice more during her Seattle stay. We worked on how I could complete that old life and deal with anger more effectively in this one. At her suggestion, I bought red clothes and claimed my soul color. The discomfort left, never to return. Now I have the courage and the will to claim all my feelings, and my life is more exciting than it has ever been.*

Mars rules our basic need to achieve our wants and desires, and sexuality is one of those basic needs. Thus Mars encompasses our sexual motivation and gratification. Its energy manifests as our need for physical excitement and stimulation, whether through exercise, physical assertion, or sexuality. It drives our primordial need to physically connect with another person on a sexual level. Our Mars energy contains the ingredient that drives us toward the erotic and to consummate our desire through sexual relations. In many ways it represents what we find physically attractive and sexually exciting in another person. Once we are stimulated by a carnal desire for someone, we use our Mars energy to take the actions necessary to become sexually active with that person.

Mars also symbolizes sharp objects and people who use those objects in their work: surgeons and soldiers, for example. Mars rules warfare, whether it occurs internally or externally. As the male archetype, it has a strong need to manifest its male energy through forward, directed action. Mars colors how we motivate ourselves, and how we initiate action.

In a woman's astrological chart Mars is one of the planets that symbolizes her animus (the hidden male side of herself). It is also the energy that romantically stimulates her and draws her sexually to another person. If a man's Mars is in a female astrological sign, he may manifest his Mars energy in a more feminine, passive-aggressive manner. The following story from Stacy, 34, will give you an idea of how this Mars energy can cause conflicts in a relationship until it is understood.

*My husband Steve and I were having serious problems in our marriage. We were always angry at each other. I would get so irritated with him that I would literally scream at him. He would respond by staring at me, saying nothing. That made me madder; I would scream more. He would get colder and more remote. The cycle seemed irreversible.*

*Things were so bad that we had even thought about divorcing. But with three young children, an expensive house, and plenty of bills, divorce didn't seem like a viable solution. I knew about Linda from other friends who had seen her. Steve refused to go with me, saying that it was a waste of time and money. However, he did let Linda do his chart in preparation for my appointment.*

*She and I spent the first half hour discussing the problems Steve and I were having. Then Linda explained that Steve and I had chal-*

*lenging Mars placements. My Mars was in Sagittarius; Steve's was in Cancer. My Mars was definitely male-oriented, while Steve's was more female. It had never occurred to me that a part of me could be "male-like" and that my masculine husband could have a female side.*

*That revelation in itself made seeing Linda worthwhile. I have to admit that I was usually the protagonist of our arguments. When I'm angry, I just say so. Having more male energy than Steve meant that I was blunt, more aggressive, impulsive, and direct than he was. For his part, he was more responsive, sensitive, and defensive of my male anger. He would close down and hide inside himself, because he felt so scared and unsafe. His inability to speak to me honestly and directly when he was upset about something would drive me nuts. I wanted him to be more like me. Learning that he had a different orientation toward anger helped me. I could stop expecting him to be a mirror image of me. I could also begin to appreciate his fears and insecurities and how abused he felt.*

*I told Steve about the session. Surprisingly, he decided to go with me to our next appointment. Linda explained our Mars placements to Steve and told him how he must have felt when I was so loud and forward. He was amazed. He later told me that Linda had very accurately described how he felt and why he felt so paralyzed during those moments. We spent several sessions striving to understand our differences and learning how to better deal with each other's anger styles. It worked. I have learned to think before I speak in anger, and Steve has learned to be a little more expressive. We slip once in a while, but the change in our marriage is dramatic because we're able to understand our reactions, and we have a better chance of altering them.*

In this life we handle our past life Mars conflicts, or past life issues surrounding anger, in one of three ways:

**1. Project our anger onto someone else.** We create a soul contract with someone to help us unravel a past life conflict. Remember, the stronger the reaction, the more vital the information it contains. Suppose your husband's angry words to you are sarcastic and biting. Your reaction is to become extremely angry with him. Intellectually, you know you are overreacting, but it's automatic on your part. When you realize your reactions form this pattern, you can see that your husband is reflecting a residual conflict involving anger from a past life of yours. In the past, you yourself probably were very sarcastic and used your rapier wit to wound people.

**2. Continue to exhibit negative aspects of our Mars energy.** The "Mars Placements" chart will show you how you may be handling issues relating to anger and other Mars issues. As I've said earlier, we often repeat our mistakes—or create them—until we learn from them and resolve them.

**3. Avoid positive aspects of our Mars energy.** Normally people tend to avoid confronting their Mars energy in this life because of the way they've handled it in the past. In other words, when we've taken an aggressive action in the past, its negative consquences often foster a fear of assertion in this life.

## MARS PLACEMENTS: SOURCING YOUR ANGER

Each astrological sign in Mars articulates its anger issues differently. Knowing your Mars sign will help you understand what you are angry about, so you can take responsibility for it. Your anger issues in this life are directly correlated to the conflicts you've created in the past. Until you discover and handle your past life conflicts, you won't be able to fully use the positive, assertive energy from your Mars placement. You'll find yourself unable to make a major decision that needs to be made quickly, to take a new action, to create a new beginning, or to take a risk. Your unconscious fear of repeating old behaviors caused by impulsivity, aggression, and rage may lead to immobilization and passivity in this life. In an effort to learn more about your anger as well as other aspects of your Mars energy, find your Mars sign by looking up your birth date in this chart.

## Mars Placements

| If you were born: | Your Mars is in: | If you were born: | Your Mars is in: |
| --- | --- | --- | --- |
| Jan. 22–Feb. 28, 1900 | Aquarius | July 28–Sept. 12, 1906 | Leo |
| Mar. 1–April 8, 1900 | Pisces | Sept. 13–Oct. 30, 1906 | Virgo |
| April 9–May 17, 1900 | Aries | Oct. 31–Dec. 17, 1906 | Libra |
| May 18–June 27, 1900 | Taurus | Dec. 18–Feb. 5, 1907 | Scorpio |
| June 28–Aug. 10, 1900 | Gemini | Feb. 6–April 1, 1907 | Sagittarius |
| Aug. 11–Sept. 26, 1900 | Cancer | April 2–Oct. 13, 1907 | Capricorn |
| Sept. 27–Nov. 23, 1900 | Leo | Oct. 14–Nov. 29, 1907 | Aquarius |
| Nov. 24–Mar. 1, 1901 | Virgo | Nov. 30–Jan. 11, 1908 | Pisces |
| Mar. 2–May 11, 1901 | Leo | Jan. 12–Feb. 23, 1908 | Aries |
| May 12–July 13, 1901 | Virgo | Feb. 24–April 7, 1908 | Taurus |
| July 14–Aug. 31, 1901 | Libra | April 8–May 22, 1908 | Gemini |
| Sept. 1–Oct. 14, 1901 | Scorpio | May 23–July 8, 1908 | Cancer |
| Oct. 15–Nov. 24, 1901 | Sagittarius | July 9–Aug. 24, 1908 | Leo |
| Nov. 25–Jan. 1, 1902 | Capricorn | Aug. 25–Oct. 10, 1908 | Virgo |
| Jan. 2–Feb. 8, 1902 | Aquarius | Oct. 11–Nov. 25, 1908 | Libra |
| Feb. 9–Mar. 19, 1902 | Pisces | Nov. 26–Jan. 10, 1909 | Scorpio |
| Mar. 20–April 27, 1902 | Aries | Jan. 11–Feb. 24, 1909 | Sagittarius |
| April 28–June 7, 1902 | Taurus | Feb. 25–April 9, 1909 | Capricorn |
| June 8–July 20, 1902 | Gemini | April 10–May 25, 1909 | Aquarius |
| July 21–Sept. 4, 1902 | Cancer | May 26–July 21, 1909 | Pisces |
| Sept. 5–Oct. 23, 1902 | Leo | July 22–Sept. 27, 1909 | Aries |
| Oct. 24–Dec. 20, 1902 | Virgo | Sept. 28–Nov. 20, 1909 | Pisces |
| Dec. 21–April 19, 1903 | Libra | Nov. 21–Jan. 23, 1910 | Aries |
| April 20–May 30, 1903 | Virgo | Jan. 24–Mar. 14, 1910 | Taurus |
| May 31–Aug. 6, 1903 | Libra | Mar. 15–May 1, 1910 | Gemini |
| Aug. 7–Sept. 22, 1903 | Scorpio | May 2–June 19, 1910 | Cancer |
| Sept. 23–Nov. 3, 1903 | Sagittarius | June 20–Aug. 6, 1910 | Leo |
| Nov. 4–Dec. 12, 1903 | Capricorn | Aug. 7–Sept. 21, 1910 | Virgo |
| Dec. 13–Jan. 19, 1904 | Aquarius | Sept. 22–Nov. 6, 1910 | Libra |
| Jan. 20–Feb. 27, 1904 | Pisces | Nov. 7–Dec. 20, 1910 | Scorpio |
| Feb. 28–April 6, 1904 | Aries | Dec. 21–Jan. 31, 1911 | Sagittarius |
| April 7–May 18, 1904 | Taurus | Feb. 1–Mar. 13, 1911 | Capricorn |
| May 19–June 30, 1904 | Gemini | Mar. 14–April 23, 1911 | Aquarius |
| July 1–Aug. 15, 1904 | Cancer | April 24–June 2, 1911 | Pisces |
| Aug. 16–Oct. 1, 1904 | Leo | June 3–July 15, 1911 | Aries |
| Oct. 2–Nov. 20, 1904 | Virgo | July 16–Sept. 5, 1911 | Taurus |
| Nov. 21–Jan. 13, 1905 | Libra | Sept. 6–Nov. 30, 1911 | Gemini |
| Jan. 14–Aug. 21, 1905 | Scorpio | Dec. 1–Jan. 30, 1912 | Taurus |
| Aug. 22–Oct. 8, 1905 | Sagittarius | Jan. 31–April 5, 1912 | Gemini |
| Oct. 9–Nov. 18, 1905 | Capricorn | April 6–May 28, 1912 | Cancer |
| Nov. 19–Dec. 27, 1905 | Aquarius | May 29–July 17, 1912 | Leo |
| Dec. 28–Feb. 4, 1906 | Pisces | July 18–Sept. 2, 1912 | Virgo |
| Feb. 5–Mar. 17, 1906 | Aries | Sept. 3–Oct. 18, 1912 | Libra |
| Mar. 18–April 28, 1906 | Taurus | Oct. 19–Nov. 30, 1912 | Scorpio |
| April 29–June 11, 1906 | Gemini | Dec. 1–Jan. 10, 1913 | Sagittarius |
| June 12–July 27, 1906 | Cancer | Jan. 11–Feb. 19, 1913 | Capricorn |

| If you were born: | Your Mars is in: | If you were born: | Your Mars is in: |
|---|---|---|---|
| Feb. 20–Mar. 30, 1913 | Aquarius | July 11–Sept. 4, 1920 | Scorpio |
| Mar. 31–May 8, 1913 | Pisces | Sept. 5–Oct. 18, 1920 | Sagittarius |
| May 9–June 16, 1913 | Aries | Oct. 19–Nov. 27, 1920 | Capricorn |
| June 17–July 29, 1913 | Taurus | Nov. 28–Jan. 5, 1921 | Aquarius |
| July 30–Sept. 15, 1913 | Gemini | Jan. 6–Feb. 13, 1921 | Pisces |
| Sept. 16–May 1, 1914 | Cancer | Feb. 14–Mar. 25, 1921 | Aries |
| May 2–June 26, 1914 | Leo | Mar. 26–May 6, 1921 | Taurus |
| June 27–Aug. 14, 1914 | Virgo | May 7–June 18, 1921 | Gemini |
| Aug. 15–Sept. 29, 1914 | Libra | June 19–Aug. 3, 1921 | Cancer |
| Sept. 30–Nov. 11, 1914 | Scorpio | Aug. 4–Sept. 19, 1921 | Leo |
| Nov. 12–Dec. 22, 1914 | Sagittarius | Sept. 20–Nov. 6, 1921 | Virgo |
| Dec. 23–Jan. 30, 1915 | Capricorn | Nov. 7–Dec. 26, 1921 | Libra |
| Jan. 31–Mar. 9, 1915 | Aquarius | Dec. 27–Feb. 18, 1922 | Scorpio |
| Mar. 10–April 16, 1915 | Pisces | Feb. 19–Sept. 13, 1922 | Sagittarius |
| April 17–May 26, 1915 | Aries | Sept. 14–Oct. 30, 1922 | Capricorn |
| May 27–July 6, 1915 | Taurus | Oct. 31–Dec. 11, 1922 | Aquarius |
| July 7–Aug. 19, 1915 | Gemini | Dec. 12–Jan. 21, 1923 | Pisces |
| Aug. 20–Oct. 7, 1915 | Cancer | Jan. 22–Mar. 4, 1923 | Aries |
| Oct. 8–May 28, 1916 | Leo | Mar. 5–April 16, 1923 | Taurus |
| May 29–July 23, 1916 | Virgo | April 17–May 30, 1923 | Gemini |
| July 24–Sept. 8, 1916 | Libra | May 31–July 16, 1923 | Cancer |
| Sept. 9–Oct. 22, 1916 | Scorpio | July 17–Sept. 1, 1923 | Leo |
| Oct. 23–Dec. 1, 1916 | Sagittarius | Sept. 2–Oct. 18, 1923 | Virgo |
| Dec. 2–Jan. 9, 1917 | Capricorn | Oct. 19–Dec. 4, 1923 | Libra |
| Jan. 10–Feb. 16, 1917 | Aquarius | Dec. 5–Jan. 19, 1924 | Scorpio |
| Feb. 17–Mar. 26, 1917 | Pisces | Jan. 20–Mar. 6, 1924 | Sagittarius |
| Mar. 27–May 4, 1917 | Aries | Mar. 7–April 24, 1924 | Capricorn |
| May 5–June 14, 1917 | Taurus | April 25–June 24, 1924 | Aquarius |
| June 15–July 28, 1917 | Gemini | June 25–Aug. 24, 1924 | Pisces |
| July 29–Sept. 12, 1917 | Cancer | Aug. 25–Oct. 19, 1924 | Aquarius |
| Sept. 13–Nov. 2, 1917 | Leo | Oct. 20–Dec. 19, 1924 | Pisces |
| Nov. 3–Jan. 11, 1918 | Virgo | Dec. 20–Feb. 5, 1925 | Aries |
| Jan. 12–Feb. 25, 1918 | Libra | Feb. 6–Mar. 23, 1925 | Taurus |
| Feb. 26–June 23, 1918 | Virgo | Mar. 24–May 9, 1925 | Gemini |
| June 24–Aug. 17, 1918 | Libra | May 10–June 26, 1925 | Cancer |
| Aug. 18–Oct. 1, 1918 | Scorpio | June 27–Aug. 12, 1925 | Leo |
| Oct. 2–Nov. 11, 1918 | Sagittarius | Aug. 13–Sept. 28, 1925 | Virgo |
| Nov. 12–Dec. 20, 1918 | Capricorn | Sept. 29–Nov. 13, 1925 | Libra |
| Dec. 21–Jan. 27, 1919 | Aquarius | Nov. 14–Dec. 27, 1925 | Scorpio |
| Jan. 28–Mar. 6, 1919 | Pisces | Dec. 28–Feb. 9, 1926 | Sagittarius |
| Mar. 7–April 15, 1919 | Aries | Feb. 10–Mar. 23, 1926 | Capricorn |
| April 16–May 26, 1919 | Taurus | Mar. 24–May 3, 1926 | Aquarius |
| May 27–July 8, 1919 | Gemini | May 4–June 15, 1926 | Pisces |
| July 9–Aug. 23, 1919 | Cancer | June 16–Aug. 1, 1926 | Aries |
| Aug. 24–Oct. 10, 1919 | Leo | Aug. 2–Feb. 21, 1927 | Taurus |
| Oct. 11–Nov. 30, 1919 | Virgo | Feb. 22–April 17, 1927 | Gemini |
| Dec. 1–Jan. 31, 1920 | Libra | April 18–June 6, 1927 | Cancer |
| Feb. 1–April 23, 1920 | Scorpio | June 7–July 25, 1927 | Leo |
| April 24–July 10, 1920 | Libra | July 26–Sept. 10, 1927 | Virgo |

| If you were born: | Your Mars is in: | If you were born: | Your Mars is in: |
|---|---|---|---|
| Sept. 11–Oct. 25, 1927 | Libra | July 16–Aug. 30, 1934 | Cancer |
| Oct. 26–Dec. 8, 1927 | Scorpio | Aug. 31–Oct. 18, 1934 | Leo |
| Dec. 9–Jan. 19, 1928 | Sagittarius | Oct. 19–Dec. 11, 1934 | Virgo |
| Jan. 20–Feb. 28, 1928 | Capricorn | Dec. 12–July 29, 1935 | Libra |
| Feb. 29–April 7, 1928 | Aquarius | July 30–Sept. 16, 1935 | Scorpio |
| April 8–May 16, 1928 | Pisces | Sept. 17–Oct. 28, 1935 | Sagittarius |
| May 17–June 26, 1928 | Aries | Oct. 29–Dec. 7, 1935 | Capricorn |
| June 27–Aug. 9, 1928 | Taurus | Dec. 8–Jan. 14, 1936 | Aquarius |
| Aug. 10–Oct. 3, 1928 | Gemini | Jan. 15–Feb. 22, 1936 | Pisces |
| Oct. 4–Dec. 20, 1928 | Cancer | Feb. 23–April 1, 1936 | Aries |
| Dec. 21–Mar. 10, 1929 | Gemini | April 2–May 13, 1936 | Taurus |
| Mar. 11–May 13, 1929 | Cancer | May 14–June 25, 1936 | Gemini |
| May 14–July 4, 1929 | Leo | June 26–Aug. 10, 1936 | Cancer |
| July 5–Aug. 21, 1929 | Virgo | Aug. 11–Sept. 26, 1936 | Leo |
| Aug. 22–Oct. 6, 1929 | Libra | Sept. 27–Nov. 14, 1936 | Virgo |
| Oct. 7–Nov. 18, 1929 | Scorpio | Nov. 15–Jan. 5, 1937 | Libra |
| Nov. 19–Dec. 29, 1929 | Sagittarius | Jan. 6–Mar. 13, 1937 | Scorpio |
| Dec. 30–Feb. 6, 1930 | Capricorn | Mar. 14–May 14, 1937 | Sagittarius |
| Feb. 7–Mar. 17, 1930 | Aquarius | May 15–Aug. 8, 1937 | Scorpio |
| Mar. 18–April 24, 1930 | Pisces | Aug. 9–Sept. 30, 1937 | Sagittarius |
| April 25–June 3, 1930 | Aries | Oct. 1–Nov. 11, 1937 | Capricorn |
| June 4–July 14, 1930 | Taurus | Nov. 12–Dec. 21, 1937 | Aquarius |
| July 15–Aug. 28, 1930 | Gemini | Dec. 22–Jan. 30, 1938 | Pisces |
| Aug. 29–Oct. 20, 1930 | Cancer | Feb. 1–Mar. 12, 1938 | Aries |
| Oct. 21–Feb. 16, 1931 | Leo | Mar. 13–April 23, 1938 | Taurus |
| Feb. 17–Mar. 30, 1931 | Cancer | April 24–June 7, 1938 | Gemini |
| Mar. 31–June 10, 1931 | Leo | June 8–July 22, 1938 | Cancer |
| June 11–Aug. 1, 1931 | Virgo | July 23–Sept. 7, 1938 | Leo |
| Aug. 2–Sept. 17, 1931 | Libra | Sept. 8–Oct. 25, 1938 | Virgo |
| Sept. 18–Oct. 30, 1931 | Scorpio | Oct. 26–Dec. 11, 1938 | Libra |
| Oct. 31–Dec. 10, 1931 | Sagittarius | Dec. 12–Jan. 29, 1939 | Scorpio |
| Dec. 11–Jan. 18, 1932 | Capricorn | Jan. 30–Mar. 21, 1939 | Sagittarius |
| Jan. 19–Feb. 25, 1932 | Aquarius | Mar. 22–May 25, 1939 | Capricorn |
| Feb. 26–April 3, 1932 | Pisces | May 26–July 21, 1939 | Aquarius |
| April 4–May 12, 1932 | Aries | July 22–Sept. 24, 1939 | Capricorn |
| May 13–June 22, 1932 | Taurus | Sept. 25–Nov. 19, 1939 | Aquarius |
| June 23–Aug. 4, 1932 | Gemini | Nov. 20–Jan. 3, 1940 | Pisces |
| Aug. 5–Sept. 20, 1932 | Cancer | Jan. 4–Feb. 17, 1940 | Aries |
| Sept. 21–Nov. 13, 1932 | Leo | Feb. 18–April 1, 1940 | Taurus |
| Nov. 14–July 6, 1933 | Virgo | April 2–May 17, 1940 | Gemini |
| July 7–Aug. 26, 1933 | Libra | May 18–July 3, 1940 | Cancer |
| Aug. 27–Oct. 9, 1933 | Scorpio | July 4–Aug. 19, 1940 | Leo |
| Oct. 10–Nov. 19, 1933 | Sagittarius | Aug. 20–Oct. 5, 1940 | Virgo |
| Nov. 20–Dec. 28, 1933 | Capricorn | Oct. 6–Nov. 20, 1940 | Libra |
| Dec. 29–Feb. 4, 1934 | Aquarius | Nov. 21–Jan. 4, 1941 | Scorpio |
| Feb. 5–Mar. 14, 1934 | Pisces | Jan. 5–Feb. 17, 1941 | Sagittarius |
| Mar. 15–April 22, 1934 | Aries | Feb. 18–April 2, 1941 | Capricorn |
| April 23–June 2, 1934 | Taurus | April 3–May 16, 1941 | Aquarius |
| June 3–July 15, 1934 | Gemini | May 17–July 2, 1941 | Pisces |

| If you were born: | Your Mars is in: | If you were born: | Your Mars is in: |
|---|---|---|---|
| July 3–Jan. 11, 1942 | Aries | Nov. 27–Jan. 4, 1949 | Capricorn |
| Jan. 12–Mar. 7, 1942 | Taurus | Jan. 5–Feb. 11, 1949 | Aquarius |
| Mar. 8–April 26, 1942 | Gemini | Feb. 12–Mar. 21, 1949 | Pisces |
| April 27–June 14, 1942 | Cancer | Mar. 22–April 30, 1949 | Aries |
| June 15–Aug. 1, 1942 | Leo | May 1–June 10, 1949 | Taurus |
| Aug. 2–Sept. 17, 1942 | Virgo | June 11–July 23, 1949 | Gemini |
| Sept. 18–Nov. 1, 1942 | Libra | July 24–Sept. 7, 1949 | Cancer |
| Nov. 2–Dec. 15, 1942 | Scorpio | Sept. 8–Oct. 27, 1949 | Leo |
| Dec. 16–Jan. 26, 1943 | Sagittarius | Oct. 28–Dec. 26, 1949 | Virgo |
| Jan. 27–Mar. 8, 1943 | Capricorn | Dec. 27–Mar. 28, 1950 | Libra |
| Mar. 9–April 17, 1943 | Aquarius | Mar. 29–June 11, 1950 | Virgo |
| April 18–May 27, 1943 | Pisces | June 12–Aug. 10, 1950 | Libra |
| May 28–July 7, 1943 | Aries | Aug. 11–Sept. 25, 1950 | Scorpio |
| July 8–Aug. 23, 1943 | Taurus | Sept. 26–Nov. 6, 1950 | Sagittarius |
| Aug. 24–Mar. 28, 1944 | Gemini | Nov. 7–Dec. 15, 1950 | Capricorn |
| Mar. 29–May 22, 1944 | Cancer | Dec. 16–Jan. 22, 1951 | Aquarius |
| May 23–July 12, 1944 | Leo | Jan. 23–Mar. 1, 1951 | Pisces |
| July 13–Aug. 28, 1944 | Virgo | Mar. 2–April 10, 1951 | Aries |
| Aug. 29–Oct. 13, 1944 | Libra | April 11–May 21, 1951 | Taurus |
| Oct. 14–Nov. 25, 1944 | Scorpio | May 22–July 3, 1951 | Gemini |
| Nov. 26–Jan. 5, 1945 | Sagittarius | July 4–Aug. 18, 1951 | Cancer |
| Jan. 6–Feb. 14, 1945 | Capricorn | Aug. 19–Oct. 4, 1951 | Leo |
| Feb. 15–Mar. 25, 1945 | Aquarius | Oct. 5–Nov. 24, 1951 | Virgo |
| Mar. 26–May 2, 1945 | Pisces | Nov. 25–Jan. 20, 1952 | Libra |
| May 3–June 11, 1945 | Aries | Jan. 21–Aug. 27, 1952 | Scorpio |
| June 12–July 23, 1945 | Taurus | Aug. 28–Oct. 12, 1952 | Sagittarius |
| July 24–Sept. 7, 1945 | Gemini | Oct. 13–Nov. 21, 1952 | Capricorn |
| Sept. 8–Nov. 11, 1945 | Cancer | Nov. 22–Dec. 30, 1952 | Aquarius |
| Nov. 12–Dec. 26, 1945 | Leo | Dec. 31–Feb. 8, 1953 | Pisces |
| Dec. 27–April 22, 1946 | Cancer | Feb. 9–Mar. 20, 1953 | Aries |
| April 23–June 20, 1946 | Leo | Mar. 21–May 1, 1953 | Taurus |
| June 21–Aug. 9, 1946 | Virgo | May 2–June 14, 1953 | Gemini |
| Aug. 10–Sept. 24, 1946 | Libra | June 15–July 29, 1953 | Cancer |
| Sept. 25–Nov. 6, 1946 | Scorpio | July 30–Sept. 14, 1953 | Leo |
| Nov. 7–Dec. 17, 1946 | Sagittarius | Sept. 15–Nov. 1, 1953 | Virgo |
| Dec. 18–Jan. 25, 1947 | Capricorn | Nov. 2–Dec. 20, 1953 | Libra |
| Jan. 26–Mar. 4, 1947 | Aquarius | Dec. 21–Feb. 9, 1954 | Scorpio |
| Mar. 5–April 11, 1947 | Pisces | Feb. 10–April 12, 1954 | Sagittarius |
| April 12–May 21, 1947 | Aries | April 13–July 3, 1954 | Capricorn |
| May 22–July 1, 1947 | Taurus | July 4–Aug. 24, 1954 | Sagittarius |
| July 2–Aug. 13, 1947 | Gemini | Aug. 25–Oct. 21, 1954 | Capricorn |
| Aug. 14–Oct. 1, 1947 | Cancer | Oct. 22–Dec. 4, 1954 | Aquarius |
| Oct. 2–Dec. 1, 1947 | Leo | Dec. 5–Jan. 15, 1955 | Pisces |
| Dec. 2–Feb. 12, 1948 | Virgo | Jan. 16–Feb. 26, 1955 | Aries |
| Feb. 13–May 18, 1948 | Leo | Feb. 27–April 10, 1955 | Taurus |
| May 19–July 17, 1948 | Virgo | April 11–May 26, 1955 | Gemini |
| July 18–Sept. 3, 1948 | Libra | May 27–July 11, 1955 | Cancer |
| Sept. 4–Oct. 17, 1948 | Scorpio | July 12–Aug. 27, 1955 | Leo |
| Oct. 18–Nov. 26, 1948 | Sagittarius | Aug. 28–Oct. 13, 1955 | Virgo |

| If you were born: | Your Mars is in: | If you were born: | Your Mars is in: |
|---|---|---|---|
| Oct. 14–Nov. 29, 1955 | Libra | June 4–July 27, 1963 | Virgo |
| Nov. 30–Jan. 14, 1956 | Scorpio | July 28–Sept. 12, 1963 | Libra |
| Jan. 15–Feb. 28, 1956 | Sagittarius | Sept. 13–Oct. 25, 1963 | Scorpio |
| Feb. 29–April 14, 1956 | Capricorn | Oct. 26–Dec. 5, 1963 | Sagittarius |
| April 15–June 3, 1956 | Aquarius | Dec. 6–Jan. 13, 1964 | Capricorn |
| June 4–Dec. 6, 1956 | Pisces | Jan. 14–Feb. 20, 1964 | Aquarius |
| Dec. 7–Jan. 28, 1957 | Aries | Feb. 21–Mar. 29, 1964 | Pisces |
| Jan. 29–Mar. 17, 1957 | Taurus | Mar. 30–May 7, 1964 | Aries |
| Mar. 18–May 4, 1957 | Gemini | May 8–June 17, 1964 | Taurus |
| May 5–June 21, 1957 | Cancer | June 18–July 31, 1964 | Gemini |
| June 22–Aug. 8, 1957 | Leo | Aug. 1–Sept. 15, 1964 | Cancer |
| Aug. 9–Sept. 24, 1957 | Virgo | Sept. 16–Nov. 6, 1964 | Leo |
| Sept. 25–Nov. 8, 1957 | Libra | Nov. 7–June 29, 1965 | Virgo |
| Nov. 9–Dec. 23, 1957 | Scorpio | June 30–Aug. 20, 1965 | Libra |
| Dec. 24–Feb. 3, 1958 | Sagittarius | Aug. 21–Oct. 4, 1965 | Scorpio |
| Feb. 4–Mar. 17, 1958 | Capricorn | Oct. 5–Nov. 14, 1965 | Sagittarius |
| Mar. 18–April 27, 1958 | Aquarius | Nov. 15–Dec. 23, 1965 | Capricorn |
| April 28–June 7, 1958 | Pisces | Dec. 24–Jan. 30, 1966 | Aquarius |
| June 8–July 21, 1958 | Aries | Jan. 31–Mar. 9, 1966 | Pisces |
| July 22–Sept. 21, 1958 | Taurus | Mar. 10–April 17, 1966 | Aries |
| Sept. 22–Oct. 29, 1958 | Gemini | April 18–May 28, 1966 | Taurus |
| Oct. 30–Feb. 10, 1959 | Taurus | May 29–July 11, 1966 | Gemini |
| Feb. 11–April 10, 1959 | Gemini | July 12–Aug. 25, 1966 | Cancer |
| April 11–June 1, 1959 | Cancer | Aug. 26–Oct. 12, 1966 | Leo |
| June 2–July 20, 1959 | Leo | Oct. 13–Dec. 4, 1966 | Virgo |
| July 21–Sept. 5, 1959 | Virgo | Dec. 5–Feb. 12, 1967 | Libra |
| Sept. 6–Oct. 21, 1959 | Libra | Feb. 13–Mar. 31, 1967 | Scorpio |
| Oct. 22–Dec. 3, 1959 | Scorpio | April 1–July 19, 1967 | Libra |
| Dec. 4–Jan. 14, 1960 | Sagittarius | July 20–Sept. 10, 1967 | Scorpio |
| Jan. 15–Feb. 23, 1960 | Capricorn | Sept. 11–Oct. 23, 1967 | Sagittarius |
| Feb. 24–April 2, 1960 | Aquarius | Oct. 24–Dec. 1, 1967 | Capricorn |
| April 3–May 11, 1960 | Pisces | Dec. 2–Jan. 9, 1968 | Aquarius |
| May 12–June 20, 1960 | Aries | Jan. 10–Feb. 17, 1968 | Pisces |
| June 21–Aug. 2, 1960 | Taurus | Feb. 18–Mar. 27, 1968 | Aries |
| Aug. 3–Sept. 21, 1960 | Gemini | Mar. 28–May 8, 1968 | Taurus |
| Sept. 22–May 6, 1961 | Cancer | May 9–June 21, 1968 | Gemini |
| May 7–June 28, 1961 | Leo | June 22–Aug. 5, 1968 | Cancer |
| June 29–Aug. 17, 1961 | Virgo | Aug. 6–Sept. 21, 1968 | Leo |
| Aug. 18–Oct. 1, 1961 | Libra | Sept. 22–Nov. 9, 1968 | Virgo |
| Oct. 2–Nov. 13, 1961 | Scorpio | Nov. 10–Dec. 29, 1968 | Libra |
| Nov. 14–Dec. 24, 1961 | Sagittarius | Dec. 30–Feb. 25, 1969 | Scorpio |
| Dec. 25–Feb. 1, 1962 | Capricorn | Feb. 26–Sept. 21, 1969 | Sagittarius |
| Feb. 2–Mar. 12, 1962 | Aquarius | Sept. 22–Nov. 4, 1969 | Capricorn |
| Mar. 13–April 19, 1962 | Pisces | Nov. 5–Dec. 15, 1969 | Aquarius |
| April 20–May 28, 1962 | Aries | Dec. 16–Jan. 24, 1970 | Pisces |
| May 29–July 9, 1962 | Taurus | Jan. 25–Mar. 7, 1970 | Aries |
| July 10–Aug. 22, 1962 | Gemini | Mar. 8–April 18, 1970 | Taurus |
| Aug. 23–Oct. 11, 1962 | Cancer | April 19–June 2, 1970 | Gemini |
| Oct. 12–June 3, 1963 | Leo | June 3–July 18, 1970 | Cancer |

| If you were born: | Your Mars is in: | If you were born: | Your Mars is in: |
|---|---|---|---|
| July 19–Sept. 3, 1970 | Leo | June 7–July 17, 1977 | Taurus |
| Sept. 4–Oct. 20, 1970 | Virgo | July 18–Aug. 31, 1977 | Gemini |
| Oct. 21–Dec. 6, 1970 | Libra | Sept. 1–Oct. 26, 1977 | Cancer |
| Dec. 7–Jan. 23, 1971 | Scorpio | Oct. 27–Jan. 26, 1978 | Leo |
| Jan. 24–Mar. 12, 1971 | Sagittarius | Jan. 27–April 10, 1978 | Cancer |
| Mar. 13–May 3, 1971 | Capricorn | April 11–June 14, 1978 | Leo |
| May 4–Nov. 6, 1971 | Aquarius | June 15–Aug. 4, 1978 | Virgo |
| Nov. 7–Dec. 26, 1971 | Pisces | Aug. 5–Sept. 19, 1978 | Libra |
| Dec. 27–Feb. 10, 1972 | Aries | Sept. 20–Nov. 2, 1978 | Scorpio |
| Feb. 11–Mar. 27, 1972 | Taurus | Nov. 3–Dec. 12, 1978 | Sagittarius |
| Mar. 28–May 12, 1972 | Gemini | Dec. 13–Jan. 20, 1979 | Capricorn |
| May 13–June 28, 1972 | Cancer | Jan. 21–Feb. 27, 1979 | Aquarius |
| June 29–Aug. 15, 1972 | Leo | Feb. 28–April 7, 1979 | Pisces |
| Aug. 16–Sept. 30, 1972 | Virgo | April 8–May 16, 1979 | Aries |
| Oct. 1–Nov. 15, 1972 | Libra | May 17–June 26, 1979 | Taurus |
| Nov. 16–Dec. 30, 1972 | Scorpio | June 27–Aug. 8, 1979 | Gemini |
| Dec. 31–Feb. 12, 1973 | Sagittarius | Aug. 9–Sept. 24, 1979 | Cancer |
| Feb. 13–Mar. 26, 1973 | Capricorn | Sept. 25–Nov. 19, 1979 | Leo |
| Mar. 27–May 8, 1973 | Aquarius | Nov. 20–Mar. 11, 1980 | Virgo |
| May 9–June 20, 1973 | Pisces | Mar. 12–May 3, 1980 | Leo |
| June 21–Aug. 12, 1973 | Aries | May 4–July 10, 1980 | Virgo |
| Aug. 13–Oct. 29, 1973 | Taurus | July 11–Aug. 29, 1980 | Libra |
| Oct. 30–Dec. 24, 1973 | Aries | Aug. 30–Oct. 12, 1980 | Scorpio |
| Dec. 25–Feb. 27, 1974 | Taurus | Oct. 13–Nov. 21, 1980 | Sagittarius |
| Feb. 28–April 20, 1974 | Gemini | Nov. 22–Dec. 30, 1980 | Capricorn |
| April 21–June 9, 1974 | Cancer | Dec. 31–Feb. 6, 1981 | Aquarius |
| June 10–July 27, 1974 | Leo | Feb. 7–Mar. 16, 1981 | Pisces |
| July 28–Sept. 12, 1974 | Virgo | Mar. 17–April 25, 1981 | Aries |
| Sept. 13–Oct. 28, 1974 | Libra | April 26–June 5, 1981 | Taurus |
| Oct. 29–Dec. 10, 1974 | Scorpio | June 6–July 18, 1981 | Gemini |
| Dec. 11–Jan. 21, 1975 | Sagittarius | July 19–Sept. 1, 1981 | Cancer |
| Jan. 22–Mar. 3, 1975 | Capricorn | Sept. 2–Oct. 20, 1981 | Leo |
| Mar. 4–April 11, 1975 | Aquarius | Oct. 21–Dec. 16, 1981 | Virgo |
| April 12–May 21, 1975 | Pisces | Dec. 17–Aug. 3, 1982 | Libra |
| May 22–July 1, 1975 | Aries | Aug. 4–Sept. 20, 1982 | Scorpio |
| July 2–Aug. 14, 1975 | Taurus | Sept. 21–Oct. 31, 1982 | Sagittarius |
| Aug. 15–Oct. 17, 1975 | Gemini | Nov. 1–Dec. 10, 1982 | Capricorn |
| Oct. 18–Nov. 25, 1975 | Cancer | Dec. 11–Jan. 17, 1983 | Aquarius |
| Nov. 26–Mar. 18, 1976 | Gemini | Jan. 18–Feb. 25, 1983 | Pisces |
| Mar. 19–May 16, 1976 | Cancer | Feb. 26–April 5, 1983 | Aries |
| May 17–July 6, 1976 | Leo | April 6–May 16, 1983 | Taurus |
| July 7–Aug. 24, 1976 | Virgo | May 17–June 29, 1983 | Gemini |
| Aug. 25–Oct. 8, 1976 | Libra | June 30–Aug. 13, 1983 | Cancer |
| Oct. 9–Nov. 20, 1976 | Scorpio | Aug. 14–Sept. 29, 1983 | Leo |
| Nov. 21–Jan. 1, 1977 | Sagittarius | Sept. 30–Nov. 18, 1983 | Virgo |
| Jan. 2–Feb. 9, 1977 | Capricorn | Nov. 19–Jan. 11, 1984 | Libra |
| Feb. 10–Mar. 20, 1977 | Aquarius | Jan. 12–Aug. 17, 1984 | Scorpio |
| Mar. 21–April 27, 1977 | Pisces | Aug. 18–Oct. 5, 1984 | Sagittarius |
| April 28–June 6, 1977 | Aries | Oct. 6–Nov. 15, 1984 | Capricorn |

| If you were born: | Your Mars is in: | If you were born: | Your Mars is in: |
|---|---|---|---|
| Nov. 16–Dec. 25, 1984 | Aquarius | Oct. 17–Nov. 29, 1991 | Scorpio |
| Dec. 26–Feb. 2, 1985 | Pisces | Nov. 30–Jan. 9, 1992 | Sagittarius |
| Feb. 3–Mar. 15, 1985 | Aries | Jan. 10–Feb. 18, 1992 | Capricorn |
| Mar. 16–April 26, 1985 | Taurus | Feb. 19–Mar. 28, 1992 | Aquarius |
| April 27–June 9, 1985 | Gemini | Mar. 29–May 5, 1992 | Pisces |
| June 10–July 24, 1985 | Cancer | May 6–June 14, 1992 | Aries |
| July 25–Sept. 10, 1985 | Leo | June 15–July 26, 1992 | Taurus |
| Sept. 11–Oct. 27, 1985 | Virgo | July 27–Sept. 12, 1992 | Gemini |
| Oct. 28–Dec. 14, 1985 | Libra | Sept. 13–April 27, 1993 | Cancer |
| Dec. 15–Feb. 2, 1986 | Scorpio | April 28–June 23, 1993 | Leo |
| Feb. 3–Mar. 28, 1986 | Sagittarius | June 24–Aug. 12, 1993 | Virgo |
| Mar. 29–Oct. 9, 1986 | Capricorn | Aug. 13–Sept. 27, 1993 | Libra |
| Oct. 10–Nov. 26, 1986 | Aquarius | Sept. 28–Nov. 9, 1993 | Scorpio |
| Nov. 27–Jan. 8, 1987 | Pisces | Nov. 10–Dec. 20, 1993 | Sagittarius |
| Jan. 9–Feb. 20, 1987 | Aries | Dec. 21–Jan. 28, 1994 | Capricorn |
| Feb. 21–April 5, 1987 | Taurus | Jan. 29–Mar. 7, 1994 | Aquarius |
| April 6–May 21, 1987 | Gemini | Mar. 8–April 14, 1994 | Pisces |
| May 22–July 6, 1987 | Cancer | April 15–May 23, 1994 | Aries |
| July 7–Aug. 22, 1987 | Leo | May 24–July 3, 1994 | Taurus |
| Aug. 23–Oct. 8, 1987 | Virgo | July 4–Aug. 16, 1994 | Gemini |
| Oct. 9–Nov. 24, 1987 | Libra | Aug. 17–Oct. 4, 1994 | Cancer |
| Nov. 25–Jan. 8, 1988 | Scorpio | Oct. 5–Dec. 12, 1994 | Leo |
| Jan. 9–Feb. 22, 1988 | Sagittarius | Dec. 13–Jan. 22, 1995 | Virgo |
| Feb. 23–April 6, 1988 | Capricorn | Jan. 23–May 25, 1995 | Leo |
| April 7–May 22, 1988 | Aquarius | May 26–July 21, 1995 | Virgo |
| May 23–July 13, 1988 | Pisces | July 22–Sept. 7, 1995 | Libra |
| July 14–Oct. 23, 1988 | Aries | Sept. 8–Oct. 20, 1995 | Scorpio |
| Oct. 24–Nov. 1, 1988 | Pisces | Oct. 21–Nov. 30, 1995 | Sagittarius |
| Nov. 2–Jan. 19, 1989 | Aries | Dec. 1–Jan. 8, 1996 | Capricorn |
| Jan. 20–Mar. 11, 1989 | Taurus | Jan. 9–Feb. 15, 1996 | Aquarius |
| Mar. 12–April 29, 1989 | Gemini | Feb. 16–Mar. 24, 1996 | Pisces |
| April 30–June 16, 1989 | Cancer | Mar. 25–May 2, 1996 | Aries |
| June 17–Aug. 3, 1989 | Leo | May 3–June 12, 1996 | Taurus |
| Aug. 4–Sept. 19, 1989 | Virgo | June 13–July 25, 1996 | Gemini |
| Sept. 20–Nov. 4, 1989 | Libra | July 26–Sept. 9, 1996 | Cancer |
| Nov. 5–Dec. 18, 1989 | Scorpio | Sept. 10–Oct. 30, 1996 | Leo |
| Dec. 19–Jan. 29, 1990 | Sagittarius | Oct. 31–Jan. 3, 1997 | Virgo |
| Jan. 30–Mar. 11, 1990 | Capricorn | Jan. 4–Mar. 8, 1997 | Libra |
| Mar. 12–April 20, 1990 | Aquarius | Mar. 9–June 19, 1997 | Virgo |
| April 21–May 31, 1990 | Pisces | June 20–Aug. 14, 1997 | Libra |
| June 1–July 12, 1990 | Aries | Aug. 15–Sept. 28, 1997 | Scorpio |
| July 13–Aug. 31, 1990 | Taurus | Sept. 29–Nov. 9, 1997 | Sagittarius |
| Sept. 1–Dec. 14, 1990 | Gemini | Nov. 10–Dec. 18, 1997 | Capricorn |
| Dec. 15–Jan. 21, 1991 | Taurus | Dec. 19–Jan. 25, 1998 | Aquarius |
| Jan. 22–April 3, 1991 | Gemini | Jan. 26–Mar. 4, 1998 | Pisces |
| April 4–May 26, 1991 | Cancer | Mar. 5–April 13, 1998 | Aries |
| May 27–July 15, 1991 | Leo | April 14–May 24, 1998 | Taurus |
| July 16–Sept. 1, 1991 | Virgo | May 25–July 6, 1998 | Gemini |
| Sept. 2–Oct. 16, 1991 | Libra | July 7–Aug. 20, 1998 | Cancer |

| If you were born: | Your Mars is in: | If you were born: | Your Mars is in: |
|---|---|---|---|
| Aug. 21–Oct. 7, 1998 | Leo | July 6–Sept. 2, 1999 | Scorpio |
| Oct. 8–Nov. 27, 1998 | Virgo | Sept. 3–Oct. 17, 1999 | Sagittarius |
| Nov. 28–Jan. 26, 1999 | Libra | Oct. 18–Nov. 26, 1999 | Capricorn |
| Jan. 27–May 5, 1999 | Scorpio | Nov. 27–Jan. 4, 2000 | Aquarius |
| May 6–July 5, 1999 | Libra | | |

After you have found your Mars sign, or the Mars sign of a person you want to better understand, refer to the description of that Mars sign in the following section. It will identify the archetypal images and potential past conflicts associated with that sign, as well as the possible oppositional responses or behaviors you may be experiencing in this life.

## MARS IN THE ASTROLOGICAL SIGNS

### MARS IN ARIES

Mars in Aries manifests itself through directed, focused physical action. Its physical energy is fueled by movement and confidence. Your positive characteristics include being action-oriented, assertive, ambitious, competitive, courageous, energetic, enthusiastic, and optimistic. You are a natural athlete, competing against yourself. You strive for new beginnings and possess an eagerness to try new things and take risks.

#### POSSIBLE PAST LIFE CONFLICTS/ARCHETYPES

- A Native American warrior who was alone most of his life, fighting overwhelming odds
- A solitary explorer or adventurer, who died alone
- Someone whose impulsive angry actions accidentally led to a death
- A military leader who led soldiers into battle, causing them to die
- A person whose impatience led to conflict
- A person injured by a sharp object, which led to the loss of much blood

- A male who was unable to have a relationship due to his self-centered, selfish nature
- Someone who died from inflammation or fever

### REACTIONS/PHOBIAS THAT MAY HAVE SURFACED

Fear of being openly angry, impulsive, impatient, and spontaneous. . . . Aversion to war, fighting, blood, and any form of violence. . . . Fear of sharp objects, including scissors and knives. . . . Desperate need for a committed relationship. . . . Dread of dying alone. . . . Terror of taking action, any action, because it could lead to conflict or someone's death.

### RESIDUE OF KARMIC ANGER IN PRESENT BEHAVIOR

Karmic anger can manifest as impatience, frustration with physical limitations, irritability at being restricted, and anger at authority figures. You deal well with anger because you are able to access it and then can express it quickly: You get angry, take action, and then forget it. You don't hold a grudge. Your propensity to act is motivated by your strong will to fight for your ideals. As a result you are courageous and eager.

Sexually, you are assertive, ardent, and strong. Your challenging characteristics are being accident-prone, combative, easily bored, uncooperative, domineering, abusive, impulsive, and arrogant.

### YOUR TRANSFORMED SELF-ASSERTION

Spiritual self-awareness leads you to be willing to take the actions necessary to perform your soul's mission.

### HOW TO HANDLE ANGER

Because you are able to understand anger as a physical emotion, you are able to release it more effectively. You claim your anger and are responsible for it. Because you are not inherently afraid of your own anger, you are able to transform it into physical energy, stamina, and power.

## MARS IN TAURUS

Mars in Taurus manifests itself through practical, concrete success requiring creativity, patience, and endurance. Its physical energy is fueled by discipline, hard work, determination, and the acquisition of valued possessions. Your positive characteristics include building slowly, thoroughly, and patiently, and finishing what you start in a persistent, dependable, earthy manner.

### POSSIBLE PAST LIFE CONFLICTS/ARCHETYPES

- A wealthy woman who was greedy and materialistic because she was obsessed with security
- A Native American who loved his land and had it taken away by U.S. soldiers
- Someone whose unrelenting resistance to change caused conflict with others
- Someone whose desires for material possessions interfered with his/her spiritual goals

### REACTIONS/PHOBIAS THAT MAY HAVE SURFACED

Need for land as vital to security. . . . Need for security and possessions at all costs. . . . Fear of being materialistic and greedy, leading to overgenerosity. . . . Fear of being too fixed or stubborn, leading to "going with the flow." . . . Denial of any material success or stability.

### RESIDUE OF KARMIC ANGER IN PRESENT BEHAVIOR

Karmic anger can manifest as a tacit refusal to alter your views or accept change. You dig in your heels and will not budge, especially when it comes to financial and security matters. You are slow to anger, but when you are angry, you have a temper and become furious. Because of your practical nature, you seek to resolve your anger, but it takes time. Your willingness to take action is fueled by your need to be enlightened by strong material and spiritual values.

Sexually you are romantic, earthy, sensual, and sensitive, and you may be possessive. Your challenging characteristics are being self-indulgent, stingy, stuck in old patterns, and resistant to change. Your physical movements may be slow and lazy. You can be argumentative and prone to temper tantrums, and you tend to either over- or undervalue your own worth.

### YOUR TRANSFORMED SELF-ASSERTION

By synthesizing your spiritual and material values, you can create serenity and peace in your life.

### HOW TO HANDLE ANGER

Develop a habitual routine to assess anger, dealing with it when it shows up on a regular basis. Use your sensory experiences, including doing gardening, arts and crafts, and home repair, to utilize your anger in a constructive manner.

## MARS IN GEMINI

Mars in Gemini manifests itself through the expression of ideas, and active communication, either verbal or written. You have an inertia driven by mental challenges, and a vast supply of ideas. Your positive characteristics include being endlessly curious, needful of a constant exchange of ideas; being an information gatherer, inquisitive in thought and action, mentally alert, and quick to grasp an idea. You are a writer or lecturer. You often try to integrate your thoughts and ideas into action. You are versatile and multi-faceted as well as adroit at doing more than one thing at a time.

Sexually, you are versatile and imaginative. Your need for sexual diversity, however, impinges on your ability to remain faithful to one partner. You need to overcome your tendency to be mercurial, fickle, gossipy, overly talkative, restless, scattered, and inconsistent. At times you lack commitment, and sometimes you get lost in the moment. You tend to spread yourself too thin and become unfocused, because you are interested in so many things at one time.

### POSSIBLE PAST LIFE CONFLICTS/ARCHETYPES

- An angry writer, journalist, or lecturer who spewed judgments or wrote for effect but not necessarily truth
- A salesman who skewed his words to sell anything to anybody

- Someone whose lack of commitment in a relationship led to infidelity
- Someone whose distracted, restless temperament caused conflict with others
- A liar who wasn't aware he or she was lying

### REACTIONS/PHOBIAS THAT MAY HAVE SURFACED

Writer's block to such a degree that writing a simple letter is a chore. . . . Tactlessness, truthfulness at all costs, even when saying nothing would be more appropriate. . . . Fear of speaking out to such an extent that necessary communication fails. . . . Aversion to gossip. . . . Unexplained dislike of salespeople.

### RESIDUE OF KARMIC ANGER IN PRESENT BEHAVIOR

Karmic anger can manifest as incredible restlessness and inattentiveness. You can be argumentative and caustic. When angry, you may be sarcastic and petty, using vituperative words to attack; you are quick to gossip about a person who has incurred your wrath. When confronted about your mode of anger, you will say anything to absolve yourself, including lying. Your anger can yield sarcasm and a manipulative streak.

### YOUR TRANSFORMED SELF-ASSERTION

A more focused and committed effort to integrate thought and action will enable you to express new creative ideas.

### HOW TO HANDLE ANGER

When you use your anger constructively, you deal with thought, words, and interactive communication to seek clarity, insight, and information. Anger inspires you to want to discover more about your environment. Be honest, and report conflicts with fairness and precision.

## MARS IN CANCER

Mars in Cancer manifests itself in emotional tenacity, sensitivity, and connection with the emotional needs of others. Its physical

energy is fueled by feeling needed by others, and by being sensitive. Your positive characteristics include being supportive, sympathetic, receptive, nurturing, and maternal. You collect valued
items from the past and are devoted to your family, affectionate,
and loyal. Your motivations are based on kindness, with a strong
sensitivity to the emotional needs of others.

#### POSSIBLE PAST LIFE CONFLICTS/ARCHETYPES
- A brooding, insecure, guilt-inducing mother who smothered
  her children, causing them to leave
- A healer so obsessed with being needed that he created codependent relationships that hurt his patients
- A person who was so hypersensitive, moody, and emotional
  that he or she felt childish, fragile, and pathetic
- A woman who clung to the past, became lost in it, and lost
  opportunities to enjoy her current life

#### REACTIONS/PHOBIAS THAT MAY HAVE SURFACED
Fear of children's leaving. . . . Phobias relating to parenting
issues. . . . Anger at mothers and other nurturing women, who
remind you of what you once were. . . . Hypersensitivity to any
guilt. . . . Paranoia about being overly emotional. . . . Avoidance of
commitment in a relationship for fear of being codependent. . . .
Strong desire to be serious, to overcompensate for past life child-
ishness. . . . Dismissal of all connections to the past.

#### RESIDUE OF KARMIC ANGER IN PRESENT BEHAVIOR
Karmic anger can manifest as frustration and discord with family
members, especially women. You may become passive-aggressive.
When angry, you may get sulky, moody, and depressed.

Sexually, you are gentle, loyal, faithful, and romantically sentimental. Your challenging characteristics include being possessive,
smothering, sullen, overly cautious, brooding, and too nostalgic.
Because you are ultrasensitive emotionally, you may be timid, tem-
peramental, too easily hurt, and sometimes childishly pathetic.

When you aren't feeling secure emotionally, you close down and withhold your feelings.

### YOUR TRANSFORMED SELF-ASSERTION

Destruction of past illusions yields emotional freedom.

### HOW TO HANDLE ANGER

Value anger as a normal, healthy emotion not to be feared or repressed. You are aware that to be angry with another means there must be some attachment. Use your sensitivity to nurture that attachment, even when you are angry.

## MARS IN LEO

Mars in Leo manifests itself in inspired and charismatic leaders who pour out their heart-centered energy to others. Your energy is fueled by your affectionate, dramatic, loving, and creative connections with others. Your positive characteristics include being commanding, dignified, prone to take action zealously, and needful of the limelight. You perceive yourself to be a commanding and inspired leader. Your alacrity to take action relates to your ambitious and exuberant nature. You love to have fun, and you may be a born entertainer.

### POSSIBLE PAST LIFE CONFLICTS/ARCHETYPES

- An aging actor who was terrified of getting old
- An autocratic king who was totally self-centered, demanding of adoration, and in complete disregard of his kingdom
- A bombastic male who had to be on center stage at all costs
- A performer who was assassinated onstage
- A childish, vulnerable adult who was obsessed with being loved and adored, never taking anything seriously, preferring to play and have fun

### REACTIONS/PHOBIAS THAT MAY HAVE SURFACED

Discomfort with being too visible or the focus of any type of attention. . . . A fear of being assassinated by imagined enemies. . . . Excessive responsiveness to other people, compensating for the need never to be accused of disregarding anyone.

### RESIDUE OF KARMIC ANGER IN PRESENT BEHAVIOR

Karmic anger can manifest as an attempt to dominate. You easily slip into the role of king or queen, barking demands to your subordinates. When angry, you may be melodramatic, even cruel. You don't back off from a fight.

Sexually, you are warm, dynamic, dramatic, and generous. Although you love to be in love, you may be inhibited in your expression of it. Your most challenging characteristics include being self-centered, self-absorbed, and demanding of love, adoration, and acknowledgment. You expect to be appreciated. You may be boastful, conceited, and childish, becoming belligerent when you are not getting the attention you think you deserve.

### YOUR TRANSFORMED SELF-ASSERTION

Being enthusiastic and enjoying life will lead to inspirational spiritual leadership.

### HOW TO HANDLE ANGER

Use anger to buttress your confidence. Anger can inspire your powerful leadership nature. Realize that through your innate generosity, you can be a catalyst for helping others deal with their anger.

## MARS IN VIRGO

Mars in Virgo manifests itself in your need to create order and high standards, in your efficient use of logic, and in your ability to analyze and discern. Your energy is fueled by a strong devotion and concern for service and a health orientation. Your positive characteristics include being scientific, discriminating, industrious, dependable, and conscientious. Your challenging characteristics include being too obsessive, too result-oriented, nervous, hypochondriacal, perfectionistic, judgmental, and critical. You project the impossibly high standards you have for yourself onto others. But you are also methodical, practical, organized, and thorough. You seek a perfect blend of mind and body, and you support that pursuit by being studious and exacting in your search for information.

## POSSIBLE PAST LIFE CONFLICTS/ARCHETYPES

- A doctor or nurse whose entire motivation was martyrdom to his or her patients
- A doctor or nurse who overlooked an important detail that might have led to a patient's death or injury
- A workaholic obsessed with perfection, whose life was filled with pettiness, detail, and negative thoughts
- A leader of workers who was controlling, hypercritical, and pedantic
- A hypochondriac driven by fear of illness

## REACTIONS/PHOBIAS THAT MAY HAVE SURFACED

Terror of making *any* mistake lest it damage self or others. . . . Eschewal of healers to avoid being positioned as a martyr. . . . Obsession with or abhorrence of details and order. . . . Strong bias toward being self-critical with impossibly high standards. . . . An overarching desire to have the "perfect" body.

## RESIDUE OF KARMIC ANGER IN PRESENT BEHAVIOR

Karmic anger can manifest in a picky, petty attitude when life is not going exactly as planned. When angry, you may be critical and judgmental. Anger brings out your pettiness. You will analyze your anger and at times discriminate about whether you should be angry. Therefore you are not spontaneous but are rather studied in your expression of anger. You are loyal and loving sexually, although not terribly passionate.

## YOUR TRANSFORMED SELF-ASSERTION

A disciplined mind delivers practical service with compassion.

**HOW TO HANDLE ANGER**

Utilize your anger to hone your logical abilities, in order to produce a clearer understanding of the essence of a conflict. Value conflict and the anger associated with it as a learning experience.

## Mars in Libra

Mars in Libra manifests its energy in harmonious, cooperative, and satisfying interactions with other people. Your energy is fueled by social connections, diplomacy, balanced communication, and a strong desire for justice. Your positive characteristics include a pleasant social manner, a desire to please, an ability to see both sides of a situation, and an appreciation for beauty, as well as refinement and peacefulness. You act based on your need for social fairness and compromise.

**POSSIBLE PAST LIFE CONFLICTS/ARCHETYPES**

- A self-serving judge whose partial decisions led to injustices in his court
- A vain society matron whose life revolved around status, superficiality, and phoniness
- A woman whose obsessive passion in a love affair created serious emotional and physical imbalances in her life

**REACTIONS/PHOBIAS THAT MAY HAVE SURFACED**

Obsession with fairness and justice. . . . Need for peace at any price to create harmony and balance. . . . Aversion to superficiality and need for status. . . . Anger with any person who appears disingenuous. . . . Strong commitment to the needs of others to the extent of unfairness to self.

**RESIDUE OF KARMIC ANGER IN PRESENT BEHAVIOR**

Karmic anger can manifest as disgust with injustice, unfairness, and a lack of social refinement and grace. You dislike anger in any form, believing it disrupts the peace, disturbs harmony, and interferes with social interaction. You repress your angry feelings and may get depressed by turning your anger inward. You also have the ability to transform your anger into compromise.

Sexually, you are very affectionate and enjoy planning a romantic setting for lovemaking. Your challenging characteristics include being indecisive, ambivalent, willing to obtain peace at any price, superficial, cloying, and phony. Because you are so interested in what others think, you sometimes devalue yourself and do what will make someone else happy. You may allow others to define how you feel and what you think.

#### YOUR TRANSFORMED SELF-ASSERTION

Your will to support balance and harmony in all relationships creates social and spiritual justice.

#### HOW TO HANDLE ANGER

Recognize that anger is a natural by-product of all human relationships, and that discord is a way to move a relationship to a higher level of resolution and harmony. Understand the true meaning of constructive conflict.

### MARS IN SCORPIO

Mars in Scorpio manifests its energy in an intense desire to seek deeper meaning by transforming and regenerating emotions. Your energy is fueled by a passionate, probing need to understand the mysteries of life and death. Your positive characteristics include magnetism, as well as strength, resourcefulness, willfulness, and inquisitiveness. You are devoutly loyal, determined, idealistic, and imaginative, and you may be a powerful and convincing leader. Your initiative stems from your need to understand all levels of spiritual and emotional transformation.

#### POSSIBLE PAST LIFE CONFLICTS/ARCHETYPES

- An intense, brooding man whose passion, extremism, and jealousy lead him to stalk someone with whom he was involved

- A magician who performed black magic
- A dark, vengeful woman whose single-minded anger created volatile emotional reactions between herself and others
- A detective whose work centered on his suspicious and paranoid nature
- The head of a company whose controlling, manipulative, and unyielding personality stifled his employees' creativity and freedom

### REACTIONS/PHOBIAS THAT MAY HAVE SURFACED

Fear of intensity and passion. . . . Repression of anger lest it become too much to handle. . . . Aversion to any type of controlling or manipulating behavior. . . . Passivity and stoicism, rather than risking the expression of feelings.

### RESIDUE OF KARMIC ANGER IN PRESENT BEHAVIOR

Karmic anger can manifest as a deep, all-consuming rage. You feel you must control this rage for fear of its potential damage to yourself and others. When angry, you gravitate toward very dark internal places that manifest as cold, remote, and intense demeanors. Your anger can turn vengeful and vindictive; you do not easily forget.

You are highly sexual and passionate. You view sex as a mystical, magical transforming experience, one of the mysteries of life. Your challenging characteristics include being secretive, jealous, possessive, intimidating, resentful, distrustful, and unforgiving. You have a tendency to be controlling and manipulative when you feel threatened.

### YOUR TRANSFORMED SELF-ASSERTION

The courage, passion, and will to understand death and transformation creates spiritual leadership.

## HOW TO HANDLE ANGER

Be unafraid to go as far as is necessary in order to transform the experience of the conflict. Transmute anger into power and creativity. Know that it can be transformed into passion and internal control.

## MARS IN SAGITTARIUS

Mars in Sagittarius exhibits its energy in a search for philosophical truth, expansion, and freedom. Your energy is fueled by traveling, nature, teaching, and exploring new horizons. Your positive characteristics include optimism, enlightenment, ethics, openmindedness, charm, and athleticism, as well as energy and boldness. You are motivated to take action by your desire and courage to fight for what you perceive as your visionary truth.

### POSSIBLE PAST LIFE CONFLICTS/ARCHETYPES

- An itinerant preacher who traveled the country proselytizing his beliefs in the form of fire-and-brimstone sermons
- A cowboy who rode into town, had a love affair, and left without any commitment
- A traveler who led a peripatetic existence fueled by intense claustrophobia
- A philosopher who was pedantic and pushed his truth down the throat of his followers

### REACTIONS/PHOBIAS THAT MAY HAVE SURFACED

Fear of open spaces. . . . Dislike of traveling, especially long distances. . . . Fear of expressing truth and philosophy, in the event of misunderstanding or misperception as pedantic. . . . Apprehension at being abandoned in relationships. . . . Preference for city to country. . . . Aversion to intense religious doctrine.

### RESIDUE OF KARMIC ANGER IN PRESENT BEHAVIOR

Karmic anger can manifest as frustration with travel, especially at long distances, irritability with religious authority, and any perceived limitation on freedom. You may be argumentative and preachy.

You are also an enthusiastic, open-hearted lover who can be charming and carefree. Your challenging characteristics include being bored by details, aggressive, extravagant, irresponsible, claustrophobic, dogmatic, afraid of commitment, and a gambler. Because you are interested in a multitude of journeys, you may often lack direction and follow-through.

## YOUR TRANSFORMED SELF-ASSERTION

The will to search for universal truth through an optimistic vision creates an inspired teacher.

## HOW TO HANDLE ANGER

See anger and conflict as an opportunity for expanding your philosophical horizons; convert it into a quest for truth, freedom, and a symbolic open road. You can release anger quickly because of your optimistic nature.

## MARS IN CAPRICORN

Mars in Capricorn manifests its energy in the achievement of practical success as an archetypal good father and executive. You perpetuate your energy by persevering, and you will not stop until you reach your goals. Your positive characteristics include thrift, efficiency, independence, and loyalty, as well as an appreciation for integrity, history, and tradition. Your initiative and drive are based on your internal requirement to climb steadily to established heights.

## POSSIBLE PAST LIFE CONFLICTS/ARCHETYPES

- A dictatorial, ruthless, demanding father who alienated his children because he was insensitive, cold, and inflexible
- An authoritarian businessman who dominated his subordinates, was indifferent to their emotional needs, and rigidly enforced all the rules

- A Scrooge-like personality who was stingy and selfish
- A person mired in self-righteous anger

### REACTIONS/PHOBIAS THAT MAY HAVE SURFACED

Anger at dominant father or other authority figure. . . . Dissatisfaction with rules and regulations. . . . Obsession with issues of being too successful. . . . Leniency with children, failure to set boundaries. . . . Oversensitivity and emotionalism.

### RESIDUE OF KARMIC ANGER IN PRESENT BEHAVIOR

Karmic anger can manifest in a stern, unyielding, and punitive authority figure. You have difficulty expressing all emotions, particularly anger, so you rarely have angry outbursts. You're slow to anger, but when you're angry, you become cold, calculating, domineering, and inflexible. You transform your anger into severe discipline. You believe that your anger must be righteous in order to be justified.

You tend to be traditional and somewhat inhibited sexually, but you are very loyal and faithful in your sexual behavior. Your challenging characteristics include being compulsive about rules, intolerant, and rigid, as well as having an obsessive drive toward materialism.

### YOUR TRANSFORMED SELF-ASSERTION

Being responsible and self-disciplined will create a wise, more mature social organization.

### HOW TO HANDLE ANGER

Be aware that there are appropriate, righteous times to be angry, and when those times come, you shouldn't hesitate to be assertive and strong. You tend to argue in a socially acceptable manner by imposing rules and structures onto a conflict.

## MARS IN AQUARIUS

Mars in Aquarius manifests itself in a tendency toward inventiveness and independence. Your energy is fueled by your fierce protection of your individuality, as well as your yearning for universal truth and equality. Your positive characteristics include your willingness to get behind a cause you believe in; you are humanistic, altruistic, progressive, and innovative, and you may be blessed with a refreshingly distinct thought-process. You lend your support for the ideals of freedom, equality, diversity, cooperation, and brotherhood. You may be highly imaginative and visionary. You may create a group dynamic to accommodate your cause-based existence. You take action based on the creative, revolutionary power of your mind.

## POSSIBLE PAST LIFE CONFLICTS/ARCHETYPES

- An erratic rebel who led a revolution against his government for the sake of rebelling
- A lawless nonconformist who hurt others with his egocentric attitudes and his unwavering belief in a cause
- An inflexible, detached individualist who was unable to connect with others on an emotional level
- A brilliant yet tormented scientist who hid in his laboratory, far from society
- A leading-edge philosopher who was ostracized for his nonconforming beliefs.

## REACTIONS/PHOBIAS THAT MAY HAVE SURFACED

Fear of anything that seems radical or revolutionary. . . . Aversion to causes requiring dedication. . . . Fear of adopting unorthodox views that could lead to ostracism. . . . Fear of standing alone behind a principle. . . . Need to fall in line with others.

## RESIDUE OF KARMIC ANGER IN PRESENT BEHAVIOR

Karmic anger can manifest as an erratic rebelliousness and irritability with any rules and regulations. When angry, you may become cold, remote, and detached, as well as argumentative with firm ideas that you refuse to modify. Sexually, you can adopt a more experimental approach, sometimes having somewhat radical ideas. Your challenging characteristics include being impersonal, intolerant, too logical, radical, internal, shy, remote, erratic, and rebellious. You tend to observe life rather than participate in it.

### YOUR TRANSFORMED SELF-ASSERTION

A progressive and distinctive approach will lead to group leadership that best serves the universal order and humanity.

### HOW TO HANDLE ANGER

Focus your anger on community, political, and humanitarian concerns. Understand that anger can manifest on intellectual, emotional, and spiritual levels. You are detached enough to observe yourself when you are in those situations.

## MARS IN PISCES

Mars in Pisces expresses its energy in a devoted quest for emotional and spiritual connections with all people. You understand others with your superb intuition and compassionate nature. Your energy is fueled by kind actions, charitable acts, and sympathetic reactions to those who need them. Your positive characteristics include being forgiving, flowing, humble, imaginative, artistic, musical, unselfish, devoted, and spiritual.

### POSSIBLE PAST LIFE CONFLICTS/ARCHETYPES
- An alcoholic unable to handle the practical realities of the world
- A religious leader who martyred himself to his religion
- An early Christian who died at the hands of the Romans
- A woman who was totally codependent, naive, illusionary, escapist, and unable to care for herself
- A person who believed that to be "good," one must sacrifice himself or herself to others
- Someone who took actions on intuition without incorporating thought and reason

### REACTIONS/PHOBIAS THAT MAY HAVE SURFACED

Aversion to any type of drugs and anger at those who are addicted to them. . . . Aversion to martyristic behavior. . . . Unexplained approach/avoidance issues with Christianity. . . . Fear of psychic experiences and distrust of intuition.

### RESIDUE OF KARMIC ANGER IN PRESENT BEHAVIOR

Karmic anger can manifest as self-doubt, vulnerability, and distrust of emotional power. You're also afraid of anger, sometimes turning it inward, resulting in escapist and addictive behaviors toward food, drinking, and drugs. You may become depressed. Because you believe anger is not a spiritually correct feeling, you will refuse even to acknowledge it, perhaps resorting to passive-aggressive behavior.

Sexually, you are a sensitive romantic and poetic lover who craves the mystical experience that the sexual act can create. Your challenging characteristics include being overly sensitive, melancholy, martyristic, impractical, too submissive, self-pitying, and timid. Because of your kind nature and naiveté, you may be taken in by other people's hard-luck stories and be easily manipulated.

### YOUR TRANSFORMED SELF-ASSERTION

Devotion to an intuitional and compassionate will creates spiritual communion and leadership.

### HOW TO HANDLE ANGER

Understand anger as a natural emotion, using your energy to drive you to be imaginative and creative. You know that anger can have intrinsic spiritual value; utilize it to understand your karmic past and conflicts for spiritual growth and resolution.

## MARS AND CHILDREN

Many of us were taught not to be angry—not even to feel anger and certainly not to express it. As children, we were often punished for getting mad. Needless to say, our parents didn't know about our Mars energy! But your knowledge of your children's Mars placements will help you better understand how your child feels when he's angry and how he can transform his anger. Since you know the karmic anger buttons that your child may have, you can help her understand why certain behaviors or circumstances trigger her anger. Because you are a circle-one relationship in your child's life, you may even carry some of those triggers in your own personality.

Parents, please use the "Expressing Anger" techniques on page 175 with your children. Model them in your own life. Buy a punching clown, and use it with your kids. They'll love it. Teach them how to remove anger from their bodies naturally and safely. They will learn to value their anger as a teaching tool, to discuss it, and they will learn more about themselves in the process.

Marty is 5 years old. Her Mars is in Pisces. Her mother, Irene, 38, is a lovely, forgiving woman who is devoted to her spiritual pursuits. Irene's Soul Pattern sign and her Mars are both Pisces. Irene can also be timid and shy, fearing intense feelings, especially anger. Because she believes that anger interferes with love and compassion, she has effectively erased it from her conscious emotional life. Irene is also a hundred pounds overweight, having struggled with a food addiction since she was a small child. Given the strong influence of Pisces in her Soul Pattern, she has spent much of her present life struggling with Pisces's challenging attributes: she is addictive, escapist, sacrificing, and overly sensitive.

Marty is very angry at her mother and has been since she was old enough to talk. Irene is devastated that her only child feels such hostility toward her and is totally perplexed by its intensity. She adores Marty with all her heart and in fact gave up a successful, lucrative career to stay home with her. From Irene's perspective, the more she did, the more cantankerous Marty got. When Irene brought her situation to me last year, I explained that Marty had her Mars in Pisces, which gave her an addictive escapistic personality, a personality like a Christian martyr who sacrificed herself for her spiritual beliefs, who put everyone else's needs before her own. I knew that Marty would one day be able to identify with that past life.

Marty's unconscious reactions were not to her mother so much as to what her mother symbolized: her own past life themes.

Whenever Marty perceived her mother giving in to her food addiction, on an unconscious level it reminded her of her own past addictions. Nor could Marty tolerate her mother sacrificing for her. Because of her own lives of self-sacrifice, it rankled her that her mother was so martyristic. Thus, the more Irene gave to Marty, the more it reminded her of lives where her sacrifice had been to her own detriment.

I convinced Irene that however painful her relationship with her daughter was, it was also spiritually perfect. Marty created her relationship with her mother to deal with her Mars in Pisces past. Irene, for her part, needed a strong motivation to leave problematic Pisces behind, in order to achieve her Soul Potential in Virgo. The more balanced Irene became in her life, the less angry Marty would become. Irene understood this immediately, telling me the message resonated deeply in her body and soul. She saw the beautiful spiritual dance that she and Marty had created in their mutual soul contracts.

My advice to Irene was to learn to take care of herself. Her first step would be to return to work, something she had missed terribly for five years. The second would be to acknowledge and deal with her own anger and see it as an emotion given to her by God. She needed to understand that by repressing anger, she was in fact escaping it through food. Third would be to honor her physical body by creating a new approach to diet and exercise. Lastly, she would talk to her daughter about the value of taking care of herself, then model that for her in a positive way. Irene was nervous about this program, but her love for Marty gave her the courage and the will to begin.

One year later, I am happy to report that Irene is back at work, has lost twenty-five pounds, and has actually been able to claim her anger and express it a few times. Marty, in the first grade, is far less angry at her mother and is very happy that Irene is happy at work. Even though Marty was too young to understand or describe her anger at Irene, her mother was clearly a constant reminder of her past life conflict. Whenever Irene was kind and sacrificing, Marty hated it because it unconsciously provoked her own memories of martyrdom and self-effacement in a previous incarnation. Seeing her mother taking better care of herself gave Marty hope for herself. She wanted and needed her mother to show her how to deal with Mars in Pisces. Irene's progress gave Marty a wonderful role model that would help her alter her old problematic Piscean behavior early in her life.

# CHAPTER 9

# Pluto: Overcoming Guilt and Fostering Forgiveness

Every day, whether we care to accept it or not, most of us are motivated by the desire to avoid feeling guilty. This unfortunate grounding is reflected in the way we act toward others and the decisions we make. For example, when faced with the prospect of doing something you'd rather not do, like visit a family member, how do you decide whether to do it? Do you call your mother, or perhaps the sibling who is causing you angst? Chances are the avoidance of guilt will play a central role in whatever action you take. Perhaps the following thought processes sound familiar to you:

- Mother's all alone, and if I don't call her, who will? After all, she depends on me.
- We have to go see him this weekend. If we don't, he'll make me feel guilty that we "don't see our nieces and nephews enough."
- Everyone else is putting in extra hours at the office on the project, and if I don't, I'll look like I'm slacking off.

All of these sentiments above are contaminated by the perception that if we don't take action, someone or something else will "make us feel guilty." Thus, instead of being motivated by want or need to some perceived beneficial end for others or ourselves, we are motivated to do something in order to avoid feeling guilty.

By allowing guilt to skew our thought processes and decision-making ability, we're manifesting negative, lose-lose thinking. If you cede control of what you truly want to a value system based on guilt, you will never do what you *want* to do, but rather what you *should* do. Sometimes, of course, you are confronted with things you *have* to do. But whether you follow through should be based on the perceived benefits or opportunity cost of taking action, not on the ramifications of possible guilt. We become frustrated and dissatisfied when we know we are doing something primarily to appease someone and avoid guilt. Yet if we don't take that action, we are forced to confront our guilty feelings. Thus if we fall victim to the demands of a guilty conscience, then ultimately we will be dissatisfied and frustrated, because we will resent whatever decision we make.

We all allow guilt to contaminate our decision-making processes to some degree, but those of us who have learned to absolve our guilt-laden inclinations are leading healthier, more productive, and more stress-free lives.

## DISTINGUISHING BETWEEN GUILT AND SHAME

As a legal term, *guilt* means one's culpability in a court of law. But guilt is also a counterproductive phenomenon that we create ourselves, independent of other people and events. This definition clashes with most people's perception of guilt: they perceive it as generated by someone else's disappointment in them. In fact, *Webster's New World Dictionary* defines *guilt* as "a painful feeling of self-reproach resulting from a belief that one has done something wrong or immoral." By contrast, *Webster's* defines *shame* as "a painful feeling of having lost the respect of others because of the improper behavior, incompetence, etc., of oneself or another."

Interestingly, guilt is defined as being based on a *belief*, while shame is based on an actual *behavior* or *event*. Taking it a step further, we may say that guilt is based on a perception, while shame is based on something that has actually transpired. Shame is an emotion, like fear or sadness, while guilt is a *perceived* emotion.

Most people use the words interchangeably, failing to see any difference. But distinguishing between guilt and shame is essential to the effort to eradicate guilt from relationships and daily behavior. Guilt subverts our purest intentions to do what makes us happy. It causes us to abdicate responsibility for our shame to somebody else whom we claim "is *making* us feel guilty." Getting to the source of our guilty feelings by confronting our shame enables us to take responsibility for our actions and learn from them.

Shame is an emotion that we own. When we feel ashamed, it's because of an action we've taken or a behavior we've exhibited. We can't shift the onus onto anyone else. But "feeling guilty" implies that someone or something else made us feel that way, thus shifting the burden of responsibility away from us. Once we understand that we are the source of our guilt and the reasons why, we can take the steps necessary to correct it.

Let's say you're at the dinner table with your fiancée's parents. You pick up an intricately designed wine decanter cut from crystal, to admire its workmanship. Suddenly it slips from your hands and falls to the floor, spilling wine all over their Oriental rug. The hundred-year-old family heirloom is fractured into a dozen pieces. Picture this, and pay attention to your body's reaction. My guess is that you will experience *shame*. It's a hot emotion that you feel in your heart or stomach. Your face may get red, and you want to crawl away as quickly as you can. That strong emotion produces a need to apologize and do whatever it takes to rectify the situation. Assuming your hosts are gracious, you will live through the moment and will forget about it. Shame is normal.

Now let's take the same experience, but let's change your age. You're 6 years old when the decanter breaks. The adults immediately scream at you for being "stupid and clumsy." They send you from the table in disgrace. You feel inadequate and embarrassed, and you have no chance to apologize. Two months later, you break something else—getting the same reaction. Now you feel shame, plus all the judgments that have been heaped upon you since the first time. The guilty feelings internalize and grow over time. The original experience is long forgotten, but the guilt remains. It builds over time and is paired with an emerging belief that you are bad.

The primary difference between guilt and shame is that guilt impedes us and keeps us stuck, while shame teaches us what we need to know about being in the world in an appropriate manner. Shame marks an experience or event in which you really did something wrong; guilt is based not on an actual experience but on a perception or belief that you did something wrong. If you are ashamed of something, you can deal with it, but guilt can fester in perpetuity. Ironically, most people have no compunction about acknowledging their feelings of guilt: "I'm feeling guilty; my cousin called two weeks ago and I've yet to return her call." But you hardly ever hear someone say they're ashamed of a specific behavior or action they've taken: "I'm ashamed of the way I've treated my cousin lately." Because once we say we're ashamed of something, we are more likely to take responsibility for it and do something about it.

## GUILT AND OUR PAST

Many of my clients say that they were born feeling guilty. They have memories from their earliest years of feeling deeply guilty about something, but they are unable to pinpoint it. That ineffable feeling is actually the karmic guilt that transcends our lives, waiting to be dealt with and resolved. I believe that our souls use this very uncomfortable sensation to remind us of a karmic experience that needs handling. It is a cosmic two-by-four that keeps hitting us over the head until we take responsibility for it.

Mary had an extremely close relationship with her mother. They enjoyed the same interests and saw each other almost every day. They went everywhere together. Then Mary, who was in her late thirties, met a man, Chris, of whom she became very fond. They began spending a lot of time together. Mary's mother felt somewhat betrayed and tried to pull Mary closer to her—just when Mary needed space to explore her budding relationship with Chris. In an effort to maintain the relationship they once had, the mother made demanding requests of Mary. Mary felt a miserable sense of guilt when she could not accommodate her mother. In fact, she found herself racked with guilt. Mary's guilt became so intense that it had a deleterious effect on how she related to her mother: she found herself lying or pretending not to be home when the phone rang, to avoid having to talk to her. Her torment was not lost on Chris, who became concerned that Mary would never have the autonomy to take part in a normal, healthy relationship. "It's tearing me apart," Mary cried one day in my office. "I love this man, and I love my mother. I can't stand this awful feeling in the pit of my stomach when I have to say no to her. I'm afraid of what this is doing to me and to my relationship with both of them."

After Mary told me her story, my first question to her was: "What are you ashamed of?" Mary looked at me, obviously miffed. "I didn't say I was ashamed of anything. I do feel guilty about abandoning my mother." I explained that her guilt feeling is a prostitution of an old shame that she hadn't confronted, and that in order to remove the guilt, we had to find the old shame.

Mary absorbed the words, ruminating over them in silence. I waited for her to collect her thoughts. "You know my dad left us when I was only ten," she finally replied. "The night he left, I was standing in the hall, listening to him screaming at my mother. I felt so scared, but now that I look back, I remember feeling something else too. Maybe it was shame. I felt bad that I was listening, and real bad that my mother was being humiliated like that."

Mary had sourced a feeling of shame, for hearing something she shouldn't have heard. "I know that I have always felt guilty for not standing up for my mom. Or to use your word, maybe I felt ashamed that I wasn't strong enough to tell my dad to stop yelling at her." I asked Mary if she had ever told her mother what she had just told me. She shook her head. "What if you did, Mary? Don't you think it would alter some of the guilty feelings you have?"

Mary agreed that she had nothing to lose and everything to gain. She left the session determined to talk to her mother.

A week later Mary came back. "We talked about that night," she reported to me. "My mother was shocked to learn that I had overheard the fight she had had so long ago with my father. She was amazed that I had spent all this time feeling so bad over not intervening. Then I told her that I felt guilty when she had asked me to do something that would interfere with a date with Chris. She told me about the guilt she had always felt when her mother had wanted her to do things with her. We actually laughed about it. I felt as if the weight of the world was lifted off my shoulders. My mother and I decided that guilt was one of the less desirable traditions that had been passed down from mother to daughter. We decided that it would stop here."

I wish I could count the number of clients who attribute some source of guilt to their families: sons feeling guilty about not pleasing their fathers, daughters about not being what their mothers want. Most of us have a story about guilt that includes our mother or father.

We often joke about "Jewish guilt" or "Italian guilt," by-products of cultures that are as traditionally enmeshed as matzo ball soup and Sunday pasta. But we can't all rectify our familial guilt as cleanly and neatly as Mary did. Our souls have often chosen our parents in order to help us deal with old karmic guilt. We created those circle-one parental relationships and soul contracts in order to discover the sources of our deepest shame. If no original shame exists in this life, then it exists somewhere in the past.

Think of a situation with your mother that produces guilt regularly. Is there something you are ashamed of that might be at the heart of it? Talk to her about the shame you're feeling, and see if the guilt dissipates. If it doesn't, chances are the source of the guilt is older than your relationship with her. For example, maybe you always feel guilty when your mother says you are mean-spirited toward your younger brother. You know that you've always been kind or at least neutral toward him. Perhaps your mother is reminding you of a time in a previous incarnation when you were hateful toward this person who is now your brother. Now you'll have the opportunity to apologize to your brother, therefore resolving the conflict and fulfilling your karmic obligation.

## GUILT AS A CONTROLLING MECHANISM

As essential as it is to understand our propensity to foster guilt and to work toward ridding ourselves of it, we must also be aware of how we ourselves wield guilt as a tool to control others.

Becoming acutely aware of our history of fostering guilt in this life and in past lives gives us a chance to change our ingrained guilt-laden patterns so we don't perpetuate them in our children. Whenever we don't give our children an opportunity to deal with their shame and apologize for it, we are perpetuating guilt in them. Whenever we've paired their accidents with unintentionally harmful and demeaning statements—"You're always so clumsy" or "Didn't I teach you how to hold a glass? You never pay attention"—we're not allowing them to handle shame and say they're sorry. We're contaminating the shame process and creating problems with their self-esteem, self-worth, and sense of adequacy.

Can you recall any instance from your childhood when you felt humiliated and had no chance to resolve it? Give your children the time and the coaching they need to deal with shame in a healthy way. Let them feel complete with the process. Never allow them to leave a broken dish feeling broken themselves. Give them a chance to feel good about taking responsibility for things that they've done, and teach them the value of saying "I'm sorry." Watch how you might be using guilt to control your child's behavior. Think about how you were controlled by guilt, by either your teachers, parents, or other close relatives. Write down the situations in your early childhood that perpetuated that horrible belief. Try not to forget those times, especially when dealing with your own children. I have noticed that rarely do parents say they're sorry to a child. You're their role model. If you can't say you're sorry, you can't expect them to do it. As adults working through our guilt, taking responsibility for our shame, and becoming free of old thought patterns, we can keep our children from having to experience the same problem.

## LIVING WITHOUT GUILT

Try to conjure what your life would be like without guilt. You would be free to discriminate among life's choices without someone's expectations or judgments weighing heavily on you. You would be free to be prosperous; free to take risks; free to explore your feelings; free to feel good about yourself; free to be happy; free to realize your potential. You would be less restrained in your dreams and aspirations. Being free to do things because you want to do them, not because you should, would clearly promote more honesty in your relationships.

At the age of 39, Cindy went through a difficult divorce, feeling as though the entire experience was her fault. Once she shed her sense of overwhelming guilt, she was able to turn her life around.

*Five years ago, my marriage of fifteen years imploded. I had been a dutiful, stay-at-home wife to a successful business owner. In fact, my relationship with Phil very much resembled that of an employee and a boss, with me in the subordinate role. Now I felt that my world was collapsing. I had done nothing to deserve this. I was scared to death. Yet I also felt this overwhelming sense of guilt. Had I done something to cause him to say it was over? He had been suffering from depression for years and had systematically closed off all sources of discomfort from his life: his job, his mother, our church, certain friends. I felt that I had been supportive, but perhaps he was right; it really was my fault. While I know intellectually that that couldn't be the whole truth, emotionally I felt consumed with dread, remorse, and guilt. About exactly what, I wasn't sure.*

*I underwent therapy with a Christian psychologist. I attended Alanon meetings to develop a sense of detachment. I went to monthly support meetings for families of manic-depressives. (My husband had been properly diagnosed by now.) And I thought I had begun to heal.*

*My first several sessions with Linda were filled with my bitching about Phil and his problems. But Linda gently steered me toward another perspective. What if all I was experiencing was my soul creating exactly the events I needed in order to learn and grow in this lifetime? I had certainly made great headway in my personal work, yet I still blamed my soon-to-be ex for my lack of internal peace. His leaving had made me sad, and I had the illusion that only his return would make me happy.*

*After almost two years, things were finally getting better in my life. Yet I still had a vague sense of guilt, as though I had done something I had forgotten but that I should feel sorry about. Linda took me through some exercises in which I visualized two past lives, which allowed me to recount experiences that were the source of my guilty feelings. I do not proclaim that the two "lives" I glimpsed actually occurred. Perhaps they did, perhaps not. But both shed light on my relationship with my ex-husband. Could the events I "saw" really be memories of past lives? I don't think those questions are nearly as important as the results of the session itself.*

*I experienced an immediate physical relief from that pervasive sense of guilt. In fact, I had nothing to feel guilty about any longer. My ex and I had done what we had done and had been doing for lifetimes. I began to feel a sense of internal strength unlike anything previously experienced in my life. I had a soul that was greater than circumstances, more powerful than emotions, unlimited by earthly time, and not limited to my earthly form.*

*Now I experience joy daily and in abundant quantities. I have a strong sense of purpose and a passion for life. I have remarried, and most importantly, I have healed the relationship with my former husband. I see him as a valuable part of my life, a man worthy of respect. I've also imbued this attitude in my two sons, who last year began living with their father when I moved to Toronto.*

*Last month, almost five years to the day since our split, my boys, my ex-husband, my new husband, and I spent time on an island on vacation. It was a truly remarkable experience. I have learned that I have the power to create any experience of life that I wish, and that honoring the soul's path is the most effective approach to a truly empowering joyful journey. I don't remember the last time I felt really angry—I believe it was about a year ago. I no longer live under the influence of guilt, a development that has propelled me forward in an exponential way. Life is indeed what we choose to make it.*

Guilt is so pervasive that it often obfuscates how we really feel. Absolving ourselves of guilt gives us the opportunity to investigate and express our true feelings, allowing us to experience relationships with more profundity. But some find the unknown—life without guilt—so problematic and scary that they prefer the guilt. Many of my clients have voiced their concern that life without guilt would be chaos. Their reasoning is that guilt controls us on a societal level. But I think of all the issues from the Age of Pisces that have haunted us for the last two thousand years: our need for redemption, our inadequacy, our need for perfection, our extremism, our mutual exclusion, and perhaps most of all, our guilt. I think about walking through a door into the world called Aquarius and closing that door behind me, leaving the Age of Pisces behind.

Let's assume for a moment that guilt was simply a belief system that we needed during those two thousand years, as a means simply to grow and evolve: to become more aware of the consequences of our actions and to gain more control over our impulsive behavior. As we move into the Age of Aquarius and evolve as loving, sensitive, responsible adults, we don't need guilt anymore to provide a social and moral boundary.

Now we must learn to appreciate what taking responsibility for our shame can do for us. Being ashamed is not just a sentiment reserved for childhood, but rather an emotion that allows us to resolve experiences that we feel bad about, so they don't fester into guilty feelings. If we determine what we did that made us feel ashamed and overcome it by making amends, then we learn not to take that action again. It sounds so simple, and it is. Yet most of us still don't follow that process. We are so uncomfortable with the feeling of shame that we will repress it, disregard it, blame someone else for it, and in time create our own guilt over it. Becoming more responsible for our actions is the cornerstone philosophy of the dawning Age of Aquarius. Guilt will dissipate as we become more conscious and more aware of our own feelings and actions. As we leave the Age of Pisces and enter the Age of Aquarius, we want to leave behind these parts of the Piscean personality, even as we take other parts with us.

Leave Behind . . .
• **A need to prove we can be redeemed for something.** This underpinning belief of the Piscean personality holds that something is inherently wrong with us and that we need some external influence to "fix" us. We have believed for centuries that if we prayed enough, some force of God would forgive us and make it all better. Perhaps it is the atavistic belief that we were born with sin and that only God would exonerate us and forgive that sin. Hence we join churches, synagogues, and mosques that promise us forgiveness and redemption.

• **A need to understand the difference between good and evil.** Our preoccupation with good and evil is thousands of years old. I believe that our souls created this dichotomy as a projection of ourselves. Each of us has a shadowy side that we may perceive as evil. Since most of us can't bear to confront that painful part of our psyche, we create it outside ourselves. When we are prepared to explore those unseemly aspects, we can work on changing them. Then our need to externalize what we see as evil will wane.

• **A need to aspire to heaven and avoid hell.** Each religion has its own teachings about the afterlife and its own specific "requirements" for admission to that ethereal bastion that Christians call heaven. Going to hell is unthinkable. Interestingly, the *Random House Unabridged Dictionary* defines heaven as "the abode of God, the angels, and the spirits of the righteous after death." In turn, hell is defined as "the place or state of punishment of the wicked after death; the abode of evil and condemned spirits." In today's more complex world, where would the spirits of those who are considered neither particularly righteous nor evil go? Once again, most religions supply us with an either/or philosophy of extremes, with no room for alternatives.

• **A strong need to value ourselves as victims and a symbolic desire to be martyrs.** I equate the failure to choose to make a change that we know is beneficial for us with self-martyrdom. Even though we know that the change will make us happier, we don't do it. We are more comfortable with the suffering that staying "stuck" brings. You might, for example, have a skewed belief that *you don't deserve* to feel good.

• **A strong need to value Godliness and devalue earthly concerns, including personal gratification.** "My reward will be heaven." A traditional Piscean way of thinking holds that living a comfortable life on earth will keep us from entering heaven. We must not love the earth and what it can give us, because to do so means we are hedonistic, materialistic, and ungodly. The Piscean personality sees things as either black or white, good or bad, right or wrong. Through this filter they would have to choose either earth over spirit or conversely spirit over earth, when in fact they can have both. How many times have you heard someone say, "I just want to have enough money to be comfortable. That's all I need." Many of us perpetuate the religious belief that God wants us to live a spartan existence and for doing so will reward us. But God has given us the earth and all it contains. God wants us to be happy.

• **A need to feel guilty to remind us of what is bad.** Clients have told me that guilt represents their personal border of acceptable behavior. Several have said that the absence of guilt would foster immorality. Guilt becomes their moral barometer.

Take with Us . . .

• **A strong need to be introspective: to have quiet moments to find inner peace.** Increasing numbers of people are turning to some form of meditation and introspection to find quiet and inner peace. Self-help books abound, offering great ideas to help us center and regroup in a world of noise, chaos, irritability, and confusion. People are taking these ideas to heart and putting them into practice. Solitary exercise is also becoming more popular, because it gives us time to be with ourselves. We're also seeking various forms of coaching to better analyze our behavior and its effects on others. Through Pisces we learned we have a spirit, and now, as we move from the Age of Pisces to Aquarius, we are learning how to understand it and communicate with it.

• **A need to value our feelings.** We need to understand our feelings: how they affect our life, how to express them, how they can control our lives, and how to integrate them into the totality of our personality. Our five basic emotions are mad, glad, sad, scared, and ashamed. Yet we have hundreds of words that mean the same thing. We can say that we feel frustrated, irritable, peeved, annoyed, enraged, irate, exasperated, and furious, but they all boil down to feeling angry. Many of us use these other words instead of simply saying "I'm angry; I'm ashamed; I'm sad; I'm scared." We even have trouble saying "I'm glad." If we honor and understand our basic feelings, we take responsibility for them. Taking responsibility for our feelings can be frightening. After a few years of denial, we lose touch with most of our emotions. Few of us, in any given moment, stop to ask the question, "How am I feeling right now?"

Use the five fundamental basic emotions to get more in touch with your own feelings. Stop a few times a day and ask yourself how you're feeling. Discriminate among the different sensations. Anger and fear can feel very similar. Sadness and shame may also feel nearly the same. The more you practice gauging your emotions internally, the more likely you will be to express them externally.

• **A need to control your aggressive and impulsive actions that could hurt yourself and others.** Aggression flares when we ignore our anger over time and it escalates. News reports chronicle the most extreme examples: those tormented people who have leaped out of their quiet, controlled personas to commit unspeakable acts of random violence. Taking the time to source our anger, understand it, and be responsible for it helps put us in control and makes us less prone to lashing out. As we understand how to act more constructively, we will have fewer causes of shame and hence guilt.

## LEARNING MORE ABOUT GUILT THROUGH PLUTO

The planet Pluto in your astrological chart can help explain your guilty inclinations. The interesting component of Pluto is that it rules not only our individual past, but our generational past. Those of us born within twenty years of each other may share deep memories that seem similar.

Pluto urges us to focus on personal transformation and our Soul Potential. It helps us face our deepest desires and obsessions and alter them. It gives us a strong motivation to let go of past guilt so we can be reborn, spiritually and emotionally. In order to become free of past life karma and the need to resist changing our Soul Patterns, we must understand what Pluto represents.

The astrological sign in which your Pluto is placed can suggest how you can act on your desire for personal transformation. The following discussion of Pluto will help you answer the following questions: How do you develop the courage to confront the parts of yourself about which you feel guilty? What do you need to do to transform your old fears into internal strength and confidence? How do you delve into your deepest obsessions and destroy them?

This chart begins with Pluto in Cancer in 1914 and ends with Pluto in Sagittarius in 2008. It covers Pluto in only six of the twelve astrological signs—the ones that pertain to the generations living now.

## *Pluto Placements*

| If you were born: | Your Pluto is in: |
|---|---|
| June 27, 1914–Oct. 7, 1937 | Cancer |
| Oct. 8, 1937–Nov. 25, 1937 | Leo |
| Nov. 26, 1937–Aug. 3, 1938 | Cancer |
| Aug. 4, 1938–Feb. 8, 1939 | Leo |
| Feb. 9, 1939–June 14, 1939 | Cancer |
| June 15, 1939–Oct. 19, 1956 | Leo |
| Oct. 20, 1956–Jan. 15, 1957 | Virgo |
| Jan. 16, 1957–Aug. 19, 1957 | Leo |
| Aug. 20, 1957–April 12, 1958 | Virgo |
| April 13, 1958–June 10, 1958 | Leo |
| June 11, 1958–July 30, 1972 | Virgo |
| July 31, 1972–Nov. 5, 1983 | Libra |
| Nov. 6, 1983–May 18, 1984 | Scorpio |
| May 19, 1984–Aug. 28, 1984 | Libra |
| Aug. 29, 1984–Jan. 17, 1995 | Scorpio |
| Jan. 18, 1995–April 21, 1995 | Sagittarius |
| April 22, 1995–Nov. 10, 1995 | Scorpio |
| Nov. 11, 1995–Jan. 26, 2008 | Sagittarius |

## PLUTO IN THE ASTROLOGICAL SIGNS

### PLUTO IN CANCER

Members of the Pluto in Cancer generation share past lives of fear, insecurity, and loss. You may have experienced lives where you had no permanent home or roots and no emotional or financial security. You probably lived in passivity or subordination, with little power to effect change. Others changed their life circumstances with little regard for what it did to you. In some dire circumstances you could have lost your family or those closest to you. An archetypal Pluto in Cancer lifetime would be that of a slave, with no home and no power, whose family could have been sold and sent away. In this life, you and the rest of your generation are terrified of change because of your powerlessness in other incarnations. The karmic guilt you experienced by being subject to the whims of the powerful, and being powerless and fearful to do anything about it, has created obsessions for you in this life. You fight for your family and hold it together at all costs. You value home, tradition, and foundations. You cling incessantly to what feels secure, haunted by issues that you perceive as having a debilitating impact on your family. You are obsessed with the immediate past because it represents cohesiveness and stability. You are loyal to government, your employers, and your religion because they represent a part of your stable "family." You were born into the Depression or thereabouts and survived it by being frugal and cautious. You learned about the value of families sticking together to survive. If you were born early in this generation, you fought in World War II to defend all that is important to you: home and country.

## PLUTO IN LEO

The Pluto in Leo generation shares past lives of understanding power and control. You've been in various roles of power, ranging from rulers of small countries to owners of land. Your vainglorious and self-centered approach kept you from seeing other people's needs. You ignored your subordinates, seeing them as having little meaning other than as workers or servants, an attitude that has no doubt fostered unconscious guilt in this life. This unconscious guilt could create a need for service, a karmic symmetry that could lead you to want to dedicate your life to others. Each person you meet in this life could potentially have been one of those poor servants with whom you have an unresolved obligation. What better way to resolve your obligation to them than to care for them as a doctor, nurse, counselor, teacher, or social worker. Many people who are healers in this life have had past lives of opulence, during which they held a blatant disregard for others. For hundreds of years those in power were born into power. They were royal and were trained to be separate from the lower classes. Now, as a member of the Pluto in Leo generation, you feel ashamed and even guilty for the way you were. Thus you've created a life to redeem yourself from the insensitivities and abuses you so ruthlessly exhibited from a previous incarnation.

## PLUTO IN VIRGO

The Pluto in Virgo generation shares past lives of being God-like healers, well ordered, and structured. As a member of this generation, you judged those who were not as ordered and rigid as you were. The archetype here is the doctor or other medically prominent member of the community who could do no wrong. You were adored, lionized, and revered. You were the healer, and everyone needed you. You believed yourself infallible: you did not make mistakes. Your mission was to be a perfect healer and to be respected as such. But one day you did something imperfect. You made a terrible mistake that cost someone their life—and you your reputation. Your shameful responsibility for the demise of someone who had placed their trust in you has manifested itself in an intense guilt yielding the type of personality that overanalyzes every move and seeks internal and external perfection to the point that it is immobilizing. Terror of making a mistake, no matter how small, keeps you and your generation in procrastination and caution. The guilt also creates a strong need to do service, but you don't derive any satisfaction from it unless you perform it flawlessly.

## PLUTO IN LIBRA

Members of the Pluto in Libra generation share past life memories of being codependent in relationships, a tendency that has weakened you and led to your indecisiveness and ambivalence. Because of your inability to articulate your needs, you constantly find yourself in situations that seem unfair to you. Your cloying ways undermine your quest for independence, yet at the same time satisfy your perverse need to climb the social ladder. Socially adept to the point of being phony, you are currently very sensitive to situations and people that appear disingenuous or dishonest.

Guilty about your own relational superficiality, you are intensely absorbed with justice and honesty in all your human relationships. You and other members of this generation often created your parents to be divorced, which allowed you to view the destruction of marriage firsthand. Your task is to transform relationships so they will endure through fairness, equality, cooperation, and balance.

## PLUTO IN SCORPIO

At this writing, the Pluto in Scorpio generation are children, several of whom I have already seen in my practice. From what I have observed so far, they share past life memories of intensity and chaos, fueled by a tendency toward extremes. Deeply paranoid, they are secretive about their innermost feelings and have difficulty trusting. They have memories of being totally in control and are relentless in their approach to getting what they want but vindictive if thwarted. They passionately love mystery, especially pertaining to sexuality and death. Their guilt feelings over their anger and fear will fuel their quest to play a major role as transformational healers. They will help others understand and transform themselves in the areas of emotions, sexuality, and fear of death. They will relentlessly strive to alter the power structure. Because of their past life guilt about sexual misuse, they will learn to honor sex. Because of their past life paranoia, they will hone their insights into human nature and help the healing process by probing and investigating the human condition. Because of their preoccupation with death, they might even overcome their fear of it. Because of their guilt over controlling others in other lives, they will learn the true meaning of controlling their own lives and creating their destiny. This generation—even at age 3, 4, or 10—knows exactly what it wants and will do whatever it can to get it.

## PLUTO IN SAGITTARIUS

Members of this generation are the youngest set among us, just now finding their way into this life in the last couple of years. They share past lives of total freedom and adventure, symbolized by the archetype of the cowboy wandering the Old West in happy solitude on his only reliable friend, his horse. They will value nature, space, and their own thoughts. They will not be interested in committed relationships, although they like experiencing other people. They will wander into a relationship, have a brief affair, and move on, unencumbered. They may have claustrophobia in big cities, and they may be restless when not on the move. They will probably be brutally honest and outspoken, possessing little diplomacy. They will learn how to thrive in society and still appreciate nature. They will transform their need for physical space and freedom into a need for spiritual regeneration and freedom of thought. They will learn to share their thoughts by teaching and inspiring others. Only babies now, this generation will be thrilling to watch as they grow into their awesome potential.

## GUILT AND FORGIVENESS

Religion preaches the importance of our being forgiven by God. We go to our respective houses of worship to pray for that forgiveness. We ask our spiritual leaders to forgive us and are significantly buoyed when they do. We confess our sins and take our penances with faith, in hope that we will be freed from our guilty impulses. We open our mind, heart, and spirit to God's forgiveness. It is a receptive process: we are the recipients of that holy forgiveness. After being forgiven, we feel cleansed, revitalized—as if a weight has been lifted off our chests. In the Lord's Prayer, Christ asked us to pray to forgive others who "trespass against us, as we are forgiven by God for our sins." Asking to be forgiven and forgiving others liberates us from the weighty throes of guilt. Both are equally important. If we are unable to forgive, we are holding back and continuing to feel guilty because we haven't been living "in forgiveness."

I believe it's easier to ask for forgiveness than to grant it. To ask for forgiveness requires acknowledging your guilt or shame. Moreover, waiting for acceptance of your bid can be wrenching. However, the most challenging aspect of the forgiveness process is forgiving someone else who either denies that they did anything to hurt you in the first place, or who shows no remorse for their action. Taking the first step and forgiving that person—before they've sought your forgiveness—is an emotional risk. Still, just because they aren't contrite—or deny they transgressed at all—doesn't mean you should abandon your gift of forgiving and the liberating qualities it can have. By forgiving, your soul is making peace with that person and the hurtful experience they conjured, regardless of whether they agree to be willing participants. But if you refuse to forgive someone based on *their* attitude, you are ceding your power—to heal and to move on and live a healthy and productive life—to them.

Living in forgiveness gives us a sense of completion and resolution. When we're not living in forgiveness, we tend to hold on to our grief and sadness, which can later manifest themselves as depression. Probably three hundred people in my practice over the years have written letters to those dearest to them—some alive, some long departed—asking for forgiveness. Often they shed tears of relief when they burned their letters, thereby sending their poignant messages out to the respective souls for whom they were intended. One of my clients, Claire, wrote a letter of forgiveness to her father, who had been dead for more than twenty years. She burned it in my office in a brass pot. As it was turning to ash, she broke out into contagious, unbridled laughter. Her father had always made her laugh. In this moment she had remembered a funny story he used to tell her. Since she had been angry at her father for so long, she had forgotten his humorous side. She wrote her letter to ask him to forgive her for being so selfish and angry. She had not visited him in the hospital when he was dying and had not said good-bye to him. She had been furious that he was dying at the age of 40. She was only 15. When she remembered the funny story and laughed, she knew he had heard her and forgiven her. She felt renewed and giddy, free from the nagging pain of guilt and incompletion. She had a clean slate and was on her way to healing that place in her heart that had been so wounded.

This exercise will help you learn more about sourcing your own personal guilt via Pluto. Part of the process of letting go of guilt is to be able to elicit forgiveness, as well as to give it.

## Pluto Exercise

1. My Pluto is in the sign of: _____ (refer to the "Pluto Placements" chart).
2. Words for that sign from the Soul Pattern Energetics Model (Chart 2 in Chapter 4) that bother me are:

Remember that for this exercise the words that create the deepest emotional reaction in you are the vital ones. They are most likely to symbolize situations in which you did something that you might be ashamed of, things you'd consider "bad" or "wrong."

For example, if your Pluto is in the sign of Leo, you might use the following words from the Energetics Model: *melodramatic, self-centered, disdainful, autocratic, dictating,* and *needs attention.*

3. Using these words, write a story about yourself living the kind of life you could have had where guilt conceivably could have surfaced. Each word from the Energetics Model can symbolize a lifestyle, a career, an interaction with others, a relationship—a total mode and philosophy of living during a particular time in history. Use your imagination to figure out what you might feel guilty about. Relax and allow your imagination to flow. Have fun with the story and see what happens.

Again supposing your Pluto is in Leo, here's how a story might unfold:

The source of my guilt comes from a life where I was in a position to *dominate* others. I was probably a ruler of some kind with many servants. I believed that my power was all that mattered, so I was *disdainful* and *autocratic.* I was *self-centered* and *needed attention.* When I did not get what I wanted, I could be *melodramatic.*

4. Having considered the kind of life you could have had, the source of your guilt may be:

## Exercise: Eliminating Guilt

Here is how you can deal with an experience that has taken place in another time, in another place, and through another personality.

**Step 1:** Become conscious. You cannot confront something if you don't know what it is.

**Step 2:** Take responsibility for the behavior you feel guilty about. Nothing will change if you blame someone else for your own behavior.

**Step 3:** Forgive yourself by asking someone for forgiveness.

Let's explore Step 3. How do you ask for forgiveness from a person who is from your past? You may not even know who that person is. Review the story you wrote in the Pluto Exercise. Meditate on that life; think of one person who could embody all the people you might have hurt in that life. Now make that image more real: give it a sex, a name, a physical identity, and a personality. Now create a situation between both of you that would necessitate an apology from you. The following Forgiveness Exercise will help you do your own.

## Forgiveness Exercise

1. I karmically wish to be forgiven for (refer to the Pluto Exercise, Step 3):
   *Example:* I wish to be forgiven for using my position of power to dominate others. In my arrogance, I disregarded people who served me well. I was autocratic and did not listen to anyone. I am so sorry that I did not understand the depth of my self-absorption and self-centeredness. It makes me ashamed that I expected and required people to bow before me and surrender their dignity for my need for con-

stant adoration. I wish to be forgiven for my childish use of power.

2. Someone in that past life whom I need to ask to forgive me is:
   *Example:* I had many servants whom were loyal and trustworthy and truly cared about me. One young woman symbolizes them all. She was only 16 when she was pressed into service as one of my concubines. I ignored her unless I wanted her favors. She loved me, but I held her in contempt. I would ask her to forgive me.

3. Someone in this life whom I need to forgive is:
   *Example:* I need to forgive my father for being arrogant and self-absorbed. He was, in fact, showing me pieces of myself that I needed to see. I not only forgive him for his behavior, I thank him for helping me see a part of my past.

4. Someone in this life whom I need to ask to forgive me is:
   *Example:* I need to ask my older child to forgive me for being so self-involved. I had wanted his unconditional approval and would get angry when I felt he was being critical of me.

   Once you have identified someone whose forgiveness you need, write that person a letter.

### Exercise: Forgiveness Letter

Dear Someone,

It has taken me many lifetimes to write this letter. For much of that time I have felt very guilty for the way that I treated you then. I just did not know how to talk to you. I now know how poorly I treated you. I disregarded you as a human being. I accepted your love as my divine right and forgot that you might have needed something in return. I want you to know that I am so very sorry for what I did. I want you to know that I have changed and that the guilt I have felt over you has produced that change. Will you forgive me?

Love,

## Exercise: Freedom from Guilt

The following steps will help you learn to live without guilt.

• Pay attention to your feelings, especially the feeling of shame. Dealing with shame means rectifying whatever led to the feeling in the first place, in order to take responsibility for it and put it behind you. Get past your embarrassment and say, "I'm sorry." Some people will say they're sorry about everything under the sun, except when they've done something truly hurtful—then they say nothing or project the blame onto someone else. Remember, shame that is not resolved sooner or later turns into guilt. To live guilt-free, we must resolve the shame.

• Understand that you no longer need guilt to keep you on a moral road, to keep you from noxious behavior. We are capable of being good people without the specter of a negative taskmaster shaking its long, bony finger at us. We are moving into the Age of Aquarius, when guilt will be totally inappropriate.

• Love and honor yourself enough to be excited about filling the void once occupied by guilt—no matter how frightening that prospect may be.

# CHAPTER 10

# Neptune: Illusion Versus Aspiration

Over the years scores of my clients have insisted on maintaining illusions that are nonetheless destined to make them unhappy. They tell me, "If only I had more money, I'd be happier," or "If I got married, then things would be better." By perpetuating such illusions, they unwittingly set themselves up to fail.

When we feel guilty about something we've done or failed to do in the past, we foster a belief that we don't deserve to get what we want. As an unhealthy response to our guilt, we create the illusion that the thing we want is unobtainable. As unconscious belief systems, illusions are often totally irrelevant to authentic happiness. They represent our desire to accomplish or obtain something in order to rid ourselves of a specific guilt, even though we may frame the purpose as "to be happy."

All of us, to varying degrees, foster and perpetuate illusions. These illusions give rise to anxious yearnings that we feel we must satisfy in order to be happy. We live with the misguided and inexplicable feeling that only through this one thing will life be fulfilling. Our sadness comes with the realization that we can't seem to satisfy this nebulous and insatiable desire—it always exists beyond us. When I first began studying illusion, I was confounded by people's obsessions with things that lie just beyond their grasp. But once I understood that these illusions or unfulfilled dreams are created from old beliefs of inadequacy, guilt, and self-loathing, they made perfect sense.

## ILLUSIONS VERSUS ASPIRATIONS

Unlike illusions, however, hopes and aspirations are not by-products of guilt. As our conscious creations, they can indeed be fulfilled. If our illusions are what we wallow in, our aspirations and goals are what we seek to attain.

| Illusion | Hope/Aspiration |
|---|---|
| unconscious | conscious |
| a pensive longing | something we strive for |
| set up to fail | plan to succeed |
| wallow | work |
| a disappointment | a goal |

Illusions and aspirations are sometimes difficult to distinguish. We can make an aspiration or hope come true. We can set a goal or objective, then take action to accomplish it. Let's say as a child you always aspired to be a doctor; you took that dream seriously, prepared for it through years of study, and made it happen. Conversely, an illusion is a dream that does not come true, is rife with regret, and is fraught with shadowy "should haves" and "what ifs." Let's say that when you were a child, your father *told you he wanted you* to become a doctor. You felt you *should* be a doctor, and you perpetuated a myth that you wouldn't be happy unless you practiced medicine. Yet you did nothing to prepare for it. You eventually became a college professor, but your existence is plagued by the gnawing illusion that you have "failed," that you are inadequate because you didn't fulfill your father's expectation. You cultivated your own illusion by internalizing your father's dream, in the belief that being a doctor would make him happy and garner his approval. Despite the rewarding aspects of your job and your high professional standing, you continue to feel unsatisfied and vaguely discontented. We all would feel better about who we are and what we do if we could identify the illusions that torment us, confront what they represent, and resolve them.

## REALIZING OUR ILLUSIONS THROUGH NEPTUNE

A powerful and effective way to bring our illusions to consciousness is to understand the influence of the planet Neptune. Neptune is the planet that ruled the Piscean Age. Everything we have said about Pisces is true of Neptune: It is mystical, psychic, a healer, devotional, inspirational, idealistic, compassionate, empathetic, and creative. It is the energy that best symbolizes Christ. Its challenging aspects include escapism, addiction, self-indulgence, self-deception, delusion, irresponsibility, being noncommittal, and martyrdom. Neptune gives us information about Soul Patterns that keep us mired in self-deception, allowing our illusions to thrive. It sheds light on skewed belief systems and unrealistic standards that can cause serious disappointments.

Neptune also supplies us with information about how we can redeem ourselves for past life mistakes. At its best, it shows us how to become one with the universe, experience our greatest joy through spiritual awakening, and transform our illusions into spiritual experiences. It symbolizes how we can realize our ideals with great love, compassion, and vitality. Neptune urges us to move from the limitations of our personality into our spiritual selves.

Aligning ourselves with the highest energetic manifestation of Neptune gives us the spiritual faith and energy to achieve our Soul Potential. This planet exposes us to the joys and the freedom of living in our soul's experience, of gravitating toward our soul mission. It helps us realize and manifest our most poignant ideals. It pushes us to uncover our illusions and discover the truth. It helps us realize our creativity. Neptune shows us that being at one with our spirit is our most joyful experience. Knowing your Neptune placement will provide you with answers to the following spiritual questions:

- How do you create a vision that will help you connect to the universal order?
- What are your true ideals, and how do you manifest them?

- How do you live in forgiveness and be compassionate with yourself and others?
- How do you change your beliefs so that you do not always live in failed expectation and disappointment?

On a much larger scale, each generation has an illusion or belief system that constitutes a retribution for a previous life experience. You can locate your Neptune in the following chart.

### *Neptune Placements*

| If you were born: | Your Neptune is in: |
| --- | --- |
| May 22, 1902–July 19, 1915 | Cancer |
| July 20, 1915–Mar. 19, 1916 | Leo |
| Mar. 20, 1916–May 1, 1916 | Cancer |
| May 2, 1916–Sept. 21, 1928 | Leo |
| Sept. 22, 1928–Feb. 19, 1929 | Virgo |
| Feb. 20, 1929–July 24, 1929 | Leo |
| July 25, 1929–Oct. 3, 1942 | Virgo |
| Oct. 4, 1942–April 17, 1943 | Libra |
| April 18, 1943–Aug. 2, 1943 | Virgo |
| Aug. 3, 1943–Oct. 19, 1956 | Libra |
| Oct. 20, 1956–June 16, 1957 | Scorpio |
| June 17, 1957–Aug. 6, 1957 | Libra |
| Aug. 7, 1957–Nov. 6, 1970 | Scorpio |
| Nov. 7, 1970–Jan. 18, 1984 | Sagittarius |
| Jan. 19, 1984–June 22, 1984 | Capricorn |
| June 23, 1984–Nov. 21, 1984 | Sagittarius |
| Nov. 22, 1984–Jan. 27, 1998 | Capricorn |
| Jan. 28, 1998–April 4, 2011 | Aquarius |

Here is a brief description of your generational illusions:

- **Neptune in Cancer:** Only when my family loves and needs me will I be happy.

- **Neptune in Leo:** Only when I am honored, loved, and respected will I be happy.
- **Neptune in Virgo:** Only when I am perfect in the service I provide will I be happy.
- **Neptune in Libra:** Only when I am in a relationship of harmony, fairness, and balance will I be happy.
- **Neptune in Scorpio:** Only when I have power and control over myself and others will I be happy.
- **Neptune in Sagittarius:** Only when I have total freedom and space to think about what I want will I be happy.
- **Neptune in Capricorn:** Only when I have obtained wealth and success will I be happy.
- **Neptune in Aquarius:** Only when I can live by my own rules and manifest my own individuality will I be happy.

The problem with all of these belief systems is that they are impossible to fulfill. People in the various generations never have enough love, money, success, power, or harmony to be content. At some point in our past, we set up our illusions so they will never be attained, punishing ourselves and creating a lifetime of disappointment.

## THE OTHER SIDE OF THE RUBBER BAND

Picture your Pluto placement—which represents guilt—at one end of a rubber band. Your Neptune placement—your illusions—is stretching the rubber band at the other end. This image shows their relationships well. Pluto is about the source of our guilt, while Neptune is about manifesting it as illusion. Our residual guilt keeps us from creating dreams that actually come true. We feel bad about ourselves, so we create failures, resulting in further unhappiness. Our old guilt, rotting within us, sets in place a vicious and self-perpetuating cycle of illusion, ensuring that we will never have the life we want.

Taking control of and ultimately reversing this discouraging trend is a two-step process. The first step is to discover what our illusions are. Many of them are so deeply imbedded in our unconscious and so intertwined among our old belief systems that we have no idea they exist. Consciously, we realize that these illusions do not come true, cultivating an aching ambivalence. The second step is to reframe our illusions into aspirations that really can come true. Let's examine how this process played itself out with one of my clients.

Lucy harbored the illusion that unless she had a loving and romantic relationship that was "perfect," she would be inadequate. But neither of her two failed marriages nor her many relationships were what she would call perfect. She wished they had been; in fact, she had needed them to be perfect. But none of her affairs of the heart were loving enough and certainly not romantic enough to meet her lofty and virtually unattainable criteria for perfection.

Thus at the age of 45, because she had not yet found the "perfect" relationship, Lucy continued to foster a feeling of worthlessness. The cycle became self-perpetuating because the more inadequate she felt, the less likely she was to create a healthy, meaningful relationship. This illusion had kept her from exploring many potentially significant relationships because she anticipated that they wouldn't meet her demanding criteria. Her illusion also kept her from discovering the most important relationship of all: the one with herself.

In order to help Lucy deal with her illusion, we first had to discover its source. What guilt had driven her to feel that she couldn't be happy without a man in her life? On the other end of the rubber band, opposite Neptune, is Pluto, the issues related to guilt. Lucy's Pluto is in Leo, which is based on being self-absorbed and focused on oneself, so she learned that she had some past guilt about being too selfish or self-involved. This guilt activated the dynamic Neptune process, fostering the illusion that the only way to overcome that guilt was through having a relationship; without it she considered herself worthless—a common illusion for those with Neptunes in Libra. Lucy's illusion was thus a reaction to the guilt produced by an old karmic experience.

Uncovering your illusions by understanding your Neptune placement gives you another opportunity to understand Pluto and therefore issues from the past that need to be resolved. Once Lucy understood this principle, she could deal with her Pluto issues of guilt without creating severe illusions that could have kept her discontented for the rest of her life. As an extreme reaction to old guilt, an illusion is seductive, usually unconscious, and difficult to discern, because it's something we think we need to be happy. Although we may perceive it as a path to happiness, an illusion insidiously creates disappointment.

The next exercise will help you uncover your illusions. Concentrate first on your illusions sourced from your parents, since they represent circle-one soul contracts. You chose your parents to show you your unconscious illusions, based on karmic guilt left over from past life experiences. Observing and analyzing their illusions is a lot easier than consciously analyzing your own, and it allows you to uncover the illusions they've perpetuated within you. Each part of the exercise has a sample answer to give you an idea of how to respond.

## Illusion Exercise

1. When I chose my mother, I chose the following illusions (illusions that your mother perpetuated within you):
   *Examples:*
   - Peace and harmony are the most important personal values.
   - Protect the sanctity of the family at all costs.
   - Showing anger is not socially acceptable.
   - Being pretty, charming, and pleasant will get you a man who will take care of you.
   - When in doubt, don't!
   - Take care of others before yourself, and you will be rewarded.
   - It is a woman's job to hold on to her man.
   - Security comes from being married.

2. When I chose my father, I chose the following illusions (illusions that your father perpetuated within you):
   *Examples:*
   • If you don't have anything nice to say, say nothing.
   • A man's job is to support his woman.
   • Be ladylike, and people will like you.
   • Taking risks is dangerous.
   • When you're upset, drink. You'll feel better.
   • Men don't like assertive women.
   • Don't rock the boat, and you'll get along.

3. What hope/aspiration do I have that I've not yet realized?
   *Example:* I have always hoped that one day I would not have to work so hard, that a man would come into my life and support me, so that I wouldn't have to work if I didn't choose to. We would live happily ever after, travel extensively, and life would be safe, comfortable, and secure.

4. Which of my parent-based illusions supports this dream?
   *Examples:*
   • A man's job is to support his woman. (father)
   • Being pretty, charming, and pleasant will get you a man who will take care of you. (mother).
   • Security comes from being married. (mother)

5. What previous experience or belief system and resultant feeling of guilt caused me to create this present life illusion? (Analyze each illusion using this rule. Remember the rubber band theory: illusion as a by-product of guilt.)

The following are examples of possible scenarios to answer Step 5:

**Past Experience:** *One's personal value is measured by the ability to get what one wants. Aggression and war bring power and strength.*

**Associated Guilt:** *Guilt at being selfish and self-absorbed, at being warlike and aggressive, at taking what I wanted from others without remorse, and in fact being proud of my ability to do it.*
**Present Life Illusion:** Peace and harmony are the most important personal values.

**Past Experience:** *Family cohesiveness is not important. Individual wants and desires outweigh those of family.*
**Associated Guilt:** *Guilt at disregarding people who loved and nurtured me, at not honoring and valuing family relationships.*
**Present Life Illusion:** Protect the sanctity of the family at all costs.

**Past Experience:** *Expressing anger causes others to cower and makes me intimidating.*
**Associated Guilt:** *Guilt at making others afraid, at being abusive and combative with no concern about how it makes them feel.*
**Present Life Illusion:** Showing anger is not socially acceptable.

**Past Experience:** *Being commanding and dominating will get me anyone I want. I am totally independent and need no one to take care of me.*
**Associated Guilt:** *Guilt at hurting people who cared about me, at not being able to love, at dominating those who were weaker than myself.*
**Present Life Illusion:** Being pretty, charming, and pleasant will yield a man who will take care of you.

**Past Experience:** *Security comes from my personal power and my ability to control others. Relationships have no meaning other than to provide me pleasure.*
**Associated Guilt:** *Guilt at not valuing and understanding the importance of relationships. Guilt, once again, at my selfishness.*

**Present Life Illusion**: Security comes from being married.

## NEPTUNE IN THE ASTROLOGICAL SIGNS

What follows is a brief description of Neptune in the different signs, replete with the illusions that need to be understood. Chances are you are perpetuating some of the illusions listed under your Neptune sign.

### NEPTUNE IN CANCER

You become one with the universe by being sensitive to the emotional needs of yourself and your family. Family is a broad concept encompassing all that you love. You nurture everyone who is close and wishes to be needed. You are capable of extraordinary acts of devotion and sympathetic support. You redeem yourself by your preoccupation with home, family, culture, and country at the expense of your own needs and desires. But your protection of others may be smothering and disabling. You deceive yourself by staying steadfastly with the traditions of past cultures and memories, unable to relinquish them for a more productive and freer present and future. At your most illusionary, you believe you must manifest extreme acts of sacrifice in the spirit of martyrdom to be accepted as emotionally understanding. Your illusions that need to be understood:

- I must be devoted to my family to be redeemed.
- I must always be supportive of my children.
- I must be there for those who need me, or I will die.
- I must value the traditions of the past to be happy.
- I must never be disloyal to friends and family.
- I must be sensitive to others' feelings over my own.

### NEPTUNE IN LEO

You become one with the universe through inspired, courageous leadership, especially connecting to the joyful, creative, spiritual child. You share ideals of self-love and honor, drama, fun, and spontaneity, and you inspire these traits in others through your role modeling. You redeem yourself by putting aside your need for constant visibility, approval, and self-indulgence. You are probably status conscious and desperately need everyone to love you. You deceive yourself by being arrogant and overly dominating. You suffer the most when not being honored or respected. Your illusions that need to be understood:

- I must be a powerful, inspiring leader to be redeemed.
- I must be respected by everyone.
- I must never lose my youthful appearance.
- I must have everyone's approval to be happy.
- I must maintain a proud, commanding presence at all times.
- I must constantly prove that I am secure and confident, or I will die.

## Neptune in Virgo

You become one with the universe and spiritually, physically, and mentally healthy by serving others. You share ideals of purity, efficiency, discrimination, and organization. You are a practical healer. You redeem yourself by helping others to create the personal structure and organization that will produce the greatest results on all levels, especially in the area of physical health. You deceive yourself by feeling you must martyr yourself in service to be perfect enough. You strive to create external perfect order and can be judgmental and critical of others who do not conform to your high expectations. You suffer the most by being judged for not "doing it right." Your illusions that need to be understood:

- I must serve mankind's needs over my own to redeem myself.
- I must strive for perfect order in my life to be happy.
- I must be totally efficient and dependable.
- I must never make a mistake, or I will die.
- I must worry about my health to be healthy.
- I must be perfectly organized to be productive.

## NEPTUNE IN LIBRA

You become one with the universe by communicating compassion and sensitivity toward all people. You share ideals of cooperation and have a strong sense of justice and fair play. You are creative in establishing harmony and balance within yourself and for others. You believe in romance but can be codependent and illusionary in relationships. You redeem yourself by caring more for others than for yourself. You deceive yourself by believing that a relationship with another is more important than a relationship with yourself. You suffer the most when others are out of harmony with you. You abhor being the recipient of others' anger. Your illusions that need to be understood:

- I must compromise myself in order to redeem myself.
- I must always be fair.
- I must be pleasing and cooperate with everyone.
- I must maintain harmony at all costs.
- I must not rock the boat.
- I must not be angry at anyone.
- I must have a relationship to be socially appropriate.

## NEPTUNE IN SCORPIO

You become one with the universe by probing the depths of life's mysteries. You strive toward transformation and regeneration, sharing your ideals through a powerful intensity that leads to emotional insight and healing. You redeem yourself by suffering the agonies of your extremistic, paranoid, and jealous nature. You deceive yourself by believing you must be in total control of yourself and others. You can be inscrutable, secretive, withholding, and distrustful. In extreme cases, you are obsessed with the darker sides of magic and sexuality. You suffer the most when out of control. Your illusions that need to be understood:

- I must have control, or I will die.
- I must always seek personal transformation.
- I must not express any powerful feelings.

- I must have intense sexual experiences to be happy.
- I must be powerfully insightful with self and others.
- I must suffer in order to redeem myself.

## NEPTUNE IN SAGITTARIUS

You become one with the universe by exploring truth, spiritual ethics, and the law, and by being an inspired teacher of philosophical thought. You share your ideals of freedom, optimism, and serendipity and teach them. You value education and are constantly in search of more enlightened teaching methods. You redeem yourself by being too expansive and unrealistic. You are overly abstract and Polyannish, with a tendency toward claustrophobia and a fear of commitment. You deceive yourself by being too pedantic and dogmatic, believing that your truth is the only truth. You can be preachy and extravagant. You are the restless traveler seeking freedom at all costs. You suffer the most when someone else restricts you. Your illusions that need to be understood:

- I must be totally honest with myself and others.
- I must have freedom, or I will die.
- I must always inspire and teach others to be redeemed.
- I must constantly travel to expand my philosophy to be happy.
- I must be more generous with others than with myself.
- I must focus on the future instead of the present.

## NEPTUNE IN CAPRICORN

You become one with the universe by seeking practical wisdom and maturity with the responsibility and commitment of the good father. You bring spiritual values into the realm of the realistic and into the daily environment. You share traditional ideals of integrity, self-reliance, and discipline. You redeem yourself by being too cautious, inflexible, and rigid. You can be authoritarian and materialistic. You deceive yourself by being obsessed with rules that can be severe and outmoded. You can be fearful of change, addicted to the old ways of doing things. You suffer the most when your integrity is questioned. Your illusions that need to be understood:

- I must be totally responsible to be redeemed.
- I must always be disciplined and structured.
- I must live by the rules, or I will die.
- I must maintain the traditions of my family and country.
- I must always be realistic and practical to be happy.
- I must be the good father to all who rely on me.

## NEPTUNE IN AQUARIUS

You become one with the universe by communicating humanitarian and universal concepts to reestablish a peaceful world order. You represent the holistic triangle of mind, body, and spirit and the symbolic beginning of the Age of Aquarius. You share ideals of individual mastery, rationality, innovation, reformation, and cooperation. You truly believe that one committed individual can make a difference in the world. You redeem yourself by being detached and observing and sometimes by being too impersonal. You deceive yourself by being too logical, remote, and intolerant (especially of others' intolerance). At your most illusionary, you are the erratic rebel who breaks rules just because they exist. You suffer the most when you are unable to understand a situation rationally. Your illusions that need to be understood:

- I must be the detached observer to be redeemed.
- I must always be logical and rational.
- I must be impersonal to achieve reformation for myself and others.
- I must maintain the ideals of equality at all costs.
- I must always be innovative and an individualist to be happy.
- I must be self-possessed and internal to be strong.

Once you know more about your illusions and the guilt that perpetuates them, you can begin to strive for attainable hopes and aspirations, free from the burden and pain of self-deception.

# Epilogue

*"The life which is unexamined is not worth living."*
Plato

*"The actuality of thought is life."*
Aristotle

In May 1997, as players began to settle into the long grind that is the professional baseball season, one story caused a minor ripple. The sports pages, still filled with prognostications about the game's contenders and pretenders and preoccupied with their off-season comings and goings, reported that one player had announced he was retiring. Such an announcement would not have been unusual coming from a veteran who perhaps needed one more spring to convince himself that his pitches no longer stymied Major League hitters or that his bat speed had slowed just enough to prevent him from turning on an inside fastball.

But Ryan Jaroncyk's announcement was rare, in fact unheard of, in that he was only 20 years old, a promising "can't miss" prospect, to whom the New York Mets had paid a signing bonus approaching $1 million in accordance with making the shortstop their number-one pick in the 1995 amateur draft. Jaroncyk said simply he didn't like playing baseball. He had only played to please his parents, who had pressured him earlier in his career to persevere, according to a May 30 *New York Times* article that appeared after his announcement. In an age of $100 million megadeals and crass commercialism, Jaroncyk had the courage to listen to his soul, to walk away from a pursuit that in all likelihood would have paid him exponentially more than he will ever make doing anything else. One day soon after making his decision, Jaroncyk reportedly packed all the baseball equipment he had accumulated over the years into a big box and, with his wife, threw the box into a dumpster. He couldn't remember ever being so happy. He had been in conflict for a long time over baseball because of his parents' expectations, but he recognized that his soul path lay elsewhere.

We all must have the courage and fortitude to listen to our souls and follow the path that will make our hearts sing, even when that path portends substantive reframing, transformation, and tumult. This book has supplied you with tools to help you learn more about yourself and your soul in order to discover your life's purpose and live it with greater meaning and profundity.

We are beginning to understand with greater certainty how important it is to embrace and be aware of our soul. In order to become the most complete human beings possible, we must be in touch with our soul on a daily basis.

Put simply, when we strive to fulfill our soul mission, our life's work, we get what we want; when we don't, we often find ourselves mired in significant crises. Our soul missions provide us with all the things for which we yearn: happiness, fulfillment, meaning, purpose, direction, and motivation. Most importantly, living our soul mission gives us peace. We must remind those who are less spiritually cognizant that they too have a soul, and explain what it does and what it means.

In essence, we're teaching people to be more reflective, to approach their lives with honor so they mean something. We're asking them to be observers, to see the world with a broader and sharper focus. Once they've overcome their myopia, their fears and insecurities will begin to subside. If we're in love with our soul, we're in love with abundance, in love with the universe. If we're consumed with fear, we're left with scarcity. At some point in our lives, we've all felt like victims, enslaved to our families, our mates, our culture, our economy, or even our own feelings. We must first gain the perspective to envision the opportunity, then dedicate ourselves to creating the freedom in our lives where none currently exists.

In reading this book and applying its principles, you have begun an adventure in self-discovery that will bring to your life an unprecedented lucidity, focus, and fulfillment. Once you make it a priority to align your personality's desires with your soul mission, you will sense your life taking on more meaning and joy. Your life work is now beginning: using the book as a foundation, you can lay the groundwork for living your soul mission on a daily basis. It is my hope that you will continue to use *Discovering Your Soul Mission* as a reference tool, accessing it to deal with any particularly challenging relationship or experience in any given moment. Staying conscious of your soul mission is the key to success. It is all too easy to slip imperceptibly back into old behaviors and thought processes. Continue gathering pertinent astrological information relating to your Soul Potential. Journalizing your experiences and spending reflective quality time with yourself every day remain essential.

Both Evan and I would like to acknowledge you, the reader, for having the courage to look at your life from a different vantage point, and for wanting to confront issues that may be painful but from which you can evolve, grow, and even heal. We all deserve to learn our ultimate truth: who we are and why we are here. Unfortunately, many of us are too fearful of what we might unearth. We encourage you to "play" with the information you've gleaned from the book for at least a month. Then you can decide for yourself whether it has made a significant difference in your life. If you make the commitment, you will undoubtedly find more meaning and gain more strength, not to mention enjoy a more thrilling and satisfying journey than you ever imagined possible.

**anger processing**  How we deal with anger.

**astrological symbolism**  Every symbol in our world corresponds to an astrological sign, house, or planet.

**color healing/meditation/symbology**  Each color vibrates to a specific level, which corresponds to a life-enhancing energy. This energy aids us in altering our consciousness, calming or intensifying our feelings, and helps in healing our mind, body, and spirit. Bringing color into our energetic bodies helps stimulate understanding and clarity.

**cosmic two-by-four**  An experience our soul creates to stop us in our tracks and draw our attention to a behavior or habit we had been unable to detect previously.

**dream interpretation**  Every symbol in a dream comes from our unconscious minds. Our chart provides specific information regarding the unconscious process. Correlating our dream symbols with astrological symbols gives us a wealth of information not normally gleaned from a dream.

**inner child**  A memory of the children we've been. It represents information and experiences in this life that we remember upon intense introspection. It's an unconscious part of us that, when released, can cause havoc.

**journalizing**  A writing exercise that helps you elicit information that may otherwise be hidden. Often unconscious memories surface when we write.

**karma**  An energetic, universal, and physical law described by the axioms "What goes around, comes around," and "You reap what you sow." Karma continues from one life to another and is only complete when you have balanced your previous actions through consciousness, commitment, and new actions.

**karmic amalgam** An opportunity to see ourselves through the people we create; an aggregate image comprised of the people most meaningful to us.

**karmic astrology** Utilizing the information obtained through the study of our past lives, karmic relationships, and soul processes to create the lives we want.

**karmic debts** Actions you need to take in this life to balance an action you took in a past life.

**karmic forgiveness** To forgive ourselves for what we think we've done wrong.

**karmic memory** Memories of our previous lifetime experiences that are part of our unconscious mind and our soul.

**karmic retribution** When we have taken an action in a previous life, and have not balanced that action out in this life. It is what we do to balance our karmic debt.

**karmic warning bells** The heady emotions, the passionate rush, that accompanies our initial foray with someone special. What feels like "love" in many cases is really a cosmic two-by-four meant to get our attention and prepare us for a major karmic insight.

**mandala** The astrological chart circle and the symbols it represents.

**Mars** The planet that represents the way we understand and express anger. It is the energy that embodies action, forward motion, and risk taking. At its best, Mars represents focused determination and self-motivation. At its worst, it can be impulsive, reckless, impatient, shortsighted, destructive, and accident prone.

**Mercury** The planet that represents our orientation to the world. Its energy helps us determine who we are, how we receive and perceive information, and what we do with it and how we express ourselves once we have it.

**Neptune** The planet that gives us information about the Soul Patterns we have that keep us mired in self-deception, allowing our illusions to thrive. It sheds light on the skewed belief systems that perpetuate the unrealistic standards we've set that can cause serious disappointments.

**North Node (Soul Potential)** The point where the moon orbiting its way to earth's *northern hemisphere* intercepts the earth's orbit around the sun. It represents all for which you strive. Your North

Node offers you a road map of words and concepts helping you to understand whom you need to be to achieve your soul's potential. Once embraced, your North Node provides you with a clear path to a life of profound joy, purpose, and congruence.

**obsession** A negative thought we can't let go of. Something that has no basis in reality but still drives us.

**personality** Our social and emotional DNA, helping us to distinguish who we are. The part of us that responds, often impulsively, to the ebbs and flows of life. It encompasses our thoughts, feelings, senses, motivations, dreams, and the way we emote, and it carries the indelible stamp of our family and history. Unlike our soul, our personality does not transcend this life.

**Pluto** The planet that represents our guilty inclinations. Pluto urges us to have the courage to focus our will on personal transformation, enabling us to focus on our Soul Potential. It helps us face our deepest desires and obsessions and alter them.

**projection/reflection** Both Jungian concepts. Projection is a process by which we deny an ugly part of ourselves and our souls impart it to another person, so that we can observe it in them. Reflection is the process by which that other person sends this information back to us for our review.

**Saturn** Our karmic conductor on the journey to our soul mission. It teaches us the truth about ourselves and helps us create order and structure in our lives. Without it we could not accomplish our soul mission.

**serendipity** Making a commitment, taking an action, and expecting the unexpected that your soul and the universe create with you.

**soul** The essence of our spiritual core; the primary, never-ending force behind us forging our destiny.

**soul circles of life** The sum total of our relationships—hundreds or more—that are linked to us from one life to the next in order to help our soul evolve and learn the lessons it needs to learn.

**soul contracts** Agreements we make with souls we've known from other lifetimes to work through situations in this life that need special attention. Souls reincarnate with other souls they are closely related to in order to overcome conflict, repay an obligation, or perpetuate love.

**soul creation** The practice of taking ultimate responsibility for the way our lives transpire given the fact that our souls create exactly the lives we need in order for us to learn and evolve to a higher spiritual order.

**soul mates** Karmic relationships that have been resolved: deep conflicts that have been settled, obligations that have been fulfilled, and love that has replaced fear and anger.

**soul mission** Your reason for being; your grand purpose, transcending the here and now.

**soul/personality integration** The aligning and meshing of our oft-divergent soul and personality to achieve our soul mission.

**South Node (Soul Pattern)** The South Node is the point where the moon, on its way to earth's *southern hemisphere,* intercepts earth's orbit around the sun. It represents your default mechanism, the type of person you become when you regress into old, predictable patterns and behaviors. The memories of your South Node run deep within you, representing your most familiar thoughts, feelings, and beliefs.

**synchronicity** A condition allowing your soul to create perfect timing and interactions with the world in perfect ways.

**traditional astrology** The study of how planetary positions and the alignment of the stars affect human affairs.

**universal order** The opposite of randomness and existentialist theory. The philosophy that there is an order to the planets, that all things have purpose and meaning, and that there is a structure and foundation to our mind, body, and spirit and it's organized in such a way that creates perfection.

# SUGGESTED READING

Arroyo, Stephen. *Astrology and the Four Elements.* Sebastopol, CA: CRCS Publications, 1975.

———. *Astrology, Karma and Transformation.* Sebastopol, CA: CRCS Publications, 1978.

Bach, Marcus. *The World of Serendipity.* Marina del Rey, CA: DeVoss & Co., 1970.

Campbell, Joseph. *Myths to Live By.* New York: Viking, 1972.

Casey, Caroline W. *Inner and Outer Space.* Boulder, CO: Sounds True, 1996.

Cayce, Edgar. *God's Other Door and the Continuity of Life.* Virginia Beach, VA: A.R.E. Press, 1977.

Cayce, Edgar, and Mary Ann Woodward. *Edgar Cayce's Story of Karma.* New York: Berkley Publishing Group, 1994.

Erickson, Milton, et al. *Hypnotic Realities.* New York: Irvington Publishers, 1976.

Gawain, Shakti. *Creative Visualizations.* San Rafael, CA: New World Library, 1995.

Greene, Liz. *Saturn: A New Look at an Old Devil.* York Beach, ME: Samuel Weiser, 1976.

Hay, Louise. *You Can Heal Your Life.* Carlsbad, CA: Hay House, 1984.

Herbert, Nick. *Quantum Reality.* New York: Doubleday, 1987.

Jung, C. G. *Memories, Dreams, Reflections.* New York: Pantheon, 1961.

———. *The Structure and Dynamics of the Psyche.* Princeton, NJ: Princeton University Press, 1970.

Jung, C. G., ed. *Man and His Symbols.* New York: Dell, 1968.

March, Marion, and Joan McEvers. *The Only Way to Learn Astrology,* vol. 1. San Diego, CA: ACS Publications, 1980.

———. *The Only Way to Learn About Relationships.* San Diego, CA: ACS Publications, 1992.

Marks, Tracy. *The Astrology of Self-Discovery.* Sebastopol, CA: CRCS Publications, 1985.

———. *Your Secret Self: Illuminating the Mysteries of the Twelfth House.* Sebastopol, CA: CRCS Publications, 1989.

Maslow, Abraham. *Motivation and Personality.* New York: Harper, 1954.

Olney, Buster. "A Met Prospect Walks Away from Baseball." *New York Times,* May 30, 1997, sec. B, p. 7.

Schulman, Martin. *Karmic Astrology.* York Beach, ME: Samuel Weiser, 1975.

Singer, Julie, ed. *Boundaries of the Soul: The Practice of Jung's Psychology,* rev. ed. New York: Anchor, 1994.

Spangler, David. *Revelations: The Birth of a New Age.* Boulder, CO: Lorian Press, 1976.

Spiller, Jan, and Karen McCoy. *Spiritual Astrology.* New York: Simon & Schuster, 1988.

Wallace, Amy, and Bill Henkin. *Psychic Healing Book.* Oakland, CA: Wingbow Press, 1981.

Walsch, Neale Donald. *Conversations with God: An Uncommon Dialogue.* New York: Putnam Publishing Group, 1996.

Wilber, Ken. *No Boundary.* Boston: Shambhala, 1979.

Zukav, Gary. *The Dancing Wu Li Masters.* New York: Bantam Books, 1979.

———. *The Seat of the Soul.* New York: Simon & Schuster, Fireside Books, 1989.

LINDA BRADY is an internationally recognized karmic astrologer and holistic teacher with clients in 32 states and five countries. She has been in practice for 25 years and is the founder of the International Center for Creative Choices, a holistic educational center based in Baltimore, Maryland, where she has an ongoing intern training program. She also has active practices in Los Angeles, Portland, Seattle, Ocean City, Maryland, and San Francisco. Her groundbreaking approach has helped more than 2,000 clients across the United States and abroad successfully navigate their own life paths. Linda has been a regular contributor on two Baltimore radio stations, WOLB and WCBM, providing her listeners with specific information about their astrological charts on the air. Her website, www.creativechoices.com, offers additional information on karmic astrology.

EVAN ST. LIFER is an Executive Editor at *Library Journal*. He has written for such publications as the *New York Times, Crain's New York Business,* and Fodor's travel books.